Praise for *The Shamanic Soul*

"This book is a gift to any who seek access to the creative power of their own shamanic birthright ... The best of academic scholarship is offered together with powerful stories of Moler's own shamanic apprenticeship and a host of accessible 'practica' that will greatly aid one's own journey of discovery and transformation." —**Bonnie Glass-Coffin, PhD, MDiv, BCC, professor of anthropology, Utah State University, and author of** *The Gift of Life*

"*The Shamanic Soul* is a must read for any spiritual seeker. As a sanctioned teacher of Indigenous wisdom, Moler brings the mystical into our midst as he guides us through the profound, age-old wisdom, giving us practical applications to access embodied spirituality." —**Dr. Jill M. Strom, DC, CACCP, FASA, founder and director of Cura Integrative Health Care and author of** *The Cura Convergence*

"A thoughtful, well-researched, and wide-ranging exploration of shamanic magical techniques that skillfully blends indigenous wisdom, contemporary psychological ideas, and Western esoteric practices. Enriched with personal stories and anecdotes, this book provides a masterful overview of the field, as well as plenty of practical exercises for readers to try for themselves." —**Julian Vayne, author of** *Getting Higher*

"An interesting and valuable read for anyone curious to delve deeper into the world of shamanic practice." —**Melanie Marquis, author of** *Modern Spellcaster's Tarot* **and** *Carl Llewellyn Weschcke*

"Daniel Moler guides those who are ready and willing through the reality portal into the shamanic realms. If you are new to shamanism or shamanistic pursuits, this book is a valuable resource with an impressive range, explaining terms, worldviews, energy dynamics, and shamanic practices." —**Joan Parisi Wilcox, author of** *Masters of the Living Energy*

"Daniel Moler has not only provided a template and guidance for an explorer to step into the Peruvian shamanic world, but he has also provided support for the larger process we face of healing ourselves into vibrant beings of integrity, compassion, and power." —**Evelyn C. Rysdyk, internationally renowned shamanic teacher/healer and the author of** *Spirit Walking*

"Moler weaves his profound understanding of an astounding array of spiritual traditions into an illuminating tapestry and, in doing so, brings light to the Self, as well as to the practicality and relevance of shamanic practices ... Moler is a most credible voice of how being whom and what we are meant to be is the best way to heal ourselves, align with our true purpose, and prepare us for the future." —**Steve Guettermann, author of** *How to Get Even with the Universe by Getting Right with the World*

"Daniel Moler opens up his life and practice in *The Shamanic Soul* and shows the transformative power of shamanism. He blends traditional workbook structure with personal storytelling to teach the concepts you need to build your practice. Uncover your unique path using modern and ancient shamanic practices." —**Jaymi Elford, author of** *Tarot Inspired Life*

"Daniel Moler has created the most user-friendly, practical, accessible, and inviting resource for engaging in shamanic practice that I have ever seen ... He reinforces the idea that we are all shamanic regardless of upbringing, and that there is no one right way ... With Daniel's steady hand at the wheel, shamanic training is no longer something to be feared." —**Rev. Dr. Stephanie Red Feather, award-winning author of** *The Evolutionary Empath* **and** *Empath Activation Cards*

"Daniel shares his personal experiences, teachings that he has received, detailed techniques, and the practical application of those techniques with a writing style that is clear and a tone that fits the subjects ... This book is also a useful look into the process of blending systems, many of which were already mixed to begin with. The goal of the book is always evident: if you do the work, the world you know will become larger." —**Ivo Dominguez Jr., author of** *The Four Elements of the Wise* **and** *Keys to Perception*

"A practical, clearly articulated translation of the therapeutic practices of Peruvian shamanism. Enhancing the author's credibility is the manner in which he openly shares his personal growth, showing how these techniques contributed to his own spiritual quest and that the key to successful initiation lies within the reach of each and every sincere seeker." —**Douglas Sharon, PhD, director (ret.) of the San Diego Museum of Man and Phoebe A. Hearst Museum of Anthropology**

THE
SHAMANIC
SOUL

© Elaina Cochran

About the Author

Daniel Moler is a visionary creator and student of the mystical arts. He is the writer, artist, and creator of the hit comic series *Psychonaut Presents* and *The Simon Myth Chronicles* and the author of *Shamanic Qabalah: A Mystical Path to Uniting the Tree of Life & the Great Work* (Llewellyn Publications), the psychedelic urban fantasy novel *RED Mass*, and the Terence McKenna guidebook *Machine Elves 101*. He has also made contributions in Ross Heaven's book *Cactus of Mystery: The Shamanic Powers of the Peruvian San Pedro Cactus*, as well as the 2020, 2021, and 2022 editions of *Llewellyn's Magical Almanac*, among numerous other articles in journals and magazines around the world. In April 2019, he was noted as Author of the Month by best-selling author and researcher Graham Hancock. Daniel has been trained in a variety of magical and shamanic modalities, including Peruvian curanderismo. Visit Daniel online at www.daniel molerweb.com.

THE
SHAMANIC
SOUL

A GUIDEBOOK FOR
SELF-EXPLORATION,
HEALING, AND
MYSTICISM

DANIEL MOLER

FOREWORD BY JASON MANKEY

Llewellyn Publications
Woodbury, Minnesota

FIRST EDITION
First Printing, 2022

Book design by Christine Ha
Cover design by Shannon McKuhen
Cover illustration by Daniel Moler
Interior art on pages 83, 122, 147, 160, 162, 163, 172–173, and 212 by Daniel Moler
Interior art on pages 21, 38, 53, 54, 55, 56, 63, 64, 65, 68, 69, 70, 71, 72, 73, 84, 89, 94, 97, 99, 100, 103, 119, 123, 127, 130, 157, 166, 179, 180, 181, 182, 187, 190, 191, 192, 198, and 201 by the Llewellyn Art Department
The High Priestess tarot card illustration on page 121 is based on those contained in *The Pictorial Key to the Tarot* by Arthur Edward Waite, published by William Rider & Son Ltd., London 1911.

Llewellyn Publications is a registered trademark of Llewellyn Worldwide Ltd.

Library of Congress Cataloging-in-Publication Data
Names: Moler, Daniel, author.
Title: The Shamanic soul : a guidebook for self-exploration, healing, and mysticism / Daniel Moler.
Description: First edition. | Woodbury, Minnesota : Llewellyn Publications, 2022. | Includes bibliographical references. | Summary: "A training guide to universal shamanism through non-appropriative methods, including healing exercises, journeying, meditation, and divination techniques"—Provided by publisher.
Identifiers: LCCN 2022004075 (print) | LCCN 2022004076 (ebook) | ISBN 9780738770697 (paperback) | ISBN 9780738770956 (ebook)
Subjects: LCSH: Shamanism.
Classification: LCC BF1611 .M64 2022 (print) | LCC BF1611 (ebook) | DDC 201/.44"—dc23/eng/20220303
LC record available at https://lccn.loc.gov/2022004075
LC ebook record available at https://lccn.loc.gov/2022004076

Llewellyn Publications
A Division of Llewellyn Worldwide Ltd.
2143 Wooddale Drive
Woodbury, MN 55125-2989
www.llewellyn.com

Printed in the United States of America

Also by Daniel Moler

Machine Elves 101

*Shamanic Qabalah: A Mystical Path to
Uniting the Tree of Life & the Great Work*

The Simon Myth Chronicles: Broken Chalice

Psychonaut Presents: MotherVine

Psychonaut Presents: Dark Medicine

Vision Tales

Contributions In

*Cactus of Mystery: The Shamanic Powers
of the Peruvian San Pedro Cactus*

Darkest Image

Don't Walk in Winter Wood

Giant-Size '63

Llewellyn's 2020 Magical Almanac

Llewellyn's 2021 Magical Almanac

Llewellyn's 2022 Magical Almanac

Weapon Echh!

For Autumn, my Sonqo Suwa

Acknowledgments

Not a single concept in this work could have come to fruition if not for my many teachers on this path. I thank them all for their wisdom and candor. Among them are don Daniel Baxley, doña Karrie Marie Baxley, don Oscar Miro-Quesada, doña Cindy Miro-Quesada; Lee Stumbling Deer Slusher, Sharon Slusher, Gray Horse Woman, Diana Adkins, Aaron Betz, Patty, and many more. Your guidance and insight over the years have changed me and contributed to this work.

A humble bow of gratitude goes to my wife, Autumn, for contributing greatly to the editing and content of this book and for being my muse. Also, to my children Dragan, Noah, and Haven, who inspire me every day to do better by them.

I would also like to thank my editor, Heather Greene, for making this work worth its merit and for teaching me how to be a better writer.

Finally, to the invisible guides and allies that have moved on to other realms, thank you for being with me throughout this process, among them don Celso Rojas Palomino, don Benito Corihuaman Vargas, doña Isabella Cole, don Eduardo Calderon Palomino, Chief Phil Crazy Bull, Red Earth, Jessie White Deer, and Gary Red Bear Who Sees All Worlds Langston. May you always be remembered!

Contents

Practicum List

Foreword

My first experience with shamanism occurred in the late 1990s at a meeting of a Pagan student group I was a part of at Michigan State University. Our faculty advisor had arranged for a local shamanic practitioner to visit one of our weekly gatherings and lead us on a guided meditation. I remember us all being quite excited by this opportunity: our guest that night had studied with some major names in the field and had a sterling reputation in our area. Perhaps even more important, we were going to get to experience something different and from outside our usual areas of interest.

I'd like to tell you that I remember the guided meditation we did that night in detail and that it was world changing, but that wasn't quite the case. I remember the sound of a live drum in the background guiding us on our journey, and I remember lying on the stiff and unforgiving conference room floor our meeting was taking place in, but I don't remember much of the meditation itself. When the drumming stopped and I returned to our normal realty, I felt like I had experienced something, but I was unable to grasp just what that experience was.

Since that night in the late 1990s, my practice of Wiccan Witchcraft has brought me into contact with many in the shamanic community. Workshops and classes on shamanism are a staple at many of the Pagan festivals I've been to over the last twenty years, and I count many modern-day shamans among my closest personal friends. I've sat through workshops on shamanism and had numerous conversations over drinks at events with practitioners, but after my less-than-transformative first experience, I've largely steered away from any shamanic practices.

During quieter moments, I've often wondered why my initial brush with shamanism was less than I thought it would be, and in *The Shamanic Soul* I found my answer. Despite what our culture tells us about spiritual practices, they take work and they take time. To have any sort of transcendent experience, one has to truly learn about the practice they are engaging in. There's history to grasp, appreciate, and respect, and there are also techniques that have to be learned and mastered; just having a drum in the background isn't enough. *The Shamanic Soul* is the primer I wish I had read twenty-five years ago.

As a Wiccan Witch, I found plenty new in these pages but also a lot of things that felt familiar. Regardless of tradition, there's a lot here to digest. If you are a Witch, Pagan, or magickal practitioner of any stripe, this book will make you look at your magick in new ways and make it stronger. Even if you have only a passing interest in shamanism, you'll find wisdom in these pages that you'll be able to apply to your own practice.

There's a lot of debate these days over the terms "shaman" and "shamanism" and who gets to use them. One of the many strengths of this book is Daniel's openness to dealing with those questions. Daniel also has the receipts when it comes to his practice. He's done the work, he's practiced with teachers all over the world, he's put in the time, and perhaps most importantly, he's respectful of the places and cultures his shamanism is derived from.

Daniel is an exemplary guide into the worlds you are about to discover and the blessings on the journey.

Blessed be!

Jason W. Mankey
November 2021

Introduction

You have a great and ancient power inside of you, yet sometimes it is hard to see that.

We live in confusing times. Our politics are filled with mistrust, our media is saturated with misinformation, and technology is delivering it all to us so fast we don't have time to process it. Unfortunately, our civilization has not yet reached the point where art, entertainment, education, economics, and all the rest of it work together. The hope would be to encourage the fullest potential of humanity. Yet, all too often, our leaders fail in leadership. The heroes we aspire to are fictional. At the same time, many of our religious organizations have forgotten what it means to provide spiritual guidance and safety. Even some of our most reliable institutions—the scientific community—can fall short when it comes to inspiration.

In April 2019, astrophysicist Neil deGrasse Tyson shot out a rather bleak and sarcastic Twitter remark to the world: "The Universe is blind to our sorrows and indifferent to our pains. Have a nice day!"[1]

Interesting that despite how atheistic that sentiment is, Dr. Tyson still managed to capitalize the word "universe." Yet former *Saturday Night Live* comedian Norm Macdonald was quick to respond to Tyson's proclamation, which was viewed and read by millions: "Neil, there is a logic

---

1 Neil deGrasse Tyson (@neiltyson), Twitter, April 3, 2019, 8:01 a.m., https://twitter.com/neiltyson/status/1113426221038284805.

flaw in your little aphorism that seems quite telling. Since you and I are a part of the universe, then we would also be indifferent and uncaring. Perhaps you forgot, Neil, that we are not superior to the universe but merely a fraction of it. Nice day, indeed."[2]

I was honestly never a huge Norm Macdonald fan until I read that response. Dr. Tyson represents a vast movement in our culture: a growing mindset of brilliance and innovation, but sometimes dubious and grim. We live in an age when science has become the dogma of the times; our entire lives are run by technology through our homes, transportation, communication, and entertainment. Our reliance on the scientific method is undoubtedly a natural reaction. The human species has spent so many years under the fanatical heels of authoritarian religion that the consequence has resulted in a pendulum swing from one extreme to another. I don't fault the scientific community for their extremist stance in some cases. That climate change science is denied by the most powerful and wealthy (especially the top 1 percent, who could actually do something about it) is an example of a world divided by ambiguous principles rather than facts.

At the same time, my hope is that we don't fall into another type of dogmatism through scientific atheism. Norm Macdonald is right. To say that the universe is uncaring and indifferent implies that we are somehow not a part of it, that we are somehow alien to the very effluence of matter and physics that make up reality. In truth, what we have observed through scientific inquiry is quite the opposite: we live in an interconnected universe that is still so full of mystery we haven't even begun to grasp a fraction of the bigger picture.

We are human beings, *Homo sapiens*. We literally sprung from the evolutionary web woven from the dirt and waters of the planet Earth, which itself was formed from the heat and gases of the universe's cosmic brew. We *are* the universe, expressed in microcosmic form. This is no esoteric concept. Undoubtedly, it is fact. Recognizing this global and cosmic heritage is an attribute of the modern shaman. This universal

2 Norm Macdonald (@normmacdonald), Twitter, April 10, 2019, 9:03 p.m., https://twitter.com/normmacdonald/status/1116159872393867265.

awareness is a tenet of ancestral wisdom that we as a species have forgotten but need to remember and act upon in our daily lives.

Taking Back the Power

This book is a self-training in the shamanic arts. The shamanic worldview is one that has been sorely missing from our society, though there definitely has been a resurgence of interest in shamanism for the past century or so. With the blossoming of anthropology—the study of human behavior and societies, past and present—there has been a heightened curiosity and fascination with indigenous cultures, specifically their healing and spiritual practices.

In 1957, ethnomycologist R. Gordon Wasson published his article of Mazatec rituals, "Seeking the Magic Mushroom," in *Life* magazine. Ever since then, a boom of attraction toward indigenous customs has emerged and grown exponentially with each decade: for instance, such works as Michael Harner's *The Way of the Shaman* and Carlos Castenada's *The Teachings of Don Juan* became milestones in a new genre of shamanic literature; the bohemian delivery of Terence McKenna's shamanic orations bridged both academic and rave communities; tourism to other countries and receiving wisdom from indigenous communities (specifically plant medicines) has become an industry in its own right; and there are entire festivals, such as the annual Burning Man, that celebrate a shamanic way of being in the world. Even now, institutions such as Johns Hopkins Center for Psychedelic & Consciousness Research and the Multidisciplinary Association for Psychedelic Studies (MAPS) are exploring how shamanic medicine provides valid alternatives to conventional treatments for mental health and well-being. All in all, shamanism has become a viable subculture in society, an alternative to mainstream religion and healthcare.

The shamanic path is one where I personally have found great medicine: mentally, spiritually, emotionally, and even physically. Though I would not venture to call myself a shaman—a title normally given to another, not granted to oneself—I certainly have gained much insight from shamanic practices in my own life. It has helped me feel more connected to the world around me as well as helped me learn to stand on my own two feet. The shaman is a being who lives as part of an interconnected universe but also operates with great individual power.

Shamanism is a vocation of individuation: it is the human grasping ahold of fate, writing their own destiny. The shaman can be Buddhist, Shipibo, Christian, Sikh, Cherokee, Hindu, Muslim, Evenki, Jewish, Wiccan, and so on. The shaman can be all or none of these at the same time. Of every spiritual ideology, the shaman is the one who steps outside the orthodoxy of authority and rewrites the rulebook. The shaman rebels, at the same time catalyzing a new spiritual awakening.

The shaman is, and will always be, a champion of the fringe; the shaman *is* the threshold of evolutionary potential.

The wisdom and techniques of shamanism are available to all humanity. The path of the modern shaman requires looking beyond boundaries of ethnic heritage and dogma to recognize the oneness of humanity. This cross-cultural approach seeks to heal the rifts in the past and restore balance with the natural world. It doesn't matter who you are: if you live in the jungles of the Amazon or the suburbs of upstate New York, in the Australian outback or the urban sprawl of LA, shamanic knowledge is available to all as an intrinsic capability the human mind and heart are designed to facilitate. You are shamanic not because you are special and have powers like Merlin, but because you are human.

You don't have to be an indigenous tribe member living in the wilds of Africa. You don't have to have exclusive access to some ancient sage's teachings. You don't have to be born with 10 percent or more Native American blood. The access to the strange and unusual realities encompassing the shamanic worldview is open to all. Shamanism is, at its core, the egalitarian worldview bridging—as well as transcending—all religions and cultures.

Every human being has the right to have a direct relationship with the divine nature of reality. You need no priests or priestesses, rabbis, imams, or popes. You are the priestess. You are the priest. Even if you are working a nine-to-five. Even if your car keeps breaking down every other week. Even while the kids are wailing because they don't want to have a bath. Even while your boss is screaming at you about deadlines. And even while you are living in the city, breathing polluted air, and your preference is to go downtown and nosh on popcorn while checking out the latest summer blockbuster. You are, right now, the center of the universe. Being a shamanic practitioner is taking responsibility for having your own connection with the ineffable realities of the universe, no matter where you are or what conditions of life surround you.

My Spiritual Lineage

Although my genetic heritage is European, my spiritual lineage and sanctioning are rooted within the openness of universal, or cross-cultural, shamanism. Originally from Peru, one of my teachers, don Oscar Miro-Quesada, was an apprentice of the legendary *curandero* (shamanic healer) don Celso Rojas Palomino, known for his miraculous curing acts throughout the northern coastal region. Don Celso is my direct lineage ancestor of northern coastal *curanderismo*, a style of shamanic folk healing centered specifically on the northern coast of Peru. One of the most prominent townships in this region is Salas, known as "the Capital of Curanderismo" (it is even inscribed on their town sign). This tradition dates back to the pre-Incan civilization of the Chavín (1000 BCE) and is composed of folk healers who use an open-faced altar called a *mesa*, healing others through herbal techniques. These remedies can include the use of tobacco as well as the imbibing of a psychedelic plant sacrament called *huachuma*, or San Pedro, a mescaline-containing cactus that grows in the lower regions of the Andes Mountains. These plants act as psychoactive stimulants, catalysts to activate the curandero's power for divination and healing. Though these substances have a strong relationship to the mesa altar—and were integral to my own apprenticeship—one can practice shamanism without them.

When his apprenticeship with don Celso was complete, don Oscar sought tutelage from don Benito Corihuaman Vargas, a renowned *paqo* (shaman-priest) of the Quechua people in the high peaks of the Andes. Here he learned the shamanic practice of sacred reciprocity with the natural world. Being an innovator coupled with a distinct call to service, don Oscar fused these two traditions into a singular model to help transmit the ancient wisdom of these traditions to the modern world. He called this fusion the Pachakuti Mesa Tradition.

I go to great lengths to describe the Pachakuti Mesa and how to use it in my book *Shamanic Qabalah*. There are other sources, such as don

Oscar's own book, *Lessons in Courage*, as well as his apprenticeship series, which you can search for online. In this book, the primary tradition I will be focusing on will be the mesa of the northern coastal curanderismo lineage, for it was this particular training I received directly from my maestro don Daniel Baxley—himself a student of both don Oscar and another pristine curandero, don Jason Blaesing—that contributed greatly to my own personal practice.

Both my wife, Autumn, and I are sanctioned teachers and facilitators in the Pachakuti Mesa Tradition and the northern coastal curanderismo lineages. I believe that recognizing lineages is important; honoring those who have come before is vital to supporting the evolution and growth of these ancient teachings. Many of the exercises in this book were inspired by the teachings of don Daniel Baxley, as well as all the others in this family tree.

A Note on Psychedelics

A vital aspect of my lineage involves using the psychoactive huachuma medicine, and there are parts of this book that refer to its use in my stories. It is important for the reader to understand that this book in no way is promoting the use of this or any other psychoactive substance. One does not need to use these substances in order to engage the shamanic path. The exercises and spiritual ideas expressed in this book do not rely on the use of psychoactive medicines, and any stories relating to these substances are meant only to provide anecdotal examples to express an idea or message related to the material.

Also, I highly recommend readers not use these substances unless it is legal in your area and under strict guidance or tutelage. In fact, I would caution anyone who may have interest in using psychoactive substances for healing or spiritual purposes to tread carefully; these medicines are not to be used lightly and have ancient lineages attached to their usage. They are spirits themselves and should be treated respectfully. Again, proper guidance and tutelage is crucial!

A Note on Gender and Terminology

The terms "shaman" and "curandero" are used throughout this book to describe the spiritual healer role at the center of these practices. The terms "shaman" and "curandero" are often ascribed to the masculine identification of this term, whereas "shamaness" and "curandera" are the feminine identification. As a species, we are growing to a level of evolution where gender is an important area of identification but also fluid. Being a father of a transgender child, I am highly aware of the value of one's gender identity.

For the purposes of avoiding any confusion, I am using the terms "shaman" and "curandero" only for simplification of reading the material. When referring to one as a shaman or curandero, I mean any gender with which one identifies. It is important to note that anyone of any gender identification can step into the shamanic role and should feel safe in their circles to refer to any usage of the term or create their own. We can only grow as a species if we allow evolution to move forward, discarding any boundaries of the past that may have prevented us from stepping into our true power.

Self-Training

Shamanic training and practice starts with you.

At some point in time in history, the first shaman had to start from scratch. They didn't have a teacher or guide except for those invisible forces and inclinations to guide them through the treacherous waters of the unseen realms. All they had was their own dreaming. However, sometimes we need a little guidance along the way.

As a teacher (both academically and spiritually), I have always seen my role of instructor not as a figurehead of authority, but as a friend who is learning material along with you. You are the one in the driver's seat; I am in the passenger seat holding a map. You can choose to follow my suggestions, or you may very well know a better way to get there.

This book is itself a class, a training, a shamanic apprenticeship. It is a guide for anyone to pick up and have as a support in discovering your own soul path using shamanic practices as they were taught to me (and that I have adapted along the way). Completing the practices in this book will not initiate you into a shamanic tradition but will assist you in your soul growth and evolutionary potential. It will provide concepts and exercises that support your shamanic journey going forward. In appendix C, there is a list of shamanic resources where you can find teachers to help you along the way to initiation into a tradition, if that is your calling.

It is the job of every teacher to lift their students above even themselves. With each generation, we are hopefully refining these practices and working toward a harmonious evolution. The shamanic path is not a rigid doctrine or set of rules—it is an artform. Shamanism is jazz. I invite you to take what I have to offer and make it your own, make it better.

In this work, I will be incorporating teachings and information from all parts of my life: my shamanic apprenticeships, my own daily practices, my personal history, my liberal arts background, and even my nerdiness. Being shamanic, uncovering the shaman that resides in you, is not about being "traditional," "tribal," or "native." Being shamanic means being you.

In this chaotic world, there is still a way to forge your own path and connect with the ineffable mystery of life. Shamanic practice has fostered my own soul's growth, aiding me in overcoming many of my shortcomings, allowing my True Self to blossom in a world designed to diminish it.

This is a never-ending path. There is no graduate level of finality to aspire to. It is more about the process than result. Shamanism is a way of life, not a religion or a belief.

Now, let's have some fun.

CHAPTER ONE
Shamanic Training

I'm not exactly sure when I first felt the call to the shamanic path. There was no true deciding point where I woke up one day and thought, "Today I'm going to be a shaman!" I could pinpoint the circumstances that led me to begin my formal shamanic training, but that would be unreliable and misleading. There is no *one* thing, no magical formula, that can cause a person to go left instead of right, to make the decision to commit one's life to spiritual service.

Every decision I ever made, every life event, led me to where I am. I grew up in a small town in the Ozarks, off a rarely driven highway on thirty-some acres of land. I had the perfect Christian American upbringing in the eighties, with church potlucks and Saturday morning cartoons. Yes, I was an odd duck. When other kids wanted to play sports and work on cars, I was in the woods fighting imaginary trolls. When the churchgoers bowed their heads in prayer, I was looking up to see if God was hanging in the ceiling rafters of the chapel. I don't think I was particularly unique. Most anyone picking up this book probably had similar childhood notions. There were traumas and abuses, yet there were also fantastic experiences filled with magic.

There were numerous times when the mysterious tendencies of the supernatural nudged my quaint little world. In fact, one of my earliest memories of life centers on a witchlike figure watching me through the window, a figure no one else in my family could see, who has followed me through the years. Other occurrences have manifested over time, countless instances of ghostly specters, UFOs, and unnatural manifestations that sound more like an episode of *Supernatural* or *Buffy the Vampire Slayer* than real life. These things have always just been a part of life. I never had a moment of "waking up" to these realties; they were merely apparent. However, I was consistently interested in navigating these realms and helping others do the same. When I was young, I considered such career paths as Christian ministry, where I could perform such a role, but the restrictions of organized religion would always hinder my ability to have my own experience and relationship with the "other side." As I grew up with a vast interest in Native American lore and practices, it only became natural that my path would lead in the direction of more indigenous, archaic forms of spiritual interaction.

Finding a Definition

When most people think of a shaman, they may conjure an image of an elderly indigenous woman or man, cracked skin, maybe with some feathers in their hair, beating a drum out in the bush. Others may think of some spell-throwing video-game wizard. A folk healer, perhaps. A witch doctor. A druid. Or maybe even just your buddy Johnny tripping on mushrooms in his basement.

All of these may be true and not true at the same time.

A shaman is many things. First, a shaman is a psychonaut, a person who can direct their ordinary consciousness into and navigate altered states of consciousness. Second, a shaman is a sage and mystic, one who can establish a rapport with the invisible realities of the natural world. A shaman is also a magician, adept at transmuting the forces of the universe. And finally, but most certainly not least, a shaman is a healer.

There are many definitions that exist for the word "shaman," but let's first look at some historical understanding of the role and how we might gain some context for your shamanic walk.

Shamans have existed since the beginning of human history. According to most historians, archeologists, and anthropologists, the shamanic worldview was the primary spiritual/religious mindset of our hunter-gatherer ancestors. The Paleolithic Era is often referred to as "prehistory," a time in which civilization had not yet concreted itself as a technological pow-erhouse. We were still wandering around in loincloths and just learning to use rocks to chisel our way to the predatory half of the food chain. We developed our first notions of toolmaking: the ability to manipulate our environment to serve our own needs. It was during this time that we lived in small bands, traveling from place to place depending upon climate con-ditions and battling other two- and four-legged creatures for territory.

This was the period of our history—anthropologists theorize—when humans began to look outside themselves and toward something *other*, a supernatural cause of events or higher power. These earliest inclinations of seeking transcendent understanding of the world were entirely shamanic.

From these first predilections, all spirituality grew. We started as hom-inids scrounging through the dirt, making fire to keep warm, and watch-ing the stars at night. This was our cosmology. Before the first creeds of religion were constructed, this was the foundation of our soul's awaken-ing. Harmony, not dominance, was sought with the world around us. I am not saying there was no such thing as war or violence. There is also plenty of evidence to show how many cultures resisted the natural, rather than embracing it. However, a plethora of archaeological evidence suggests that balance with nature was an inherent value of the early human over-all. Eventually, our new way of seeking understanding brought an aware-ness that made us feel vulnerable. Something about the raw, elemental powers of nature scared us.

What happened? Maybe we took tribalism too far. Maybe some great cataclysm drove us to the brink of fear and panic, catapulting our need for control. Regardless, instead of relationship, we at some point sought dominance. Agriculture was invented. Resources were hoarded to pre-pare for the next turn in Earth's ever-shifting climate. Leaders rose to the top of societal hierarchies to dictate the labor of the masses. Lines were drawn in the sand. Thus, civilization was born.

It is the early civilizations—Mesopotamia, the Indus Valley, ancient Egypt, and so on—where we see religion become dogmatized, at one with the state, existing only to support the laws of the aristocracy. At one time, it seemed spirituality was but an individual endeavor with a collective cultural understanding. With the establishment of the city-states, spirituality was no longer for the individual but for the temples, exclusive to a priest class infused with the political bureaucracy. There was no more access to spirit by the people, for the people. Suddenly, one had to talk to the gods through a municipally designated mediator.

If you take a look around, we haven't changed much in the last ten thousand years or so. True, technology has certainly advanced, but our spiritual paradigms are still as entrenched as ever. Watching the news, it is easy to examine the religious divisions across the world and within our own country, even within denominations of the same spiritual path.

Yet again, I will repeat, every single religious institution came from, at its root, the idea of some person having a direct revelation of the gods (or God). That person then communicated their experience with the Divine and garnered a following, and that was all she wrote. That person was, in essence, a shaman. Whether it be Jesus, Gautama Buddha, Joan of Arc, Muhammad, Elijah, Paramahansa Yogananda, or whoever. Any spiritual doctrine you have ever read or received teachings on was forged by some normal, ordinary human who others claimed was extraordinary. It was a person who was flesh and blood and—via some sort of shamanic endeavor—exhibited qualities that seem supernatural to the mundane.

In my experience, these qualities are not "supernatural" at all. They are shamanic qualities: the capacity of direct spiritual experience. Every conscious being in the universe has the potential to exhibit these qualities. Therefore, it is the human being's divine right to enjoy and express their inner shamanic nature.

There are many people, I am sure, who claim to be (and very well may be) legitimate shamanic practitioners who will label me a charlatan, who will say I am making an irresponsible proclamation. It is often stated that to give oneself the title of shaman is indeed hubris, after all. Even so, there are those out there who will not even use the word "shaman." Some say it is a title that should only be bestowed, rather than taken or adopted. Others say using the term is a form of cultural appropriation. But is it really?

Being the linguistic nerd that I am, I always like to investigate the history of a word that I am going to use frequently so as to avoid any inappropriate use. I would rather know the actual history than submit to people's whims and opinions on an issue. Let's dig into this word "shaman" and find out what it really means.

The word "shaman" originally comes from the indigenous peoples of Siberia called the Tungus (also Evenki). Its original expression—*šamán*—was first noted in the fifteenth-century journals of a Russian Orthodox priest named Avvakum Petrov while exiled in the Siberian tundra. The term was written to describe the witch doctor–like priests he observed in Siberian societies. Dutch statesman and cartographer Nicolaes Witsen (responsible for one of the first known maps of Siberia) also used the term in a book of his travels, as well as introducing one of the first images of a Siberian shaman to the Western world.

The word "shaman" grew in prominence in reference to this style of priestly healer within tribal communities. Scholars agree it is probably not the correct term that the Siberian peoples would have used themselves (such as *kam, tadibei, oyun, bö, enenalan*, among others). Why this word was chosen by Avvakum and adopted by other Westerners has been up for debate. Some say there are Arabic and even Indian influences for the etymology, though prominent shamanic anthropologist Mircea Eliade concludes that the word likely stemmed from the term *samāne*, a Buddhist monk. Eliade and other scholars have mapped many strong correlations of the symbols and practices between Buddhism and Siberian spiritualist practices, which is understandable due to the geographical proximity of the two cultures: "hence we could regard Tungus shamanism, in its present form, as strongly influenced by Lamaism."[3] Regardless of the connection, it is apparent the word most likely was used either incorrectly or out of context; then it grew in popularity throughout the formative years of anthropology. Over time, "shaman" became the common term to identify a priest, medium, medicine person, or witch doctor within any sort of tribal community.

---

3 Mircea Eliade, *Shamanism: Archaic Techniques of Ecstasy*, trans. Willard R. Trask (London: Penguin Books, 1989), 499.

This is the way all languages evolve. Cultures have intermingled since the dawn of time, and words are exchanged, adopted, modified, and changed to be expressed in other languages. For instance, the words "condor" and "puma" are not English words but come from the Quechua language of the indigenous peoples of Peru. "Kindergarten" is a German word. "Karaoke" is Japanese. You get the idea. English speakers are not the only ones who do this with other languages. This is the nature of linguistics: the family tree of language is like a spiderweb weaving in and out of cultures in an ocean of adaptivity. Language is not set in stone; it is fluid. Watch a movie from fifty years ago and observe how much average speech behaviors have changed. Note how many words we use nowadays that would seem completely foreign to the average citizen from half a century ago.

I have no issue with using the word "shaman." If people ask, I refer to myself as a "shamanic practitioner" or a "shamanist," implying that I am a student of the shamanic arts. Nevertheless, the word "shaman" is now used the world over. It is a cross-cultural designation to pinpoint a specific type of spiritual practice. As I stated before, there is no institution that can box in the shamanic paradigm. In fact, it is the negation of institution.

What exactly is a shaman? Quoted earlier, Mircea Eliade wrote one of the most comprehensive anthropological studies of shamanic practices, called *Shamanism: Archaic Techniques of Ecstasy*, with the title itself providing a general definition. One of my favorite definitions is more specific, coming from psychiatrist and anthropologist Dr. Roger Walsh from the University of California. He writes, "Shamanism can be defined as a family of traditions whose practitioners focus on voluntarily entering altered states of consciousness in which they experience themselves or their spirit(s) interacting with other entities, often by traveling to other realms, in order to serve their community."[4] I have pared this definition into two parts in order to pinpoint the core concepts of shamanic practice:

Communion: "interacting with other entities"
Service: "in order to serve their community"

---

4 Roger Walsh, *The World of Shamanism: New Views of an Ancient Tradition* (Woodbury, MN: Llewellyn Publications, 2007), 15–16.

Communion consists of having a relationship between yourself and the universe, the universe being the powers and beings that exist in nature, the spirit world, God, or whatever phenomena with which you are interacting. Through this, the shaman normally engages in what are called "altered states of consciousness." An altered state can be any state of consciousness that allows you to engage with reality in a new way beyond your normal state of awareness; this can be accomplished through psychedelic states via plant sacraments, meditation, drumming, and more. There are numerous ways to do this that are perfectly safe, which we will explore later.

Service consists of retrieving information from your communion with the universe and using that information on behalf of yourself or others. This service can come in the form of supporting another person with ancient healing practices, bettering the community's way of life by volunteering for a nonprofit, creating art, and more. There is no limit to the way communion or service can be implemented.

When service is executed successfully, in the shamanic path, we call this medicine.

Training

How does one become trained in the shamanic arts? Should you book a plane ticket to Peru or Mongolia? Should you spend thousands of dollars traveling the world in search of the greatest and wisest of wizards?

Within and without shamanic history since the dawn of civilization, there have been those whose sole purpose has been to shepherd humanity into a greater understanding of our place in the universe. The seeds of these practices can be found in our indigenous roots, tribal rites of passage inaugurating children into adulthood. Over time, these practices evolved into establishments. From the mystery schools of Egypt to the Academy of Plato, from the Hermetic tradition to the Rosicrucians, our global history is populated with institutions that fulfilled this esoteric function. Even up to the twentieth century, we have had such groups as the Theosophical Society and the Golden Dawn—often taking the guise of fraternal or "secret" societies—that have offered an avenue of spiritual initiation. To this day, there are those who still keep their indigenous traditions alive, living in huts in the Amazon or adobe dwellings in the American Southwest, teaching the shamanic ways of their lineage to those willing to step up.

There is no right or wrong way to be trained in the shamanic arts. Whether you are actively involved in a formal training or merely have this book in your hand, all these traditions of initiates support you. In fact, some say there is an even higher order of spiritually advanced beings that secretly support all forms of initiation, whether you are a solitary practitioner or part of a group. Known by many names, such as the Ascended Masters, the Great White Brotherhood, the Secret Chiefs, or the Order of the Red Hand, these beings transcend all formalities of tradition and strive to support all forms of spiritual evolution within the individual. Nobody knows truly who these beings are—humans who evolved into a higher plane of existence, aliens, a different race of human entirely, spiritual guides—but most every system of initiation has a reference to their existence and role in the world.

With this centuries-long heritage of mastery supporting us, it begs the question: What is it about shamanic practice that attracts us? Indeed, what does it *do*?

Shamanic training and practice is a method of achieving a new understanding of ourselves and the world around us. It is a process by which we find a sense of purpose in our lives. In many of the indigenous communities around the world, this new understanding often takes place as a singular rite of passage from childhood to adulthood, where the individual discovers and then assumes their role within the larger community. This can take the form of elaborate ceremonies that involve vision quests into the wild, mutilation practices, and even simulations of death itself.

Even so, shamanic practice can represent a fundamental transformation in the existential condition of the trainee. Traditionally, this transformation can sometimes be an event during which the past self of the person becomes a memory, a shadow. The person emerges into the world anew, an initiate. Who they were no longer rules the desires and whims of the new self. It is an individual and spiritual transformation, a rebirth. At the same time, their social makeup has changed as well.

As observed by Allegheny College professor of religious studies Carl Olson, "There is also a change in social status for the initiate. ... The initiate is incorporated into a new social reality. He has passed from his former profane state of ignorance, inequality and irresponsibility into a sacred social position of enlightenment, equality and responsibility."[5]

The key word here is "responsibility." In our modern world, so few seem to understand the personal responsibility we have not only to ourselves, but to the wider community. The new self truly understands—not just conceptually—what their role is as a human in the world. The new self (in our case, the shamanic practitioner) embodies that role.

Shamanic training can be a singular event, a ceremonial rite of passage. At the same time, one who has gone through the ordeal of shamanic training understands that shamanic practice never ends. In fact, every moment of life is a lesson in shamanic training. The shaman understands that life itself is the teacher, no matter where you are in the world: if you are a warehouse worker in the Bronx, if you're the CEO of a tech company in Silicon Valley, if you're on welfare in a trailer in the Midwest, *you* are the center of the universe, and that universe is delivering lessons to you every single moment of every day. Shamanic training and practice centers on opening your eyes to that moment, receiving it for the wisdom, for the medicine, that it truly is.

Practicum 1: Journaling

There is no other time or place to begin, to initiate yourself, than right now. Before getting started with anything else, get yourself a journal.

It has been well proven that journaling is one of the most effective ways to process and retain information, and that will be very important in the shamanic work to come. But, before your brain goes there, do not journal on an electronic device. Plenty of studies from credible institutions have concluded time and time again that note-taking by hand, rather than typing, is by far the most successful approach to

---

5 Carl Olson, "The Existential, Social, and Cosmic Significance of the Upanayana Rite," *Numen* 24, no. 2 (1977), 155.

understanding an idea.[6] Although shamanism is an art form, it does require practical results. Because of this, paying attention to conclusive evidence of science, rather than shunning it over our own personal inclinations, is highly advised. Scientific inquiry and mysticism can work hand in hand, if we allow.

Here are just some of the many benefits of journaling, to support our work on the shamanic path:

Retention: As stated earlier, journaling boosts memory and comprehension skills. The mind of a shamanic practitioner must be sharp, and the practitioner must be able to use their brain productively.

Review: You will have many experiences exploring the shamanic arts; it will often be required to review earlier experiences. The experience of the supernatural often comes in parts and pieces; rarely will you have an experience with 100 percent clarity. The ability to review past experiences will help you put the puzzle pieces together over time.

Organization: However you would like to organize your journal is up to you. Regardless of how you do it, it is more likely to assist you in organizing your own thoughts, ideas, and emotions. It is easy in this modern world to let your thoughts and emotions get jumbled up. When this happens, we too often put ideas to the side rather than face the chaotic storm in our minds. Journaling takes that chaos and organizes it, puts it in some sort of order so your brain can better assimilate the information.

---

6 Hetty Roessingh, "The Benefits of Note-Taking by Hand," BBC, September 10, 2020. https://www.bbc.com/worklife/article/20200910-the-benefits-of-note-taking-by-hand; Pam A. Mueller and Daniel M. Oppenheimer, "The Pen Is Mightier Than the Keyboard: Advantages of Longhand over Laptop Note Taking," *Psychological Science* 25, no. 6 (2014):1159–68, https://linguistics.ucla.edu/people/hayes/Teaching/papers/MuellerAndOppenheimer2014On TakingNotesByHand.pdf.

Strengthening Your Self-Discipline: I can't tell you how many people I have counseled who felt so spiritually lost, but when inquiring into their practice, I find out they have absolutely no practice to begin with. How can one have a spiritual connection to reality if one doesn't *make* it happen? Journaling, ideally, should be done daily. If that doesn't happen, as often as you can will be sufficient. This will give you an opportunity to set up time for yourself on a regular basis to do the shamanic work ahead. Also, it makes for a good incentive to push yourself, an encouragement to devise a routine for yourself.

Sparking Creativity: One of the key aspects of a vital shamanic life is learning to flow with one's own creativity. "I'm not a creative person." You just said that in your brain, didn't you? Or you have at least met others who have said such things. Every human being has some form of inherent creativity inside of them because we are all a part of creation itself. It is our birthright, in our very DNA, to be creators. Our very existence is fueled by reproduction, by creation. Creativity doesn't have to look the way you think it does. Every person has their own creative spark. Journaling helps ignite that individual fire within each of us.

Better Knowing Yourself: This is the end result of what is known as the Great Work of all mystical and magical practices, to know oneself. To get to know the universe, you must know yourself first. In knowing yourself, you will better understand the world around you and better understand your relationships with others as well as your relationship with the transpersonal states of consciousness that a shamanic practitioner must be adept at.

Go get a journal. You can find many unique journals in your local metaphysical shop or craft store. You can also just use a composition notebook or notepad. If you are into making things, there are many suggestions online for building your own journal. Have fun with it. Use different colors and types of writing materials. Maybe you could even incorporate sticky notes or collage. Your journal can be anything, as long as you have an easily accessible way to document your experiences.

Ideally, after years of being a shamanic badass, you will have a whole library of journals chronicling your exploits. You may start looking like the crazy madman with piles of maniacal doodles around you, but that's okay. As the Cheshire Cat says in *Alice in Wonderland*: "We're all mad here!"

Practicum 2: Mapping the Monomyth

Once you have your journal, consider where you are currently in your life. Not just physically in this moment, but as a whole. Let's try to understand your current position in the greater context of your shamanic training.

In his book *The Hero with a Thousand Faces*, the famous comparative mythologist Joseph Campbell calls out a motif revealed in all myths and stories from cultures around the world, dubbed the monomyth.[7] The monomyth (commonly called the "hero's journey") is the idea that all spiritualities and mythologies have common themes and symbols that relate to the human experience. Campbell spent his academic career finding a comparative framework for this monomyth, a map of sorts tracking how the characters of these myths go through their own trials and tribulations, only to be reborn into something new.

There are many variations of this monomyth—often presented in the form of a hero on a quest, as in many myths—but I have broken it down into an easy-to-read circular representation as depicted here in this graphic:

---

7 Joseph Campbell, *The Hero with a Thousand Faces* (Princeton, NJ: Princeton University Press, 1973), 3.

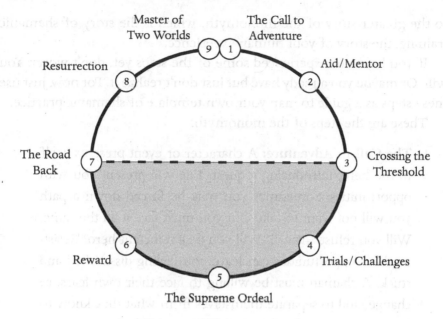

Figure 1. The monomyth

My version of the monomyth, or the hero's journey, is divided into nine steps. These steps are not just a representation of common themes in myths and folktales around the planet, but—for our purposes—they symbolize the various milestones one will encounter in shamanic practice. As we go through these, bring to mind a common story in your life that you can relate to. Think of your favorite stories, such as the Harry Potter, Lord of the Rings, or Star Wars series. In Star Wars, Luke Skywalker starts in a familiar world where he yearns for the call to adventure (bored with his farm life on Tatooine), then is aided by his mentor Obi-Wan Kenobi into a quest of the unknown, where he eventually encounters Darth Vader (the supreme ordeal) and returns a Jedi Master. This pattern, in one way or another, could be applied to many—if not most—primary characters in movies and stories in popular culture.

As you read, relate these stories to your own life's journey—specifically, you as person awakening the shaman within. Write down each step (1 through 9) and trace the description as related to the life you have lived so far. Write a good paragraph or two for each step; write more if you like. There is no wrong way to do this. Just find a way to relate to the greater story of the monomyth, which is the story of shamanic training, the story of your human experience.

If you have not experienced some of the steps yet, don't worry. You will. Or maybe you already have but just don't realize it. For now, just use these steps as a guide to map your own template of shamanic practice.

These are the steps of the monomyth:

1. **The Call to Adventure:** A character or event presents itself to the hero, introducing a quest. Life will present you with opportunities. Sometimes you may be forced down a path you will not want to take, but you must face it all the same. Will you refuse the call? Will you be a reluctant hero? Resisting life's opportunities can leave you feeling dissatisfied and stuck. A shaman must be willing to face their own fears, to change, and to separate themselves from what they know to be "normal."

2. **Aid/Mentor:** An elder, or another form of supernatural aid, will come to present the hero with some wisdom or tool to succeed. This tool could be a weapon or talisman that will assist the hero in their success. Accepting wisdom, training, and support from others will increase your chances of success. Relying on the assistance of others will help during future trials and tribulations. Sometimes having faith in those around us will be crucial to overcoming future obstacles.

3. **Crossing the Threshold:** The hero exits the known world, leaving it behind, and enters the vast unknown (hence the dividing line cut horizontally through the circle diagram). The threshold propels you fully into adventure. Like leaping off a cliff, there is no turning back once the leap is taken. Whenever you try something new, there is always fear. If you give in to the fear, you will fail at your endeavor. In order to overcome these fears and proceed in your shamanic training, you must take that leap of faith from the known.

4. **Trials/Challenges:** The hero faces a variety of challenges to prepare for the supreme ordeal, the final battle with the dragon, as it were. Trials along the way will test your mettle and therefore increase your stamina. Overcoming these challenges will make you stronger and better prepared to face the future.

5. **The Supreme Ordeal:** The hero fights the Big Bad, the dragon, in the final battle. The dragon in mythology is a symbol for the hero's adversary. Sometimes this is an external threat in the form of a person or force, but all too often it is an internal aspect of ourselves we must overcome. This internal dragon, in many shamanic traditions, is called the shadow. Defeating the shadow in your own life means conquering your own fears and weaknesses. This requires a death of the old self so that a new self can be reborn. A part of you must die. This is representative of many myths throughout the world where the hero is swallowed in the belly of the whale. This is the deepest, darkest place of the unknown, and it often seems like there is no hope, no way out. Yet, through death of the old self (as we have covered), the shaman will endure and rise anew.

6. **Reward:** Also known as "seizing the sword," the hero receives a reward for their hard work. In many tales, the hero defeats the dragon to retrieve the hidden treasures stored in the dragon's cave. Alchemy is the ancient art of transmutation, of turning lead into gold. In overcoming your own shadow, what gold did you uncover in your process of transmutation? What aspect of your life situation can be turned into a gift for the world at large?

7. **The Road Back:** The hero prepares for the journey home. This begins the path of reintegration back into the known world. Life continues after we face our deepest struggles.

This is the time to decompress and take stock of your new strengths, moving back into the world of familiarity with a new level of confidence that never existed before.

8. **Resurrection:** The hero returns home, though not as the person they were before. As a new person, the shaman is unrecognizable to the community, as they should be. This would be the time for you to use the rewards from your ordeal to change the world for the better.

9. **Master of Two Worlds:** Having returned and using their new strengths to restore the world, the hero becomes a master in their own right. One can become a mentor to others, understanding this journey is just a cycle: there is no beginning or end. The process starts again, only to be repeated in infinity forever. The shaman fully knows and embodies that the known and unknown worlds are as one. There is no actual dividing line.

Notice that the depiction of the monomyth is a circle in figure 1, not a series of steps ascending to a peak or plateau. Step 9, the master of two worlds, leads right back into step 1, the call to adventure. This is true training in the shamanic path. There is no final mode of ascension or achievement. In shamanic training and practice, everything runs in circles and cycles, not linear pathways. You may think you have found some high level of success as a shamanic practitioner, then find yourself right back at square one like a beginner. That's the way it goes in the world of soul and spirit. To better reduce your own hubris, which can lead to confusion and suffering, it's best to always approach every moment as a beginner, no matter the circumstance.

As you can see, this monomyth exemplifies the path of shamanic practice. It's not easy. It does require work and possibly some hardship. As Joseph Campbell himself states in *The Hero with a Thousand Faces*, "The agony of breaking through personal limitations is the agony of spiritual growth." He continues, "The font of life is the core of the individual, and within himself he will find it—if he can tear the coverings away."[8] Take time to sit with this information and process it; feel free to rewrite the steps or add to them multiple times. There is no reason to rush through to the next steps of shamanic training. In fact, pacing yourself through these processes will be more beneficial in the end.

Practicum 3: Engaging the Dreamtime

In the next chapter, we will begin uncovering concepts regarding the "other side," the invisible realms of the spirit world or astral realms in which the shaman travels. There is no better time than now to begin engaging with these realms by becoming more aware and intimately familiar with your dreaming.

Shamans and mystics around the world focus much of their attention on their dreaming or the dreamtime. For shamanic adepts, the dreamtime is so important that it is normally attributed to being the *actual* reality of existence, rather than the mundane reality of the waking world. Noted especially by the Aboriginal peoples of Australia, the dreamtime is the cultural ethos of the people, of creation itself. As described by mythographer Robert Lawlor, "The Dreamtime stories extended a universal and psychic consciousness not only to every living creature but also to the earth and the primary elements, forces, and principles. Each component of creation acts out of dreams, desires, attractions, and repulsions, just as we humans do. Therefore, the entrance into the larger world of space, time, and universal energies and fields was the same as the entrance into the inner world of consciousness and dreaming."[9]

Therefore, the access point to the invisible realms of soul, or the spirit world, is through the gateway of dream. Every living creature that dreams is a ready-made shaman. Therefore, being human, you already possess the natural know-how to travel into the unseen dimensions of consciousness. You dream every night, even if you don't remember it, and you do it without thinking. Shamans and psychonauts just take that subconscious skill set and make it a conscious effort. They willingly

---

8 Campbell, *The Hero with a Thousand Faces*, 190, 191.

9 Robert Lawlor, *Voices of the First Day: Awakening in the Aboriginal Dreamtime* (Rochester, VT: Inner Traditions, 1991), 17.

enter altered states of consciousness, engaging the dreamstate, in order to explore and commune with the invisible realms.

Psychoanalyst Carl Jung saw the dreamtime as a direct insight into the subconscious mind, as noted in many of his works, including *Man and His Symbols* as well as *Memories, Dreams, Reflections*. These murky depths of the psyche are where the symbolism of archetypal imagery is uncovered. Over time, with focused intention, one can learn to manipulate this imagery. Called lucid dreaming, this is a commonly accepted method in dream research of being able to control repressed notions in the psyche that often overpower us.

Journaling your dreams can help you process the imagery within the subconscious. If written down immediately upon awakening, the retention of the dream becomes clearer and clearer. Dream journaling regularly is akin to exercising certain muscles within the psyche: the more you do it, the better you will become at it, the more you will remember, and the more sense things will begin to make over time. When journaling a dream, it is best not to try to make sense out of it at all while writing. Just write whatever comes into your head, without limiting yourself by standards of grammar or sentence structure. This is a popular literary device called stream of consciousness. The terminology of this is a very helpful reminder that consciousness is like a stream, a body of water, and flowing with it naturally will help deliver to the page all the content in its purest form. You can organize later. The important thing is to get down the dream while it's raw.

Some people like to keep separate journals for dreaming and for their spiritual or magical work. You can certainly do this. Personally, I prefer to keep one journal for all these experiences. As you will learn over time, there is a very thin veil between the dreamtime and waking reality.

Journal your dreams regularly, but don't try to make sense of any of the symbols of imagery for now. That will come later with accumulated knowledge and experience. If you rush out to buy a dream symbol book (not that I blame fellow book lovers), try to not use it just yet. Just focus on recording the dreams as accurately as possible, and as you continue your shamanic work, you will be able to piece together concepts that will be meaningful to you alone, rather than what a dream expert says it means. You can always find symbol correspondences later.

Getting to know your dreamtime state takes a while. Patience is definitely a virtue. If you find it difficult to remember your dreams, don't fret. Set the intention. Be ready to journal every morning. Even if you have to write "Nothing so far," keep at it. Sometimes it can take weeks, months, even years for the brain to harness its recall. Not everyone is the same.

Keep at it. Eventually, with intention, you will begin to get snippets of your dreams. Even if they are just feelings or intimations, write it all down! Everything you can! The more you foster this practice, the more you will attune your brain to remembering more details of the subconscious state. It takes practice, discipline, and tenacity.

A Way of Life

Remember, shamanic training and practice is not a goal to achieve. There is no award for whoever is the most "shamanic." Shamanism is a way of life. It is the root of all spiritual paths because there is no intermediary between you and the universe. Shamanic practice engages us with most primal aspects of the world and the self. Therefore, building your relationship with dreamtime is vital; it is the root connection you have with the great mystery of life. As an initiate, be ready to step over the threshold and face new vistas of reality.

CHAPTER TWO
Shamanic Sight

Second sight. The third eye. Clairvoyance. ESP.

These terms describe an ability to see the world beyond mundane reality. You may assume that the first steps in shamanic training would be to learn how to see into the spirit world, as shamans around the world are said to do. You would assume correctly, though—as you will find throughout this book—the reality of a "spirit world" may be different from your preconceived notions.

Having shamanic sight means having the ability see through the veil and into the realm of soul, to see the truth lying behind consensus reality. Consensus reality is the agreed-upon version of the world among the people of society: the sky is blue, the ground is hard, water is wet, and so on. Consensus reality is important as it establishes common rules of understanding that allow us to function in the world. With all the divisions that already exist, can you imagine a world in which we cannot even agree on the solidity of ground?

The shaman, however, is an exception to the agreed-upon consensus. They can upturn the rules of physics and navigate the uncharted territories of reality. The shaman has no need for the common ruleset that governs the world; they are the rulebreaker, the trendsetter. In the shamanic worldview, reality is nothing but a configuration of smoke and mirrors that can be easily manipulated. Some manipulate the circumstances of reality for good; others, not so much. In fact, the shaman sees how everyone manipulates reality all the time—that the world is not so solid—they are just not aware they are doing it. The vast majority of the people are, in fact, *sleepwalking*: living while unaware of their true shamanic potential.

My moments of sleepwalking on this earth did not last too long. I have had numerous events in my life, layer by layer, shake off my preconceived notions of consensus reality. The first came when I was about eight years old. I lived in a small, conservative Christian town in the Ozarks, in a fundamentally religious family. My scope of the world was not very large, limited by age, experience, and geography. However, one day, the foundations of my reality cracked open.

I recall clearly one morning, my mother was driving my brother and me to school, and we were listening to a DJ on the car radio interviewing a man who professed to be a prophet of God. This man claimed that that very day would be the day Christ would return to Earth, swoop away all the Christians to heaven, and leave everyone else on the planet to suffer the fate of the apocalypse. I asked my mother if that was true and she shrugged her shoulders, saying, "Jesus could come at any time." To my young brain, this seemed to be a confirmation of the prophet's claim.

A fear welled up in my belly. The prophet had claimed the time of Jesus's return would be precisely 10 p.m. I had just this one day to say goodbye to my friends and loved ones. What would happen to those who weren't chosen? Surely, my older brother would not be selected for Christ's rapture, for all the times he had bullied me, but that notion saddened me. What about others in my family that weren't exactly "godly" in my eight-year-old mind? What would happen to them? What about me? If I were to be honest with my little self, there were times I had disobeyed my parents and—one time—even took a sip of my dad's beer during a Fourth of July party. Would I even be allowed in the pearly gates? Would Christ leave me behind?

These thoughts stacked in my tiny mind all day, racking my tummy with a twisting anxiety. By bedtime, my parents were more than ready to tuck my little nervous self into my throng of Star Wars blankets, as I had said my goodbyes to them more than once in a tearful display. I was restless. After all, the end of the world was going to happen at 10 p.m.

How could I be expected to sleep at a time like this? One way or the other, I was going to meet the Almighty God, King of Kings, Lord of Lords! The idea of meeting the creator of the entire universe paralyzed me with terror. I found I didn't really want to go to heaven—the concept of forever scared me out of my wits. The room spun around as I imagined how it was all going to play out, going from this world to the spirit world. How would reality crack open, and what would be the process of slipping away to the other side?

The clock reached 10 p.m. in what seemed to be an eternity of apprehensive moments of reimagining my death (and the death of all things) over and over again. I squeezed my eyes shut in anticipation of the big bang, the blaring of trumpets in skies, or however it was all going to play out. Moments passed. Nothing. I chanced to barely open one of my eyes to sneak a quick glance at my alarm clock: 10:01. Hmm. Maybe Jesus was late. Then 10:02 slipped past, 10:03, and so on. By the time I built up enough bravery to tiptoe out into the pending Armageddon, I walked in on my parents' evening routine of watching Johnny Carson in the living room. Nothing had changed. The world had kept on turning.

Nevertheless, something inside of me had changed.

I did not feel relief at the lack of an apocalypse. Why did these ideas of God and death and the world terrify me so? Why did I feel shammed, like this was all some grand, cosmic joke? It was like the curtain was being pulled back and the great wizard was just a shriveled, mousy old man, except this old man was the whole world laughing at me because I fell for it, fell for the illusion.

It was then that I realized that this thing we call "reality" was not all it was cracked up to be. The world became less stable, less black and white. Little me was intent on finding answers, lifting the veil of the mystery of God, the universe, the afterlife—all these things that are so integral to our existence, yet few people ever want to discuss.

From then on, I entered a period of insomnia that lasted decades. I could not sleep knowing that a veil of illusion exists between me and God. I wanted to tear that veil down and spent countless nights lying in bed and teaching myself to cross the threshold between the known and unknown. I was beginning to see that reality was actually fluid, malleable, a game to be played. Through will, imagination, trial, and error, I eventually was able to carve a pathway through regular, waking consciousness to be able to see and touch that other space of reality, what rock god Jim Morrison dubbed "the other side."

The Other Side

To the shamanic cultures of the world, the other side has many names, among them being the spirit world, the soul realm, the astral realm, the collective unconscious, and so on. The Australian Aboriginals called it the dreamtime, or dreaming, as noted in practicum 3 in the previous chapter. The ancient Chinese philosopher Lao Tzu refers to it as the Tao. Despite the terminology, most cultures speak of another reality either alongside or within the one we currently inhabit.

Shamans specifically speak of this other reality as the prime reality, the source of all things—in essence, the "real" reality. On the other hand, they refer to consensus reality as merely an illusion. This reality is integral to waking consciousness and indeed even influences it. How often do you wake up and spend the day disturbed by a dream? Or a random thought inspires you to make a life change? There is an extrasensory dimension available to us that we cannot access through cameras or test tubes, but only through the auspices of our own mind-stuff.

The psyche is even more vast that the outer universe. There was a reason "Know Thyself" was inscribed on the forecourt of the Temple of Apollo. Philosophers and mystics throughout the ages have reinforced this maxim, that in order to understand the outer world, you have to first know yourself fully, completely, and honestly. No holds barred. You must first understand your inner world—*inner* space, as it were—before ever engaging with the rest of reality.

This is the role of the shaman within us all. A shaman is a psychonaut, a navigator of the psyche, an explorer of soul. She/he is adept at traversing altered states of consciousness and coming back to tell the tale. Upon arrival, the shaman will have—in all hope—acquired a certain wisdom that can be disseminated back to the people (recall the resurrection phase of the monomyth in the previous chapter). This doesn't have to be great, guru-like, fortune cookie wisdom. I'm talking inspiration: art, music, dance, medicine, or anything that was acquired in that altered state to bring back and help make the world better, or at least more interesting.

Samuel Taylor Coleridge supposedly wrote his famous poem *Kubla Khan* while on opium. The late George Harrison of the Beatles was and current filmmaker David Lynch is a known practitioner of transcendental meditation. Salvador Dalí—as well as the other Surrealist painters—were primarily inspired by the imagery and seeming absurdity of dreams. Psychoanalyst Carl Jung willingly journeyed into the unconscious mind through dreamstates and meditation using mandalas. Steve Jobs, IT pioneer and cofounder of Apple Inc. has credited LSD for some of his most influential moments.

I—as a kid—pushed my consciousness into other vistas of reality. I wasn't daydreaming; I wasn't asleep. I learned to cross over into other states of consciousness where I encountered experiences that stimulated my imagination and creativity but above all curbed my anxiety about the fragile state of reality I encountered on Armageddon day. It helped me. It got me through the days, carried me through the fear. Tapping into this shamanic way of sight became a medicine that, as I have grown into a man, continues to support my mental health and well-being in a multitude of ways.

Obviously, the invisible realms contain a vast wealth of information to be explored. The greatest of ideas have come from revelation. "Eureka!" shouts the scientist after a great discovery, after bonking their head on the cabinet and watching stars and birds swirl around their crown for half an hour. The unseen landscape of the astral or soul dimension is a resource that humanity should cultivate and harvest. Why don't we spend more time suiting up to survey and analyze altered states, map their topography, and refine our enterprise? We do get snippets of discovery through metaphysical practices and philosophies, the psychoanalysis of Freud and Jung, as well as the recent medical developments, such as Rick Strassman's clinical research of N,N-dimethyltryptamine (DMT) and its effects on the mystical well-being. We have made a lot of gains, but we still have a long way to go.

Ethnobotanist and psychedelic connoisseur Terence McKenna was particularly interested in shamanic states of consciousness as a catalyst for evolution. In his compendium, *The Archaic Revival*, he stated, "We should admit that we know no more of the topology of the collective unconsciousness than any other culture. ...It is shamanic personalities, grand exploring souls, who somehow rise above or find themselves beyond any but a universal set of values; they explore the deep waters of our collective being. They show the way, and to be with them is to be near the cutting edge."[10]

McKenna's assertion is that we should take charge of forging our own topographies of the invisible dimension accessible to us all. The shamanic approach unveils the wild magic that exists in this world and within us. Let's explore some key concepts to understanding how we can see and interact with this shamanic reality.

Reality Is an Illusion

Take a look at your hand. What you see as a solid object of flesh and bone is actually a conglomeration of millions of cells and, even smaller, atoms that are in constant, buzzing movement and rotation. There is an entire microcosmic universe at play that we are unaware of in our conscious state. It wasn't until we invented microscopes (and then particle physics) that we could even detect this whole other perspective that expanded our understanding of life.

Now, go outside at night and look up to the sky. Whatever starlight you see with the naked eye is, in most cases, a few hundred years old (the closest being roughly four light-years away, whereas the furthest reaches the billions). By the time you are even observing them, some of those stars may have even gone nova and are currently dead. Yet they still appear before you as if they were alive today. This is of course due to the distance in light-years the star is from Earth—with light traveling approximately 186,000 miles per second. You are, in effect, seeing the past.

What you sense in the natural world is not necessarily how things *are*. The shamanic practitioner knows this as an inherent and fundamental

---

10 Terence McKenna, *The Archaic Revival: Speculations on Psychedelic Mushrooms, the Amazon, Virtual Reality, UFOs, Evolution, Shamanism, the Rebirth of the Goddess, and the End of History* (San Francisco: HarperCollins Publishers, 1991), 125.

truth of all being. Many spiritual traditions have supported this idea. The Vedic texts speak of *maya*, an illusion that all consciousness is susceptible to, where all things are not what they seem. There is an indication that reality is somehow a fraud or trick, a magic show in which the aim is to uncover the trick. If there was one thing my near-apocalypse experience taught me as a kid, it was that the world is indeed not what it seems at all. What I thought was a guaranteed fact of the end times turned out to not be true at all; in fact, it was a trauma that allowed me to become aware of the illusion of reality and to turn that awareness into medicine.

One of my favorite Buddhist texts is *The Great Medicine That Conquers Clinging to the Notion of Reality* by the nineteenth-century Tibetan Lama Shechen Gyaltsap Gyurme Pema Namgyal. It may be obvious from the title why I would appreciate this work so much. I only wish I had stumbled upon it earlier in my life. Shechen Rabjam, the modern-day abbot of the Shechen lineage of monasteries in Nepal and India, wrote an incredible commentary (of the same name) in the early 2000s. In it, he breaks down Shechen Gyaltsap's text in a concise definition of the Buddhist concept of *bodhichitta* (more commonly referred to as *bodhisattva*), which is the aspiration of attaining enlightenment for the sake of all sentient beings. When you hear anyone speak of the Mahayana path of Buddhism, this is the prime philosophy of that particular lineage of the Buddhist religion. Shechen Rabjam says, "Our sickness is the idea of self and other, the notion of a personal identity, and the belief in the reality of phenomena. This clinging is the cause of all suffering and the main obstacle to achieving reality. The medicine of compassion and an altruistic mind that aspires to free all beings from suffering is the cure."[11]

Of all of the years I have spent studying shamanism and aiming to pinpoint an exact definition, I believe none exactly hit the nail on the head quite like this statement from Shechen Rabjam. The shaman's job is to cure sickness, but that does not mean throwing a pill at a common cold. It means getting to the root of *all* sickness, which, according to *The Great Medicine*, is identifying with and clutching tightly to this thing

---

11 Shechen Rabjam, *The Great Medicine That Conquers Clinging to the Notion of Reality: Steps in Meditation on the Enlightened Mind* (Boston, MA: Shambhala Publications, 2007), 29.

we call "reality" and is what Shechen Rabjam purports is characterized by "phenomena."

A phenomenon is, put simply, the object of your perception. That perception is all we know, even though there could be other realities—other truths—associated within it. Take for instance the image of two people standing opposite each other, looking at a symbol painted on the ground. One person sees the symbol as the number 9, and the other swears they are looking at the number 6. Both are adamant in the truth in what they are seeing, but maybe neither are correct. Maybe that symbol is part of a larger paisley-like design of which they are not quite aware just yet. The goal of shamanism is to relinquish your identification with what you see and try on another perspective, and then discard that one and look wider, deeper, beyond what your original perceptions were capable of revealing.

How does one gain this perspective, this shamanic sight? Let's relinquish any previously held ideas of what "shamanic sight" may mean and take a trip to the minds of (specifically Western) humanity in the late nineteenth and early twentieth centuries. Not only were massive innovations blossoming in the arts, but also the sciences were evolving quickly. Mathematics was engaging in its own Renaissance, the profession booming as a viable occupation, and the works of such notable mathematicians as David Hilbert and Georg Cantor established many of the foundational theories that are used in mathematics today, such as set theory, calculus of variations, and the mathematical logic of Alfred North Whitehead. Mathematics became increasingly abstract—paving the way for quantum physics—attempting to quantify the as-yet unquantifiable.

During this time, Anglican priest Edwin Abbot was headmaster of the City of London School. In 1884, he published the fiction novella *Flatland: A Romance of Many Dimensions*, which achieved notoriety after Albert Einstein's theory of relativity gained traction in the scientific community about two decades later. The book contains some interesting ideas on the concept of other dimensions and how those dimensions may be perceived.

The main character of *Flatland* is a two-dimensional character named A. Square who is, you guessed it, a square. A. Square lives in a two-dimensional plane of existence. The story describes the nature of existence of such a dimension of reality. As a being on that flat plane, you would not have the perception of three-dimensional reality, as we do. Imagine yourself as a square living on a plane such a piece of paper. All you would be able to see are the other shapes of that flat plane, though you would not see them necessarily as a circle, triangle, or square as we do in our three-dimensional reality. Since your level of perception is on that two-dimensional plane, you would only see a series of lines.

A. Square describes to the reader how this effects perceptions, communications, and overall culture in the reality of Flatland among the various shapes of figures who live there (squares, circles, triangles, etc.). There is no concept of up or down, only left and right. There is no conception of a square or circle in the way we understand it, but a variation of a straight line that the denizens of Flatland distinguish through its lengths and various sides. It is an intriguing set up for a peculiar set of circumstances that changes A. Square's life forever.[12]

One day, A. Square is visited by a Sphere from the third dimension![13] Now, based upon what we previously learned of A. Square's world, how do you think this Sphere was perceived? Certainly, this Sphere would not have been perceived as a Sphere in the way we understand it, for if you were to move a ball through a two-dimensional plane (of which there is no up or down), then A. Square's perceptions would only have been able to detect the Sphere as a line (a flat circle) moving through Flatland. This circle would have grown in size as Sphere passed through the flat plane, then shrunk again as it passed all the way through, as depicted in my rendition of A. Square's experience in the following image:

---

12 Edwin Abbott, *Flatland: A Romance of Many Dimensions* (New York: Signet Classics, 2005), 15–16.

13 Abbott, *Flatland*, 102–12.

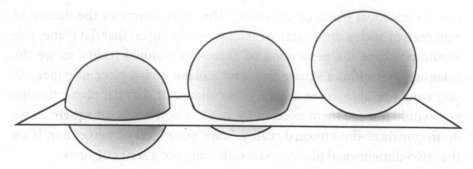

Figure 2. Flatland sphere as depicted by the author

Imagine how this phenomenon would have appeared to A. Square: he would have had no clear conception of what was happening! A Flatlander would have no foundational understanding of a third-dimensional being, but it would appear to them as an unusual occurrence within their own plane. The third dimension cannot fit within the second dimension, yet fragments of it were able to bleed through based upon the physics and consensus reality of the second dimension. Through that event, A. Square was able to build a theoretical understanding of the third dimension, but not an actual experience of it.

It is only later in the book when Sphere brings A. Square to the third dimension, Spaceland. The experience for A. Square is a disorienting, psychedelic journey that his two-dimensional psyche tries in vain to conceive: "There was a darkness; then a dizzy, sickening sensation of sight that was not like seeing; I saw a Line that was no Line; Space that was not Space: I was myself, and not myself. When I could find voice, I shrieked aloud in agony, 'Either this is madness or it is Hell.' 'It is neither,' calmly replied the voice of the Sphere, 'it is Knowledge.'"[14]

We can learn a lot from A. Square's adventures, both in how the shamanic worldview can be viewed and understood and in how perceptions of other realities can be experienced. All too often our experiences of unnatural phenomena are not what we might think them to be; what may be a vision in a dream, a UFO or ghost sighting, or a trance state may very well be just a fragment, merely a piece of a greater reality trying to make

---

14 Abbott, *Flatland*, 117.

itself known. It behooves the shaman to seek the practice of not defining or categorizing these experiences. How could A. Square have defined his first conceptions of Sphere on his flat world? Jumping to conclusions, thinking you know the answer, can lead you back to sleepwalking, where reality is fixed. Making room for the mysteries of the other dimensions to integrate within one's own consciousness will allow a greater possibility of what Sphere termed "Knowledge." One should be able to live in those spaces of madness calmly so that one may someday be that higher dimensional being shepherding others through the discord.

I fully concur with the *bodhichitta* philosophy, that every human being is capable of handling the strange realities of the universe becoming unfurled. At any moment the rug of your reality could be pulled out from underneath you: all things you believe to be true can suddenly be whisked away. It happens all the time. A divorce, being laid off, a death in the family. Major life changes can cause one to rethink the world around them. We often have to come to terms with hard truths we at one time denied or were unaware of, but sooner or later we will have to accept them. These major upheavals—called paradigm shifts—challenge us to reorient our perspective and rethink our approach to life.

The shaman accepts a paradigm shift with open arms; the shaman does not hesitantly dip their toes into the waters of change but takes a swan dive into the turbulent oceans. The shaman knows these paradigm shifts always contain lessons. As the waters of chaos rush through, the soil is kicked up, and oftentimes ugly truths rise to the surface. The shaman is above it all, calm and collected like the Buddha. There is no chaos, because the shaman knows it is all an illusion.

Practicum 4: Reality Cosplay

American author, futurist, and mystic Robert Anton Wilson was somewhat of a wily fellow. His works—the Cosmic Trigger trilogy, *Prometheus Rising*, and *Quantum Psychology* especially—aim to find a way of relinquishing our natural inclinations of clinging to reality. He helped develop and popularize the term "reality tunnel," the concept that we often experience the phenomena of reality in a limited way, as if we were looking through a tube that blocked all periphery vision. We only allow the sensory input of experiences to come into that tunnel based upon what we know; anything that does not compute with our current understanding often gets cast aside—"tunnel vision," as it were. We rarely assimilate new information. However, Wilson's goal was to help people expand their reality tunnels in order to take in more information, to expand consciousness.

Shamanic consciousness is about rising above and looking past the illusion of phenomena. One of the ways Wilson suggests doing this is an exercise I like to call "reality cosplay." This is the practice of trying to gain as much understanding of the wider reality of phenomena as possible. The more we can understand other perspectives (a 6 instead of a 9) the more likely we are able to see the wider purview of reality. As a rule, I suggest making reality cosplay a normal practice in your life that continues indefinitely. Make it a routine, like you would daily yoga or your weekly visit to the gym. You can do it anytime, anywhere, no matter what your life's schedule or situation may be like. Here are the steps:

1. Take stock of your belief system. What are your opinions and beliefs on spirituality, politics, relationships, social media, culture, economics, and so on? It is helpful to write them down, but you do not have to. Regardless, try to list and pinpoint what exactly makes up the consciousness that is you: your identity. Be fully consciousness and aware of this identity, without judgment.

2. Now, release yourself of that identity. This is not easy, but allow yourself to no longer identify with that belief system for the sake of the exercise.

3. Randomly select a new belief system that you would not ordinarily relate to or identify with. If you are a liberal, select conservatism. If you are a capitalist, select socialism. If you are Jewish, select Wicca. Research and accumulate knowledge on that belief system so you have a valid understanding of it (your own preconceived understanding doesn't count). Learn what that new belief system is from the understanding of that belief system, not your own.

4. Then, adopt that belief system. Fully. Don't just try it on for size. Accept it as your new framework of thought and belief. There is no dipping your toe in the water here. Take that swan dive into the ocean!

5. Live your life operating from that belief system for a period of time. First try it for an hour, then a day. Give it a week, maybe even a month. Try a year if you want to get really dangerous. Regardless, set up a timing that is most conducive to keeping harmony in your life (no sense in making Thanksgiving dinner even more uncomfortable).

6. Record the results in your journal.

7. Finally, go back to step one and do it all over again but with a different belief system.

The point of this exercise is not to convert you from one belief system to another. If you end up sticking with one system entirely, you have missed the point. The goal is to be able to find the validity, but also the flaws, of every system. The shaman is able to rise above all belief systems, opinions, and perspectives so that they can become accustomed to the wider reality of universal consciousness rather than the segmented pluralism that comes with human identification of phenomena.

I personally have multiple reality tunnels that I have become accustomed to using in order keep my day-to-day life going. Yet I am also always challenging those perspectives and welcome their disintegration if it serves the higher purpose of freeing myself or another of suffering. There is no point, especially in the current hostile political and social climate we find ourselves in today, of drawing a line of division between myself and any other human being. Actually, we need more harmony. The practice of reality cosplay doesn't mean I agree with another person's perspective; it just means I gain an understanding that relinquishes my desire to be right. Some of the worst suffering I have endured has been because I would not let go of a certain thought or ideal I held to be an absolute. Shamanic consciousness is fluid, oceanic. You must learn to surrender to the waves and currents rather than resisting, or you will surely drown.

Practicum 5: Breathing Basics

As noted in the observations of shamanic anthropologists Donald Joralemon and Douglas Sharon, "a true shaman is distinguished by his psychic sight, or *vista*."[15] Vista is the ability to see things as they are, to perceive the true nature of reality. Vista is a clairvoyance that is not so much about being able to "see the aura" or some other phenomenon, but more so about training the mind to see truth in all things. One way to sharpen this skill is to train the mind through some sort of meditative practice.

There are many things we do, every single day, to which we give our utmost focus. Otherwise, we wouldn't be able to drive from one place to another, to walk with one foot in front of the other. This may seem like habit, but at one point in time, it had to be learned, and you needed focused intention in order to accomplish that feat. Meditation will help you train your mind for exploring the unseen realms as a shamanic practitioner.

The most important aspect to a meditative practice is awareness. Do not worry about any kind of result coming from the practice at all; just experience it merely in order to experience it. Just as you would experience a drive through the country in order to enjoy the scenery.

A general formula for a good meditative practice is to start small and work your way up. Start anywhere from five to ten minutes if you can. If this cannot become a daily practice, that is fine. Find what works best for you. Some people meditate multiple times a day, some only once a week. As an individual, it is up to you to find the cadence that will serve your highest good.

Breathing Basics

Sit comfortably, preferably in a chair or cross-legged, with your back straight. Rest your hands gently on your knees. Don't worry about postures or motions; just sit and be present. And then, breathe.

---

15 Donald Joralemon and Douglas Sharon, *Sorcery and Shamanism: Curanderos and Clients in Northern Peru* (Salt Lake City: University of Utah Press, 1993), 29.

Breath is life. It is the engine of your body, what keeps everything pumping and going. It is also the engine of your experience of life, your consciousness. Being conscious of your breath will establish the motion that will drive your shamanic experience. But first, before having any kind of "experience," just experience breath as it is, without judging or projecting upon it. Just practice for a while breathing regularly, in a steady rhythm. Just get to know that rhythm, become familiar with it, comfortable with it. Become one with that rhythm. I recommend having quite a few sessions of just this. Knowing yourself, knowing your breath.

The most basic practice is to just focus on the way breath moves through your body. It is most efficient to breathe in through your nose and exhale out of your mouth. As you inhale, focus on the very essence of life itself entering your body, and on the exhale, imagine it moving down your spine, through your perineum, and into the earth below. This movement of the breath cycle will help cleanse out anything within you that might act as a blockage to your work ahead. It sweeps through the mind and body so that your entire being becomes a clear channel to operate with. Of course, you will naturally be exhaling through your mouth, but it is the focused intention of your imagination that counts.

Spending a chunk of time in perfect stillness, with only your focus on this breath function, will begin honing your vista skills. If other thoughts come into your mind space, gently push them aside and direct your intention back to this breath.

Try this for a few weeks and observe how it may or may not affect your daily actions and thoughts. Record your observations in your journal. This is the one practice you can do most anywhere—at work on a break, at a park—that will benefit you the most. You do not even need to have your eyes closed. This is just about observing your breath without judgment, without trying to control it. Allow the breathing to drive you, rather than you driving the breath. When it all comes down to it, the basics are the most essential ingredients to honing your shamanic prowess.

Practicum 6: Thought Tracking

After you have established a regular practice with breathing, I encourage you to try another practice to begin sharpening your vista. Learning to observe and track your thought forms is important so that when the time of receiving visions comes, you can distinguish a true vision from your own internal thoughts. All too often practitioners let their own thought forms get in the way of divinatory revelation. Like any skill set, this takes practice to refine.

One of my favorite methods for this type of thought refinement was developed by Czech Hermeticist Franz Bardon. Bardon was said to be so powerful a mystic that the Nazis tried to recruit him into their occult army. When Bardon refused, he was thrown into a concentration camp to rot away until the Soviets came to save the day. Bardon's methods are very sophisticated and require a lot of time and dedication to master. However, in his book *Initiation to Hermetics*, Bardon's exercise for the student is called "Thought Control."[16] My own preference is to refer to it as "thought tracking," but regardless, the method is still the same.

Thought Tracking

In this practice you will definitely not be able to drive or be doing anything else. You will need to block off a dedicated amount of quiet time—at least five minutes or more—in which you will not be disturbed. Seat yourself comfortably and get into a steady, relaxed breathing rhythm. Close your eyes.

Do not try to empty your thoughts (which is nigh impossible unless you are a Zen master). Merely allow your train of thought to run its course for five full minutes and observe without judgment. Do not try to control the thoughts that come in. Just track objectively and try to remember each one. At the end of the five minutes, try to record each thought in your journal in sequential order. My suggestion is to do this every day for ten days. Start at five minutes and try to build on a minute for each day. As Bardon writes, "The attentive student will notice how, in

---

16 Franz Bardon, *Initiation into Hermetics*, trans. Gerhard Hanswille and Franca Gallo (Salt Lake City, UT: Merkur Publishing, 2016), 67.

the beginning, he is besieged by thoughts, and how quickly they pass by him, so that it will be difficult for him to remember all of them. However, from one exercise to the next he will notice that these thoughts will appear less chaotically, and will abate little by little until only a few thoughts emerge in the consciousness as if from afar."[17]

I especially practice this exercise when I find my mind becomes frazzled and in a chaotic state due to stress. It is recommended to practice this daily, or at least several days in a row during stressful times. By day five, I find that I come to grips with the thought forms, and by day ten, I feel completely in tune to the barrage of information coming into my mind. The goal is not to control your thoughts (as Bardon's initial moniker for the exercise implies) but to merely get to know them. It is surprising how unfamiliar with ourselves we really are, how out of tune with the way our own brain works. Thought tracking is an excellent way to come to terms with the way information flows into your brain, to become familiar with how you understand the data coming in from the outside world going into the interior. When this familiarity becomes intimate, a level of self-control does settle within your mind. You understand the difference between a randomly generated thought form and something else entirely: a message from the soul realm.

A New Perspective

Shamanic sight, vista, is anchored in the idea of entering and re-entering the shamanic process (or life in general) with new eyes. The longer I am in this work the more I can say that when I enter every day, every ceremony, with the mind of a child—rather than an adept—my experience is a thousand times more meaningful. Try on a new way of life, a new perspective, whenever you can; it doesn't mean you have to be married to it. Breathe and track who you are. Don't obsess over your thoughts; just get to know who you really are. Life is a multifaceted diamond and the shamanic initiate is one who is ready to lift the veil of illusion and experience all aspects of existence.

---

17 Bardon, *Initiation into Hermetics*, 67.

CHAPTER THREE
Shamanic Body

I think it was the night I was lying in the hospital bed that I decided to seek extra help.

A massive boil the size of a cantaloupe was eating away the tissue in my leg. In fact, I was covered in them. It was just a year previous when my doctor had informed me that I was a chronic carrier of methicillin-resistant *Staphylococcus aureus* (MRSA). This condition gave me an unusually high susceptibility to staph infections that would surface as painful boils; it wasn't uncommon for me to be covered in blood-soaked bandages that had to be changed multiple times per day. They weren't just painful. My immune system was constantly in overdrive fighting off the infections. My body became weak and vulnerable; the slightest cold bug would knock me out for a week. A flu would be even worse.

I was living on a regular regimen of antibiotics and painkillers. I couldn't even exercise because the activity would exacerbate the host of other conditions that I developed due to my body's heightened sensitivity, including an unidentifiable type of eczema my doctor had no idea how to treat: various areas of my skin would inflame and basically burn away, the flesh eating itself in an agonizing process. Then, like on a leper, that patch of skin would rot away. It would eventually grow back, only to do the same thing again.

The physical suffering inflamed my emotional and mental state. Not only was I a single father dealing with a toxic and heartbreaking custody battle, but I was diagnosed with post-traumatic stress disorder (PTSD) due to an episode when I was physically and viciously attacked. These factors—according to my doctor—likely led to the vulnerability in my immune system. At the same time, the condition prevented me from being present for my son and other relationships. I was often irritable and impatient, my mind consistently overstimulated with all I had to juggle in order survive. It was a classic case of an event (or series of events) causing emotional and mental distress, which impacts one's physical health and in turn further hinders the ability to properly operate in the world.

That night, staring at the IV pumping a constant stream of antibiotics into my arm, I felt myself drowning in a deep, dark pool of desolation: I was sick all the time, I was weak, constantly in pain. Exhaustion overcame me, and as I slipped off into unconsciousness, I told the universe to take me away for good. If I were to wake up in the morning, then—for the sake of my son—I needed to find another way out of this. As the sun rose through the hospital room blinds, the answer was clear to me: time to live, find a way to keep going. It wasn't that I just needed an alternative way to approach my health. I needed to become whole: body, mind, and spirit.

The Wounded Healer

Sickness. Dismemberment. Death.

These are some of the more common characteristics of shamanic initiation in indigenous cultures.[18] For example, it is not uncommon for a shaman of the Yakut people in northeastern Russia to have been chopped into pieces as an initiation before being brought back to life as a newly reborn healer of the people (while we in the modern world may see this as a metaphorical experience, to the Yakut it is as real as any other life experience). A shaman of the Nganasans would be sick—sometimes with smallpox—for three days until almost dead. The Araucanians of Chile tell of their shamans (called *machis*) receiving the call of initiation by suddenly falling ill and appearing near death until their re-emergence to

---

18 Mircea Eliade, *Rites and Symbols of Initiation: The Mysteries of Birth and Rebirth*, trans. Willard R. Trask (New York: Harper and Row, 1958), 13–18, 31–40.

consciousness; they journeyed to the underworld and back to gain their shamanic power. The indigenous Pomo of California would torture initiates, often burying them underground in order to later be resurrected as medicine men or women, emulating the healer spirit they call *Kuksu*.

Why all the brutality? One can imagine there would not be many volunteers for this particular vocation. Oftentimes shamanic initiation isn't something that is sought out or chosen. It is something that befalls the initiate. Mircea Eliade, one of the most prominent anthropological contributors to the study of shamanism, explains why initiation of this type is a common feature on the shamanic path: "Those among them who had been ill became shamans precisely because they had succeeded in becoming cured. ... When the shamanic vocation manifests itself as some form of illness or as an epileptic seizure, the initiation is equivalent to a cure. To obtain the gift of shamanizing presupposes precisely the solution of the psychic crisis brought on by the first symptoms of election or call."[19]

Eliade's description of initiation helps us understand that the training and practice of shamanism should be the very thing that gives the shaman the power to heal. In order to do that, the shaman must be initiated into the very type of crisis that will indeed someday be their trademark medicine. The only way they can do this is to survive the ordeal. This means the illness—the crisis—must be transmuted. The shaman must turn their situation around, to turn the crisis into an opportunity of attaining power rather than succumbing to the crisis itself.

Even though I had felt a turnaround the following morning in that hospital bed—that I would find a way through my own pain to the path of health—I still had setbacks upon my return home. The PTSD made life circumstances particularly hard. Trauma prevents one from reading one's own senses clearly. The trigger response is hypersensitive. It was very easy for me to see the slightest interaction with another individual, particularly those close to me, as an attack.

Very often this would happen to me at work, already an environment full of anxiety. My boss and coworkers were obstacles my nervous brain

---

19 Eliade, *Rites and Symbols of Initiation*, 88.

consistently had to navigate in every moment, as if they were the MRSA bacteria itself. I was afraid for my job, afraid of failure, and afraid of the anger or disappointment that those around me might express. These triggers would create emotional responses that manifested into physical reactions: a rise in blood pressure, rapid heartbeat, hot sweats, dizziness, nausea. In essence, a full-blown panic attack!

I felt at a loss. How could I turn this emotional anxiety around so that I could focus on my mental and physical health? What was the next step I would have to take?

I was referred to a woman I'll call Patty who was known in the community as an alternative healer. I didn't really know what that meant at the time and was a little taken aback that upon contacting her, she asked me to meet her in her home. Didn't this person have an office? Living in a tiny bungalow in the middle of downtown Kansas City, the old woman welcomed me in and shuffled around her plant-covered living room in baggy sweats. Pulling back her frizzy, witchy hair into a ponytail, Patty had me lie on a massage table and began waving her hands inches above my body while she described her background to me. Having worked alongside the Crow Dog family, she was intimately familiar with Native American Lakota medicine. Further, she had traveled to Tibet to apprentice in the healing practices of the Lamas. With those credentials, Patty had also been asked to participate in numerous academic studies to identify and manipulate the energetic field of the human body. What she was going to do, she explained to me, was to locate the blockages within the energetic field of my body and remove them; this would allow greater opportunity for my life to move forward in the direction I wanted it to go.

It wasn't enough, however, to just have her do some energetic work upon me. Patty clarified that true healing comes when the person in question takes the responsibility of healing into their own hands. I needed to become a healer myself, and therefore she recruited me as an apprentice to train me in the healing arts of energy medicine within the body. Two days a week, for nine months, I was hers. Even in graduate school I did not work as hard. I had numerous scientific texts about biology and physics I was ordered to study and tons of homework and research projects, including having to acquire my own clients and document my interactions through hundreds of pages of field notes.

Although I had grown up having some supernatural experiences earlier in life, I saw more miracle work in those nine months than all the previous years combined. I saw and experienced physical injuries disappear within seconds, a child who was told by doctors she would never walk again run and play sports, and even the spectral visitation of a deceased relative. Magic, I learned, is indeed real, and it all starts with the human body.

The Energy Body

A professor of physiological science at UCLA, Dr. Valerie Hunt facilitated and participated in numerous research projects and experiments studying the electromagnetic frequencies within the physical body. Her research focused not only on the electrical activity of connective tissue but also on a more subtle field of frequency that impacted the overall health of the body. Dr. Hunt was by no means the first to make these observations, but her work greatly influenced the mainstream acceptance of healing these subtle energies through interaction with another human being (i.e., energy healing).

While examining human physiology, Dr. Hunt had found that the subtle field of energy within the body is not just some abstract or spiritual phenomenon. Even though she relates this field to the mystical concept of the aura, she consistently asserts that this field of energy is indeed a material one: "Each of us carries our elaborate biosphere within our tissues and fields. ... We enter the world equipped with five senses with which we perceive the world around and within us and from which we create an ordinary, everyday reality for living. ... Our primary reference to the world is our physical body, and from these bodily sensations we create a reality in which our body is constantly present."[20]

This "biosphere" is our body's collaborative effort to construct our conscious reality using the various mechanisms available within our physiology, such as the nervous and endocrine systems. This biosphere

---

20 Valerie V. Hunt, *Infinite Mind: Science of the Vibration of Human Consciousness* (Malibu, CA: Malibu Publishing, 1996), 60.

is known by many names: the aura, the energy field, the luminous body, the morphic field, and even the mindfield. This field is the subtle interface of our physical body and our consciousness, existing through the entire physical form. In fact, this field has often been conjectured to be the location of the mind, which is not stored solely in the brain but throughout the entirety of the body. While the brain is certainly the center of the intellect, "90% of the body's serotonin is produced in the gut" and the heart contains enough neurons to produce an electromagnetic field sixty times larger in amplitude than the brain.[21] The entire body works together as mind, a holistic and integral system that cannot be divided into disparate parts with siloed functions.

It wasn't until after my work with Patty commenced that I began my apprenticeship in the shamanic practices of Peru and everything she taught me about the biosphere/mindfield came together. We will learn more about that specific shamanic apprenticeship later. For the purposes of understanding more about the energy matrix throughout the body, I will employ the wisdom of the energetic practices of the Quechua. The Quechua of Peru are descendants of the Incas who live as farmers and llama herders in the Andes Mountains. They are a highly practical people, but at the same time very spiritually advanced. Even the Dalai Lama has spoken highly of the Quechua and their *paqos*, shamanic healer-priests who understand the intricacies of a reality based upon participation and reciprocity with the natural environment.

Author Joan Parisi Wilcox, an apprentice of the paqos in Peru who wrote one of the most thorough accounts of Quechua energy practice, *Masters of the Living Energy*, writes, "As paqos, our fundamental task is to maintain at all times the ecology of our energy environment. If our energy environment is not ordered and light, then it must be cleansed."[22]

---

21 University of California, Los Angeles, "Study Shows How Serotonin and a Popular Anti-depressant Affect the Gut's Microbiota," *ScienceDaily*, September 6, 2019, www.science daily.com/releases/2019/09/190906092809.htm; Jessica I. Morales, "The Heart's Electromagnetic Field Is Your Superpower," *Psychology Today*, November 29, 2020, https://www .psychologytoday.com/us/blog/building-the-habit-hero/202011/the-hearts -electromagnetic-field-is-your-superpower.

22 Joan Parisi Wilcox, *Masters of the Living Energy: The Mystical World of the Q'ero in Peru* (Rochester, VT: Inner Traditions, 2004), 51.

Basically, all life is energy, and we engage with energy every moment of our existence. Our goal is to become compatible with our environment. The field of living energy which runs throughout our bodies is key to maintaining a healthy interaction with our environment.

The Quechua paqos call this field of energy the *poq'po* (POHK-poh). Though I did not know this term at the time of my training with Patty, I later adopted it during my apprenticeship in Peruvian shamanism. The poq'po refers to a bubble of living energy that surrounds and flows within the body, not unlike the electromagnetic energy field.

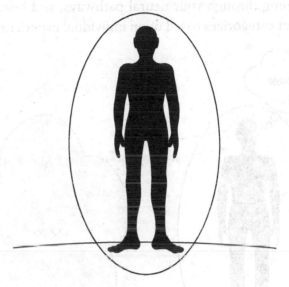

Figure 3. The poq'po

The poq'po is an information carrying system running throughout the entire body, like an internet for our thoughts, emotions, experiences, and so on. In short, it *is* our consciousness, or reality.

One of the progenitors of modern philosophy, René Descartes (the "I think, therefore I am" guy) spoke a lot about consciousness. Descartes held to the idea of a dualistic nature to reality, meaning

- consciousness resides within the realm of thought, and
- matter resides within the realm of extension (anything outside of the self).

What he means by this is that we can never really know matter in its purity. All we can know is our observation of it, which is filtered by layers of information that exist between the realm of thought and the realm of matter: tools of observation, individual experience, individual knowledge base, and so on. For instance, if you are looking at a flower, you will never truly *know* the flower you are observing in its truest form. You will know it only by how your eyes specifically receive the information of the photons bouncing off its petals, traveling through and integrating with millions of molecules in the air, then bouncing off your retinas, traveling through your neural pathways, and being interpreted by a brain that categorizes based upon individual experience.

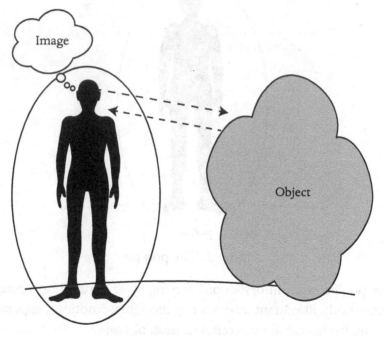

Figure 4. Image and object

It's an *idea* of the flower, but not the flower itself, you are perceiving.

This is reality. The poq'po is the interface of that information from outside of yourself. Reality, though, is different from *actuality*. If we look at the meaning of the Latin root of the word, *actualitas*, actuality is "anything that is currently happening." There is an objective world all around us; we are all experiencing similar events (air, rain, trees, traffic, conversation), but our experiences of them are often quite different, sometimes extremely so. We will never be able to fully experience this objective actuality, but we can experience bits, pieces, and interpretations of it in our personal reality.

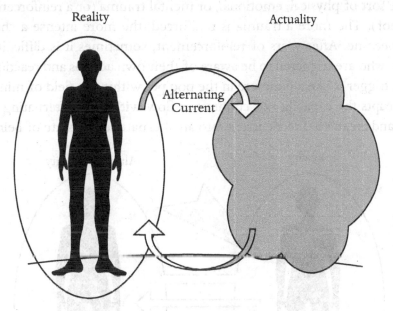

Figure 5. Actuality

Remember when I stated earlier in chapter 1, practicum 3, that the Aboriginal peoples considered the dreamtime the *actual* reality of existence—in essence, actuality? We will discuss the actuality of dreams later on. For now, our focus is on first fostering a healthy relationship with actuality, which is why it was encouraged to begin opening your awareness to the dreamtime.

What Patty showed me was that creating a continuous flow between your individual reality and this objective actuality is called creating an alternating current. It means we are participating in, not rejecting or forcing, our experience. In this state, we can understand that reality is not always what it seems, that we won't always know the full truth of any experience, and that we can participate in the game of life with good humor. This suggests a give-and-take, a reciprocal exchange with the world that is healthy, light, and freeing.

However, in terms of electromagnetism, there is also the direct current. In the human energetic field, the direct current is a nonreciprocal exchange that occurs when one's poq'po becomes triggered. A trigger is an energetic charge, an interception into the poq'po that occurs through some sort of physical, emotional, or mental trauma (or a reinforcement thereof). The more a trauma is reinforced, the more intense a charge can become. After years of reinforcement, sometimes it is difficult for those who are triggered to be aware of their own actions and reactions.

A trigger is like a puncture in the poq'po, within the field of mind. It interrupts the capability of continuous flow within the alternating current and creates a direct current into an alternate reality state of being.

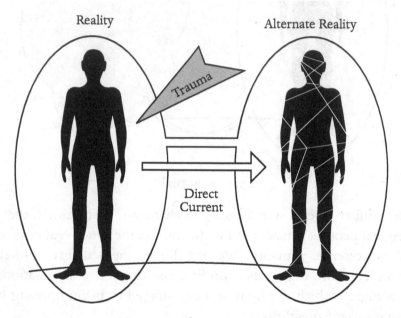

Figure 6. Alternate reality

When we are in a healthy reality state, we can perceive a potentially stressful situation or threat as an opportunity, focusing on the present moment and what it has offer us. In an alternate reality state—brought on by a trigger—one begins to live either from the past or the future. For instance, you may think, "This is how my previous partner used to treat me" or "I'm going to lose my job if I don't get this done in time." Working from an alternate reality state, you are truly operating from a supposed reality that is currently not happening in front of you; you are working within a state of consciousness that does not actually exist. Therefore, it has no basis in actuality, which is what we want to have participation with.

In my case, anytime I had a reinforcement of my negative life experience through a trigger, I was unable to be a good parent to my child or to operate healthily with friends and family. My work and creativity would be hindered, as well. In the alternate reality state, I was fractured and broken and could only see through the lens of my own suffering. Operating within that alternate reality interaction with the world around me was based upon pure illusion. Everyone was an enemy and I was perpetually a victim of circumstance. This state of mind only reinforces itself over and over, and before I knew it, I found myself in an infinite loop of despair. Body, mind, and soul—normally meant to work with each other—clashed, and there seemed to be no way back to health.

Taking the Power Back

Our goal as shamanic initiates should be to rework this alternate reality state back to a healthy participation with our environment. Getting into this work, you may think that shamanism is about hugging trees in nature and throwing down with totem animals, but all of that is just the gloss to the real work to be done: empowering yourself.

With every trigger, with every reinforcement of negative experience, you are allowing someone or something other than yourself to take away your power. Power is essential to the shamanic path. You have to hold power and yours alone. It cannot come from anyone or anywhere else. Not from me, not from this book, not from Johnny Two-Feathers or some guru you paid thousands of dollars to attend their weekend workshop experience. You and you alone are the center of your power.

Anthropologist Douglas Sharon spent years following the life of one of the most honorable and well-known curanderos in northern coastal Peruvian curanderismo, don Eduardo Calderon (also known colloquially as "El Tuno"). In his detailed accounts of don Eduardo's extraordinary life, *Wizard of the Four Winds*, Sharon explains how the "concept of power remains the pivot of shamanism" and outlines seven characteristics of power expressed through don Eduardo's philosophy and practice. These attributes of power are:

1. **Knowledge:** The accumulation of knowledge and wisdom is essential, as shamanism requires expertise in healing and ritual practices.

2. **Fate:** This denotes the idea of power coming to the shaman through a "calling" or sickness, rather than the shaman seeking it out.

3. **Individuality:** The shaman is de-cultured, their own person, unswayed by the whims and polarizations of society.

4. **Variability:** Power varies from person to person, so it is important to accept and understand one's limitations.

5. **Success:** Without power, the shaman has no ability to be successful in their endeavors.

6. **Focus:** Discipline and discernment are paramount, as distraction will diminish one's power.

7. **Balance:** It is important for the shaman to understand their power can be used equally for both good or evil, and to walk the line down the middle path between each (a subject we will cover later).[23]

Brought together, these features provide a meaningful template for what it means to have power and to exercise it accordingly. This idea of power is prevalent in other cultures as well. The Chinese call it *chi*, and the Hindus refer to it as *prana*. It is a vital life force that fuels the human energy field—the poq'po—so that the mind and body operate in harmony with the environment, rather than alternate reality. Don Eduardo dubs this force of power *magnetismo* (magnetism). Magnetismo is the curandero concept describing a force of nature channeled through both living beings and inanimate objects. As don Eduardo says, "Magnetism is the activating electrical force of the individual to unite with others.

---

23 Douglas Sharon, *Wizard of the Four Winds: A Shaman's Story* (self-pub., 2015), 66.

All have a magnetic point, a magnetic force linked with the earth, since all are elements of the earth. Thus, by forming a magnetic chain, the attraction of the individuals, the telepathic force, the intellectual effort, unites all beings along this nexus in a magnetic fashion. That is, magnetism is the thread and the telepathic force is the transmission of the elemental force along the thread."[24]

As you can see, don Eduardo's concept of an "activating electrical force" is very similar to Dr. Hunt's observations of the mindfield or poq'po. He asserts that this magnetism is prevalent in all things and that through will and effort, it can be altered or modified. The Quechua have their own term for this life force, known as *kawsay* (KAW-sai). Kawsay is that invisible force that is the essence of life itself that sustains and vitalizes the poq'po. It is the chi or prana, as it were.

Often people will refer to this force generically as "energy," but I feel that term has become too nebulous and associated with a lot of woo-woo New Age practices. Kawsay, or chi, is a very distinct force that is imperative to maintaining an unobstructed flow of movement in life. Without a continuous flow, the inevitable obstacles of life will throw you off your game and prevent you from succeeding in whatever it is you need to complete. It will block movement and curb your ability to have authentic relationships with others.

It isn't just enough that we have been given the gift of life, we must nurture and preserve it. Yoga instructor and good friend Brad Elpers—founder of Acme Human—has a creed he lives by in his own mind and body work: "stability before mobility." In order to gain power as a shamanic initiate, you must first preserve the foundation of your life force before you expand into more advanced practices and material. Otherwise, you will falter and likely crash, potentially hurting both yourself and others.

Now, let's explore some practices that will support you in interacting with actuality in a healthy way, as well as stabilizing your power.

---

24 Sharon, *Wizard of the Four Winds*, 69.

A Daily Practice

The best way of stabilizing your power is by implementing a daily practice for yourself. Shamanism may be an art, but it is also a skill set. As an artist and writer myself, I have learned that the idea of "talent" doesn't really exist. True, some people are more inclined than others toward a specific area of expertise, but you do not become an expert just by having interest in something—you have to *do* it, repeatedly! There is a lot of hard work that goes into becoming a good artist, musician, craftsman, doctor, or athlete. As the old adage says, practice makes perfect!

Now, I know what you might be thinking: A daily practice? How will I have the time? This world is not situated to give you the ample space to begin self-training in the shamanic arts, let alone any other mystical-magical practice. In my case, I have a full-time job, a wife, three kids with school and extracurricular activities, my extended family and friends, my spiritual community, and my own personal activities (writing and art) to tend to. You would be surprised how much you can juggle in one day, but if you are serious about becoming adept as a shamanic initiate, then you may need to sacrifice some things in order to prioritize. Above all, however, do not sacrifice time with your family and friends.

To begin, I suggest carving out a good half hour to forty-five minutes a day devoted to your spiritual work. You can go longer if you wish, but I believe that amount of time will give you the timing you need to exercise your shamanic prowess. You may have to give on the timing on some days, including skipping days altogether, and that is fine. There is no medal of achievement to unlock here; work at the pacing that fits you. You will need to adjust for real-world situations. Further, don't burn yourself out. Some days you will need to forgo your daily practice to just chill and watch Netflix, and that is fine too. Just remember, the results of your practice will only be as effective as the work you put into it. I would advise not making too much a habit of skipping.

Also, remember, this practice time does not include the extra work ahead in your training. Your daily practice is in addendum to the other practices in this book, unless otherwise referenced. You will find an example of a daily practice that I offer in appendix A.

Regarding cadence, my suggestion is to split your time roughly in half: about twenty-five to thirty minutes in the morning and ten to fifteen minutes in the evening. When it comes down to it, you will need to decide for yourself what is the most effective method of practice for you and how you want to implement the exercises offered in this book. Generally, it is understood that a morning practice should be about energizing you, readying you for the day ahead. An evening or night practice should center you, bringing you back to yourself, winding down from the day. See appendix A for established foundational exercises for you to begin a daily practice, which includes exercises from the previous practicums. I recommend using these practices often and ad hoc throughout the day, as they may be needed, and regularly in the morning. Often at the end of the day, our thoughts are clouded and filled with the activities of the day. Thought tracking should especially be done fresh from sleep, when your mind is clear. Breathing basics, however, I highly recommend using at the beginning of any practice or ceremony.

Let's take a look at some exercises for you to start with your daily practice.

Practicum 7: Morning Practice 1, Kawsay Activation

After you have done your breathing basics, and ideally thought tracking, you will want to begin a practice of activating your life force, or kawsay. Regarding the energy of life, we live on the greatest resource available to us: Earth. Our planet is the primal battery of life, both generating and sustaining its own existence as well as all the beings on the planet. In this sense, Earth is quite literally our mother, which is why many indigenous traditions refer to our planet as Mother Earth. In the Quechua tradition, they use the term *Pachamama* (PAH-chah-MAH-mah), literally meaning "Earth Mother."

One of the reasons we feel so drained in our daily lives is that we do not maintain a habit of consuming healthy energy. We will consume all sorts of other stuff throughout the day—social media feeds, news, greasy foods, work gossip—but none of it is sustainable. We live, walk, and sleep on the most sustainable source of life available and we rarely utilize it. As children of the earth, our umbilical cords have been cut, yet our etheric cords can always be connected if we so choose.

One of the ways in which we bring life energy, kawsay, into ourselves is through intention, will, and visualization. Now, let me make it clear that I do not adhere to the adage that just by thinking something you can make it happen. Thoughts have no power in and of themselves, it is the belief behind them that holds the power. Through your intent to draw life energy, you must summon the will to make it happen, and back it up with acute visualization of the experience so that your reality bubble, your poq'po, believes it to be true. In this sense, the greatest weapon against malevolent energy in your life is to not believe in it. Belief is everything. If you do not have belief intact, your mindfield will not truly accept something as a vital reality.

Activating Kawsay

To activate your field with kawsay, begin by closing your eyes. You can either sit or stand, though my preference is to stand for this exercise. Shut out the world around you and release any thought forms that may come in. Bring your awareness to your feet on the ground, standing with the Earth Mother, Pachamama, below you. Expand that awareness so that your attention is drawn to Pachamama's massive expanse, the giant storehouse of life that she is, ready to provide for her children if they just ask. Spend a few moments reflecting on Pachamama's amazing ability to produce life and to nurture it.

Now, allow yourself to breathe rhythmically. Remember how we created a pattern of breathing in practicum 5 in which we could follow the trail the breath is taking, like an engine to fuel your experience. Direct the flow from the inhale from below your feet, exhaling up all the way through your body and out the top of your head.

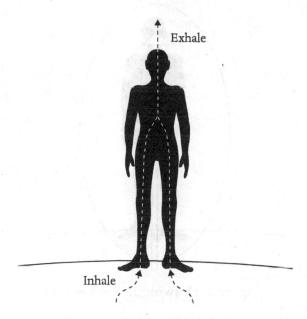

Figure 7. Kawsay breath flow

As you establish that flow after a few moments, begin visualizing the kawsay, the life energy of the planet below you. There are many ways to do this and no correct way, as long as you associate that visualization with the power of life. Kawsay is an organic energy, not etheric, not nuclear, or some other way energy may be imagined. This is essence of Pachamama, the mother of all creation on Earth. Some people imagine this energy as a shaft of light, while others will visualize a red power beneath their feet. I use the imagery of root-filled soil, a mass of organic matter, because that is what works best for me to tap into the power of kawsay.

Once that imagery is settled upon, feel it pulse beneath your feet, like a beating heart. This essence of life is ready to flow within you and fill you up completely.

Now when you inhale, visualize the kawsay being drawn up through your feet and into your body for the inbreath. When you draw it in, allow that life energy to fill you, to empower you. Feel that energy flow within and throughout your poq'po, allowing it to enliven your own energetic field.

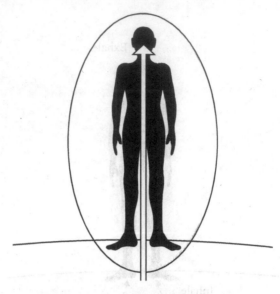

Figure 8. Drawing in the kawsay

As you exhale, push the kawsay energy out the top of your crown and let it flow out and around your poq'po, encircling you by a foot or so around your entire body. Allow your crown to be like the spout of a fountain, showering kawsay over the front of your body, back of your body, and sides. As it flows out of you, imagine the kawsay as a golden light.

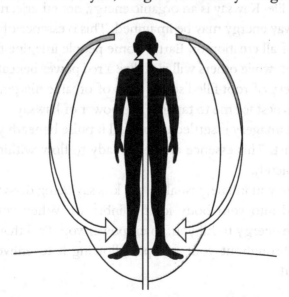

Figure 9. Kawsay encircling the poq'po

Continue this exercise for a few minutes. On each inhale, you are drawing the kawsay in from Mother Earth and into your body, and on each exhale, you are releasing that energy through your crown and allowing it to shower over your entire energetic body. With every exhale, as the golden kawsay flows down over your poq'po, envision it coating the outer skin of your poq'po with a golden layer. With each exhale, the outer layer of your energetic form should be getting thicker, stronger, and brighter. After a few moments have passed, you should have the image of a golden globe or egg surrounding you, a globe of invigorating life energy fueling you for the day as well as acting as a barrier of protection for whatever you may face ahead of you.

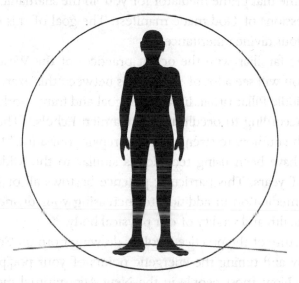

Figure 10. Barrier of protection

Sit within and bask in the radiance of this golden globe of light; this is the coalesced life force of you and the earth in harmony. I recommend practicing the kawsay activation daily for a few weeks, if you can. Make it a regular habit. You do not have to limit it to a morning routine, either. Anytime throughout the day you may feel stressed, overwhelmed, or disempowered, the kawsay activation exercise will give you that extra boost and stability you need to get through the moment.

Practicum 8: Morning Practice 2, Pillar of Light

After you have made a habit of regularly strengthening your poq'po through kawsay activation, you may begin the pillar of light exercise to give yourself that extra juice to begin tuning your mindfield to the shamanic mysteries ahead of you. Shamanism isn't just about energetic healing and revitalization; there is a mystical component to the art, as it is largely about becoming your own source of divine connection. You and you alone are the prime mediator between yourself and the Source of Creation, also known as the Great Originating Mystery, Great Spirit, Creatrix/Creator, God, and so on. Nothing and nobody in the universe should become that prime mediator for you. In the shamanic mindset, we are all expressions of God made manifest. The goal of this exercise is to remember your divine inheritance.

If you are familiar with the occult practices of the Western Mystery Tradition, you will see a lot of similarities between this exercise and especially the Middle Pillar ritual. In fact, the goal and framework are basically the same. According to occult author Damien Echols, "The Middle Pillar will teach you how to strengthen and repair your aura."[25] He explains, "Magicians have been using techniques similar to the Middle Pillar for thousands of years. This particular practice bestows all of the expected benefits of meditation in addition to increasing your divine energy and enhancing health and vitality of our physical body."[26]

The structure of the practice involves drawing from the Source of Creation directly and tuning the energetic points of your poq'po directly to that Source. Now, most people in the New Age spiritual movement and Hinduism are familiar with the chakra system of the energy body, focal points of energy with specific meanings and functions. Though there are normally chakras appointed as the primary energy centers, there are actually several points of energy throughout the entire body, in almost every section. These points act more like toroidal functions, which allow the free flow of energy throughout the poq'po.

---

25 Damien Echols, *High Magick: A Guide to Spiritual Practices That Saved My Life on Death Row* (Boulder, CO: Sounds True, 2018), 73.

26 Echols, *High Magick*, 74.

The Peruvian Quechua have an extremely sophisticated system out-lined for the poq'po, not unlike the Hindu system. The Quechua refer to these centers, similar to chakras, as *chunpis*, which is the Quechua word literally meaning "belts." Referred to in English as "belts of power," these are numerous throughout the poq'po, though there are five that are pri-mary points imperative to the pillar of light exercise.

Pillar of Light

STEP 1

To begin, I recommend starting with your breathing basics and then the kawsay activation. After you have achieved the globe of golden kawsay around you, let that imagery go and just settle into the energy of your own power for a moment. Remember that you are a divine being, a child not only of Mother Earth but also of God/Great Spirit/Creator/etc. Bring your awareness to what you imagine is the center of the entire created universe, the seat of what the mystics call the Great Originating Mystery. You may view it as the largest of all swirling galaxies, the biggest of stars, or a glowing ball of light. Whatever image you bring to it, make sure it resonates with *your* vision of the Source of Creation.

Now, imagine a beam of light emitting from this Source and traveling through the expanse of the universe to then reach you, showering over you in a shaft of brilliant luminescence. This light does not have to be understood as something literal but as a symbol representing the spark of life, the code underlying the fabric of creation. Feel the effects of this light directly from creation itself shower over your physical and etheric bodies, like a warm, gentle spring rain massaging your entire reality.

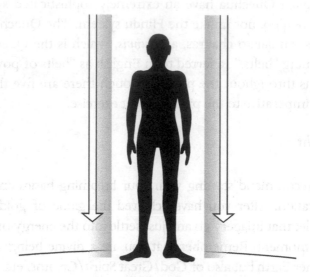

Figure 11. Pillar of light, step 1

STEP **2**

Spend a few moments basking in the radiance and connection with the essence of what you believe God to be. When you feel the strength of that connection, imagine your crown begin to open, almost like a lotus flower opening to draw in the light of the sun. On an inbreath, allow yourself to receive this shaft of light into your crown, enlivening the first chunpi of the body, the *kulli chunpi* (KOOL-ee CHUN-pee), which literally means "purple belt." As this chunpi is activated, imagine it glow into a belt of violet energy within your upper crown, including your eyes and above. The purpose of this first chunpi is to activate your vista, your second sight and mind, in alignment with your divine purpose, in alignment with the Source of Creation.

With the visualization, gently intone the words *Ñoqa kani* (nyo-KA KAH-nee) which are the Quechua words for "I am." In the Western Mystery Tradition version of this ritual, one would intone the Hebrew god name *Eheieh* (eh-HEE-yay, also meaning "I am"). You can also intone "I am" in English if that suits you. Regardless, it is the intent you are invoking, which is a direct connection with that ultimate source of universe, the great "I am," the recognition of Creator as Self and Self as Creator. You, and only you, are the direct connection; there is no intermediary.

Breathe for a few moments, pulling the light with your inbreath, and with each exhale intone "Ñoqa kani" while visualizing the kulli chunpi growing ever brighter.

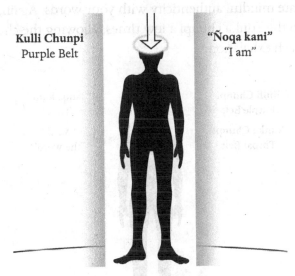

Kulli Chunpi
Purple Belt

"Ñoqa kani"
"I am"

Figure 12. Pillar of light, step 2

STEP 3

After a few breathing cycles, when you feel the connection to your crown is sufficient, now intend for the shaft of light to extend from the kulli chunpi to the next energetic center: your throat. Here resides the *kunka chunpi* (KOON-ka CHUN-pee), the "throat belt." The purpose of this chunpi revolves around language and authenticity. It is a common shamanic adage that language begets reality; what we speak into the world helps define the rules and behavior of our environment. Only by speaking the truth and being authentic to ourselves can we come into true alignment with divine purpose.

Visualize a blue belt of power forming at the end of this shaft of light, within your throat. Intone the word *simi* (SEE-mee), which means "the word" or "to speak" in Quechua. The Quechua call their language *runasimi*, which means "people-speak" or "the words of the people." It is the way in which they communicate about the world to one another. and it is constructed in such a way that uses very few possessive statements; it is a language built upon reciprocity and participation with the natural world and in community. While intoning this phrase, *simi*, intend that this light from Source and then your crown will fuel your ability to speak into the world, to create mindful authenticity with your words. Again, breathe this intention into the kunka chunpi a few times, allowing the chunpi to grow bright with each exhalation.

Kulli Chunpi	"Ñoqa kani"
Purple Belt	"I am"
Kunka Chunpi	"Simi"
Throat Belt	"the word"

Figure 13. Pillar of light, step 3

STEP 4

When you are ready, extend the shaft of light from the kunka chunpi to the center of your chest, where the *sonqo chunpi* (SAHN-koh CHUN-pee) resides, the "heart belt." This chunpi glows with a green energy and is emblematic of the true center of shamanic life: love. When all actions are performed with unconditional compassion and love for humanity, for life itself, then your actions will better be able to create the reality desired. As shamanic initiates, our jobs are to be the channels of creation, and love is the fuel of creation itself.

Intone the Quechua phrase *munay* (moon-AI), which means "love" or "to love." With each breath cycle, allow the sonqo chunpi to grow brighter, strengthening your capacity for love of all life without condition.

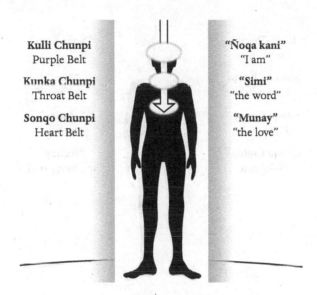

Kulli Chunpi
Purple Belt

Kunka Chunpi
Throat Belt

Sonqo Chunpi
Heart Belt

"Ñoqa kani"
"I am"

"Simi"
"the word"

"Munay"
"the love"

Figure 14. Pillar of light, step 4

STEP 5

Now draw the shaft of light down from the sonqo chunpi to your belly, where it will grow into a belt of red or reddish-orange light, the *qosqo chunpi* (KOSH-koh CHUN-pee). The qosqo is the navel, also known as the spiritual belly, where all things in life are processed, digested, and turned into vital life energy. It is the seat of shamanic power, where the soul can perform its duties to transmuting the muck of experiences from density into kawsay, the spirit of life itself. Allow this belt of energy to grow within you as you intone *nunay* (noon-AI), meaning "the living soul." Cycle through a few breaths as this chunpi grows brighter and more vital.

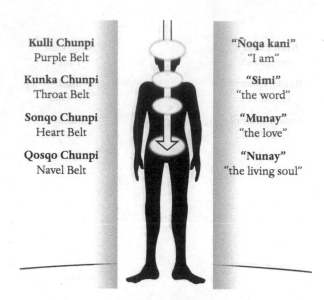

Figure 15. Pillar of light, step 5

STEP 6

Feeling that essence of soul in your belly and drawing upon the shaft of light flowing through all the preceding chunpis, allow the shaft of light to extend down to your feet. Visualize a belt of energy, much bigger than the others, growing within and around your feet, the bottom half of this belt fusing within the earth below you. Some people visualize this chunpi a deep red; others (especially in the Western Mystery Tradition) visualize it black. This is the *chaki chunpi* (CHAWK-ee CHUN-pee), meaning "foot belt." In the Hindu tradition, the root chakra (at the base of the spine) is the center of energy that connects us to the earth. However, in other traditions the feet themselves are also seen as vital portals of flow between the human body and the energy of the planet. Intone the word *Pachamama* (Mother Earth) as way to connect to the remembrance of yourself as a literal child of this beautiful planet, our one and only home in the cosmos. Breathe and with each exhalation, allow the chunpi to grow bigger, brighter.

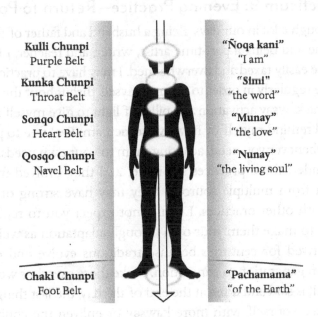

Kulli Chunpi Purple Belt	**"Ñoqa kani"** "I am"
Kunka Chunpi Throat Belt	**"Simi"** "the word"
Sonqo Chunpi Heart Belt	**"Munay"** "the love"
Qosqo Chunpi Navel Belt	**"Nunay"** "the living soul"
Chaki Chunpi Foot Belt	**"Pachamama"** "of the Earth"

Figure 16. Pillar of light, step 6

Now, extend the shaft of light beyond the chaki chunpi and down into the earth, to the core of the planet itself. Visualize and feel the power of that light flowing through each chunpi, each aspect of who you are as an incarnated being. Intone each chunpi phrase again, or speak them in English. Be mindful of their meaning. The phrases of the chunpis can be brought together into a sentence, a mantra that can align you with the purpose of the exercise:

Ñoqa kani simi munay nunay Pachamama!
I am the word, the love, the living soul of the earth!

You are a bridge between the Source of Creation and the manifest world. Bring your awareness to what the ancient mystery schools and shamanic cultures around the world have taught for centuries: as above, so below; as below, so above. You are Creator itself, formed into being as this magnificent machine, this pillar of light!

This exercise, complemented with the kawsay activation, will assist in boosting your energy for the day and setting the tone for how to walk and interact with the world.

Practicum 9: Evening Practice—Return to Power

We go through a lot in our days. Being a husband and father of three, working full-time and being a part-time artist, writer, and teacher, I know that I can become easily taxed and overwhelmed. I may have to practice breathing basics quite regularly in order to ground myself throughout the day, including using the kawsay activation and pillar of light to give myself some more energy and remind myself of how awesome I am. Feel free to practice the exercises whenever you need, adapting them to your own needs.

A reminder: these practices are mine, and they evolved from what I was taught from multiple sources. They may have strong or loose correlations with other practices. I would not expect you to replicate them exactly but to make them your own through adaptation as well. Shamanism has thrived for centuries because traditions evolve and continually change from generation to generation. Make these exercises work for you.

When all is said and done at the end of the day, the last thing you want to do is juice yourself with more kawsay or enliven the chunpis within your energy body. You're tired and exhausted and just want to let the day go. Yet sometimes we carry frustrations with us that prevent us from having our moments of peace and respite. Maybe a raged driver cut you off, a coworker took credit for a project you completed, your friend wasn't there for you like you needed, or your spouse said that one triggering thing that you know that they know really upsets you.

These are all common disturbances in our day that we allow to pull our power away from us. In truth, absolutely nobody and nothing in this world has the ability to take your power away from you. The real kicker is that we allow them to. We may not be able to control our environment around us, but the liberty of shamanism is that our job is to control our own reactions and responses to our environment. That is true power: personal accountability.

A good exercise at the end of the day—especially directly before bed—is to take a few moments, whether it be five or ten minutes, to settle down, preferably away from anyone else. Take a few moments to practice breathing basics and relax your body.

Much like in thought tracking, begin tracking your memories of the day, from beginning to end. Bring to mind your first moments of waking up and run through every action, from brushing your teeth to getting ready for work or school—all of it, in sequential order. Pay attention to moments and interactions with others or situations when you felt your power drained or taken away, moments when you may have been triggered by trauma or felt defeated, angry, or sad. None of these are bad emotions. The goal is to take these moments and transform their resonance within your memory into something new and useful, so that they do not stick around as dense refuse in your poq'po.

When you find one of those moments in retracing your day, imagine that experience is contained in a form of vapor or cloud before you. Breathe it into your body, imagining that vapor or cloud being sucked into your nostrils. Then, exhale while imagining that vapor and the experience it contains trailing down your spine. With the force of the exhale, push the vapor out through the coccyx or tailbone and into the earth below. Release the moment entirely, giving it up to Pachamama, Mother Earth.

Do this again and again, for every memory of when you felt a piece of your power was drained or pulled away. Sometimes, you may need to do it multiple times for a single memory, and that is fine. Take as long as you need.

Some students have asked me why I would give my negative stuff to Mother Earth. My answer is always this: think of compost. Mother Earth is an incredible, biological machine that takes refuse and turns it into nutritive soil, not only physically but energetically as well. Part of the human inheritance is remembering how to leverage this aspect of relationship with Pachamama. When you send this stuff to her, you are not sending it to harm her. When you send her your refuse, you send it to her with the intention that it is food she will churn and compost, transforming it into a new energy that will manifest someday in the future as a beautiful flower or tree. It is important not to be attached to an outcome, but align your intention with both yours, Pachamama's, and humanity's highest good. Mother Earth will do the rest.

You Are the Source

One's physical, mental, emotional, and spiritual health are paramount. Without them, you do not have the ability to fully experience all that life has to offer. By recognizing the energetic body, the poq'po, as the principal filament of consciousness, the shamanic initiate can incorporate these practices using the will and visualization to reinstate one's birthright of wholeness. Power (magnetism) resides in maintaining a healthy relationship with the life energy of Pachamama (kawsay) and remembering—via the pillar of light—that you are an extension of the creative source of the universe made manifest in flesh. You are the word, the love, and the living soul of the earth!

CHAPTER FOUR
Shamanic Tools

When my training with Patty was complete, it was suggested to me to seek out and discover more of the Native American path. I had no idea what that meant at the time, but thankfully I live in such a community that could support the next steps on my soul's journey. My city happens to have an extraordinary spiritual undercurrent with a wide array of alternative spiritual modalities and connections. Through this community, I was able to connect with one of the most magical mentors of my life only a short distance away from my home at the time.

It was a chilly but clear day in February when I met him. He lived on a piece of pristine land about a half hour outside the city. My car had to putter through a mile or so of gravel road before I found his white shingled farmhouse peeking out of the woods. Next to the well-kept home was a massive shed, obviously remodeled sometime recently. On the side was painted a white silhouette of a twelve-point buck deer, his shamanic sanctuary dubbed White Deer Lodge.

I had arranged the meeting beforehand, and his instructions were clear: park in front of the shed and walk around to the back. I left the car and walked through a wooded area, passing by a domed stick framework that looked to be a sweat lodge for Lakota inipi ceremonies. My heartbeat thudded in my eardrums, as I knew little of what to expect.

I didn't enter right away. There was a porch coming off the back door and I paced frantically for a few minutes, breathing deeply to get some oxygen into my head, to calm myself. Not only did I seek this man because of my growing draw to and interest in shamanism, but I needed help. Conventional medicine had failed me for the past few years; as noted in the previous chapter, I was plagued with severe health issues as a result of post-traumatic stress disorder. With nowhere else to turn, I needed some relief from the suffering, and I had heard through the grapevine in the Kansas City metaphysical community that this man was a legitimate healer using the shamanic arts. I gulped down as much of the anxiety as I could and—with all the courage I could muster— knocked on the back door.

A tall, brawny frame loomed in the threshold. Long raven-colored hair reached down to the middle of his back. Aging, droopy eyes glinted through a wrinkled face, which pulled back to reveal a surprisingly comforting grin. Even more surprising was that my guard immediately dropped. The Spider-Man sense of anxiety racking my psyche began to dissolve. Everything about him resonated a gleaming kindness.

"Hello, brother," he greeted in a deep, resonant tone. He reached out for a hug, his large brown hands held out to either side of me. This was unexpected. He spoke as if we had known each other for quite some time, like I was just stopping by for a casual visit with an old friend.

I was inclined to oblige the greeting and an invisible force moved me to him, hesitantly giving him a half-embrace. Though my PTSD had interrupted my ability to be close and intimate with others, it was fairly easy to allow this physical connection between us, even though I didn't know him. A quality of magnetism emanated from his being.

"Come on in." He motioned me through the doorway. "Take your shoes off please, but you may want to keep your socks on. I haven't quite warmed up the lodge yet." He bowed as we entered a large room. It was about forty by thirty feet, with curtained windows lining the opposite wall. Indigenous paintings and masks, drums, dream catchers, and other esoteric paraphernalia hung on all available space. The wooden flooring was covered with deerskin and wool rugs.

To my left, I noticed the most magnificent thing I had ever seen: a large altar-like compilation of various artifacts on the ground, composed of stones, crystals, staffs, owl wings, candles, antlers, bottles full of mysterious concoctions, as well as photographs of Catholic saints and other unknown individuals. It looked and felt so raw, unbridled, pulsing with power. Copal filled the air. There was a chair behind the altar and a chair in front of it, in the center of the room. He nodded toward the chair in the center.

"Go ahead and have a seat there," he suggested cordially, ambling to the seat behind the altar and sitting to face me. He leaned over to the altar and picked up an incredibly long feather, which I could only imagine came from a condor or other large bird. He waved it in the air, flitting the smoke of the incense billowing from a small cauldron on the altar. I took my seat gingerly. The scent was intoxicating. I felt light-headed but at ease.

"This is a *mesa*." He pointed to the altar with the condor feather. "It is an arrangement of ceremonial medicine pieces on a sacred cloth. I use it like a tool set, designed to assist me in shamanic healing with clients. The mesa is my primary way of working with the unseen realms. It will help me diagnose your issue as well as cure it."

"Okay." I nodded timidly to show that I had some semblance of understanding what he was telling me. Somehow, I did get it, though. Somehow, it all felt so familiar. He flicked the feather a couple more times over the mesa. The incense smoke made spirals in the air.

While working with me, he had me tell my story. For the first time, I was able to speak about all the things that had happened over the years to put me in the state of sickness I was in. He asked questions to gain clarity of my story. He counseled me. This went on for about half an hour.

"Come to the altar," he told me after the counsel. I stood and approached the mesa.

The shaman then began to take objects from the mesa and scrape them across my body or put them in my hands. At other times, he would place them on my forehead or heart and blow into them. He did these strange things called *limpias* and *floreciendos* and *singado*. When he was finished, the shaman cleared his throat and leaned over to grab something from his mesa cloth on the ground. It was a bottle of yellow liquid. He took swigs of the yellow liquid and then spit it on me in an aromatic spray. As soon it hit me, the floral essence floored me. The relief was immediate! The mixture of flowery sweetness and cinnamon uplifted me in a way I had never before experienced. I was hooked. Whatever that was, whatever he just spit into my face, I knew in that moment this mesa stuff was going to be something I would never walk away from.

"What is that?" I asked, feeling immediately lighter, less anxious.

"*Agua de florida*," he answered, his eyes squinting in a jovial grin.

That flowery aroma soothed me, a sure sign in that moment that I would now willingly be on a path from which I would never turn back. What ensued from there was a shamanic apprenticeship that lasted seven years.

The Mesa

The mesa is a spiritual altar, the shaman's gateway into the soul realm. In Spanish, *mesa* literally means "table," which is fitting because it is the place where the shaman comes to feast on the fruits of spirit, where the shaman invites the invisible forces of the universe to commune. As noted by author and shamanic practitioner Matthew Magee, the mesa is "a living control panel, co-created by Spirit and the curandero, to become a vehicle for experiencing the ineffable."[27] As a "control panel," it is a tool to help you navigate the invisible realities on the shamanic path. The mesa is the vehicle from where the spiritual practices of the shaman as well as their curanderismo (curing) and divinatory techniques are performed.

Can a person be shamanic without a mesa? Yes, absolutely. It is not required, but any altar of some sort is a helpful tool that can act as your own intermediary (rather than another person, such as a priest or guru) between you and the unseen realms of the shamanic experience. Shamanic training can, at times, be daunting. You are opening your world into a whole new experience of being, even if you've been at it a very long time. The real and the surreal can sometimes begin to blend into

---

27 Matthew Magee, *Peruvian Shamanism: The Pachakuti Mesa* (Kearney, NE: Morris Publishing, 2005), xvi.

one another. The varieties of experience are limitless. It is best to have some sort of filtration system in place, a dam so to speak, so as to not open the floodgates and be overcome by the deluge. A mesa is a perfect tool for just such a foundation, as well as being able to assist you, as Magee says, in being a "vehicle" for your shamanic experience.

Although there are many versions of shamanic altars around the world that are similar, the mesa is specifically South American in origin. Every region of South America, and even traditions within families, will use the mesa in different ways. There are common threads of course, but the use of a mesa can easily be catered toward the individual's personal inclinations. Truly, this is how shamanic lineages stay alive throughout the ages: they grow and evolve with each passing generation. Take for instance your own family traditions. Various holidays or religious rites were likely imparted to you, but as each generation of society changes, so do these traditions. You may do things slightly differently—in your own style—but still carry on the core tradition or value.

In the case of the mesa, there is no difference. There are some mesas that are used as open-faced altars placed on the ground, some which are used literally on a table. Others may be wrapped into a bundle and used in this way. There are some that honor basic symbol sets based on the cardinal directions, and some focus primarily on the dualistic nature of the universe. It always depends upon which lineage of mesa carriers you bump into from Peru, Bolivia, Ecuador, and so on.

The mesa, in form and function, is a syncretic tool, meaning it incorporates a union of ideas normally at odds with one another. This is apparent in its historical evolution through the centuries. Currently, many of the shamanic practices regarding the mesa incorporate Catholic iconography; however, the native ceremonial rites of the mesa pre-date Spanish colonization. Some of the mesa practices still seen in curanderismo can even be traced back to thousands of years BCE. Elements of these practices are found in archeological evidence throughout ancient civilizations of South America up to the Incas. When the Tawantinsuyu (Incan Empire) fell under the brutality of the conquistadors, the people not only adopted the religious symbolism of the Spanish in order to avoid persecution but also accepted the monomythic correlations between their indigenous cosmological heritage and the symbols of the Church. The traditions of Voodoo and Hoodoo in the Americas are similar in their syncretic fusion. Due to this savvy incorporation, the shamanic practices of curanderismo are cross-cultural in nature; thus, they have been able to thrive and evolve over the centuries, while other traditions around the world have struggled to survive.

This blending of traditions apparent in the mesa generates a unique teaching itself in shamanic practice: to accept and integrate equals life; to resist is extinction.

This spiritual combination also creates an extraordinary ritual experience. Imagine being in a candlelit room with a great altar of objects before you: bottles of herbs, ancient stones, skulls, crucifixes, and staffs carved into figures of owls or jaguars. The shaman rattles over the mesa and then invokes the Lord's Prayer. It is a peculiar experience, especially for a guy raised in the Ozarks under the holy-rolling auspices of Southern Baptist and Assembly of God evangelicals. However, it is the syncretic nature of curanderismo (the shamanic art of curing, specifically within the mesa lineage) that has drawn me to it and allowed me a space to bring my own religious past into union with the spiritual path that would eventually cure me.

Coincidentally (or rather, synchronistically), the shaman I visited that day was named Daniel as well—don Daniel Baxley—and he became my maestro (teacher) in the Pachakuti Mesa Tradition and northern coastal curanderismo. Once a firefighter in the Kansas City area, don Daniel spent much of his free time in life traveling around the world learning the shamanic healing practices from many traditions, called to be of service to humanity. This also included the ceremonial rites and teachings of the Lakota from Chief Phil "Crazy Bull" and Red Earth. Upon encountering the maestro curandero don Oscar Miro-Quesada, don Daniel jumped fully into the curandero arts. He became one of the first sanctioned teachers of the Pachakuti Mesa Tradition, as well as the carrier of the curanderismo practices of the northern coastal lineage.

Figure 17. Don Daniel Baxley and his mesa, drawn by the author

Even more than a maestro, don Daniel Baxley became my *padre* (father), my spiritual parent guiding me fully out of my suffering and into the man I am today. As noted earlier in the introduction, the practices of the shamanic mesa in this book have a lot of crossover with the Pachakuti Mesa Tradition but are more aligned with the northern coastal curanderismo lineage as taught to me by don Daniel.

The Campos

The mesa is normally constructed using a cloth laid either upon the ground or a table of some sort. It is composed of sacred objects, called *artes*, to represent various ceremonial or healing powers which augment the overall power of the mesa. Each arte has a specific ceremonial purpose depending upon where it is placed on the mesa. The mesa itself is a representation of the shaman's cosmos, a map of the originating powers of the universe itself. Typically, the mesa is divided into multiple parts, or fields, that represent these universal powers. As pointed out by anthropologist Douglas Sharon, "The mesa, as a reflection of Andean cosmology, is a mediating space between the levels of the cosmos with the sides... representing the two primary cosmic forces and levels, while the apex (the shaman's seat) represents the unification of opposed principles linked to a central, mediating cosmic axis (cross)."[28] Essentially, the curandero is the mediator between two primary cosmic forces that create the universe as we know it today, those forces represented on the mesa as corresponding fields.

In curanderismo, these fields are called *campos* in Spanish. Every lineage of curanderismo represents these campos in their own way, but generally they are portrayed as three vertical fields upon the cloth of the mesa extending from top to bottom: one on the left, one in the middle, and one on the right. They are known primarily as the *campo ganadero*, the *campo medio*, and the *campo justiciero*. Figure 18 shows how these fields are depicted in the mesa.

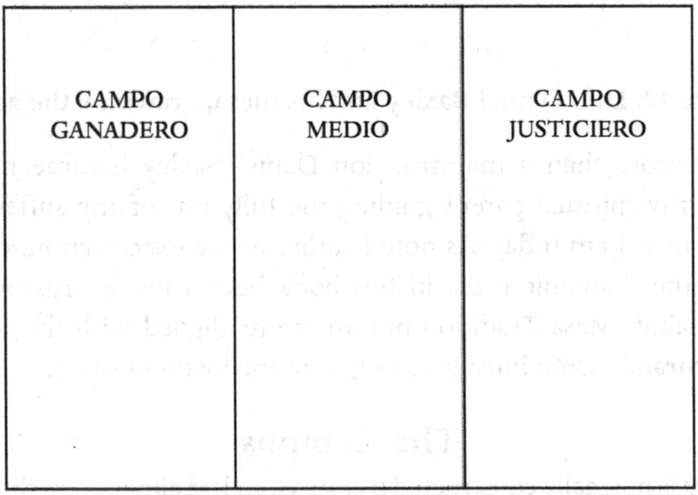

CAMPO GANADERO	CAMPO MEDIO	CAMPO JUSTICIERO

Figure 18. The campos

28 Joralemon and Sharon, *Sorcery and Shamanism*, 186.

The way the mesa operates, any arte that is laid on a particular field will take on the powers and energies of that corresponding field. Therefore, any artes you may have in the campo ganadero will naturally take on the attributes of the campo ganadero, and so on. Let's examine what each of these fields means and how it represents the ideology of the shaman's work.

The Campo Ganadero

The field on the left is called the campo ganadero—in Spanish meaning the "field of the rancher"—otherwise known as the field of the magician. A rancher controls his flock of cattle, and so too the shaman is also a magician controlling the forces around him. The tradition of curanderismo is a superstitious one, and there is a prevalence of sorcery, manipulation, and bad luck (*mala suerte*) that is wielded against others. A true curandero is one who knows how to contain these types of forces and use them for beneficent, rather than malevolent, purposes. The purpose of the campo ganadero is to contain these forces and leverage their power for a constructive outcome in harmony with the other forces on the mesa.

Due to its proficiency in magic, the campo ganadero is the field of the feminine. By referring to the feminine, I am not attributing anything to gender, as we all have masculine and feminine aspects within our soul. The feminine is a form of energy we can all tap into, regardless of identity, and it is one of majestic protection. The idea of the womb is a perfect symbol for the containment necessary to wield the forces of magic. The curandero uses the campo ganadero to dispatch negative energies or malevolent forces, as the womb protects and nurtures the child within. Also, it is attributed to the field of the dark arts and some sorcerers in Peru certainly use it for those means.

Each field on the mesa has its own patron saint or deity that is honored, governing the powers of that particular campo. Traditionally, these deities will herald to Catholic iconography, but they do not have to. Each person chooses their own deity or saint, and this entity is an inspirational container of power for that campo. For this reason, it is common for San Cipriano (Saint Cyprian) to be the patron saint or deity of the campo ganadero, and his origin can tell us much about the resonance of the left field of the mesa.

Not to be confused with Saint Cyprian of Carthage, this particular story arises from a legend started around the fourth century wherein San Cipriano was a notorious dark magician in Antioch (in Turkey). One day, a would-be suitor came to Cipriano to purchase a charm to woo a beautiful woman named Justina. However, Justina had made her vows of chastity and was highly pious. Cipriano's charms were useless on Justina, as her bond with Christ was so strong that his magics had no effect. Inspired by her faith, Cipriano became a devotee of Christ himself and, because of his mastery of the dark arts, became one of the most balanced and effective bishops of that region.

There is another version of the story, in which Cipriano himself was in love with Justina and attempted to charm her for that reason. Regardless of the interpretation or whether or not you are religious, Cipriano provides an excellent teaching for the campo ganadero: that only by being a master over the dark arts—not a slave to them—can one hold a proper position of service as a shamanic practitioner. San Cipriano is often invoked in this campo to help dispatch anything in the unseen realms that may not serve the higher purpose of curanderismo. Many markets in Peru will have prayer books to San Cipriano, which are used frequently to call his presence in from the heavens to assist the curandero. Oftentimes, both San Cipriano and Santa Justina (Saint Justina) will be used together in the campo ganadero, but again, the choice is yours to represent the energetic quality of your mesa. Maybe another myth from a different culture applies to you that aligns with the principles of this field: for instance, Isis of Egyptian lore, the Roman Saturn, or especially Kali of the Hindu tradition. The choice is yours.

The three campos together represent the concept of time and the life span of the human. Therefore, the campo ganadero represents the past, our personal history and place of our ancestors. We learn from our past in order to reorient to the present and future; it is here where the shadowy aspects of past history reside, which we may reconstruct to serve the present day.

The Campo Justiciero

On the right-hand side of the mesa is the campo justiciero, the "field of divine justice," the divine judge. This field embodies the mystical quest of seeking connection with the Divine, generally associated with white magic or beneficial energies. The path of the mystic is not about changing what is (such as through magic) but raising and lifting forth the potential of a situation. This is the true essence of communion with the Source of Creation, to uplift the already divine nature of the world around us. For this reason, one of the primary governors of the campo justiciero is the black saint San Martin de Porres, the son of a Spanish nobleman and a freed African slave. A native of Peru, San Martin is often depicted holding a broom, as he considered all work sacred, even the most menial of tasks, a most mystical and monastic attribute to be sure. He is also portrayed feeding multiple animals out of the same dish, a sign of harmony between differing groups and races.

Another patron deity in the campo justiciero is the mother of Christ herself, Madre María (Mother Mary). Madre María is often the prime mediator between God and the people, seeking blessings on their behalf. It is because of the purity of Madre María that she was fit to carry the son of God in her womb. Though there is no judgment of piety in the shamanic arts, it is understood that these practices stem from a long line of priests and priestesses from various cultures through history, a certain amount of conduct within one's character may be relevant in seeking connection with the Divine. Other divinities to be recognized in the campo justiciero could be Kuan Yin from the Buddhist tradition, Jupiter from the Roman pantheon, or even Hanuman of the Hindu myths.

Interestingly enough, the campo justiciero is primarily a masculine field, the field of force or pushing energy out into the world, a channel of creative force. Whereas the feminine side centers on protection, the masculine side is a movement in a direction conducted by the shaman. Therefore, the healing powers of raising the potential of an individual and helping create their own future is vital within this campo.

The Campo Medio

Now finally the campo medio, the middle field, also known as the field of equilibrium. This campo is not so much a field in its own right as it is a fusion of the campo ganadero and campo justiciero. This is where the two opposing forces of the universe come together in harmony, which may not always be a pretty sight at first, but through time, effort, and will they are stabilized into a cohesive union or balance.

This represents fully the shamanic paradigm: a shaman wields magic (campo ganadero), connecting to the mystical qualities of the universe (campo justiciero), in order to bring medicine to others (campo medio). Medicine is absolutely the result of magic and mysticism conjoined in equilibrium. Medicine is the true goal and is not something that can be given from one person to another; medicine is found within oneself. It is the initiate aligning with the true intent of their soul's purpose on this planet. Therefore, any healing practice in association with the campo medio is a transmission only to align a person with their soul's intent, and nothing else. It is the place where the chaotic waters of either of both poles of existence (the campos of the mesa) come to be calmed, to be depolarized and no longer swayed by one side or the other. Due to this, the concepts of masculine and feminine energies fail to exist, and the campo medio becomes a truly androgynous state. Not one or the either, but both and neither at the same time. This is where you become you: the human soul in its most pristine state. There are many other names for this in other cultures: the Middle Pillar of Qabalah, the Middle Path of the magical traditions, or the Red Road of Northern Native American spirituality.

Jesu Cristo (Jesus Christ) holds governorship over this campo, as well as San Pedro (Saint Peter), keeper to the keys of heaven. Divinities that can be recognized in the campo medio from other traditions include Brahman from Hindu tradition, Gautama Buddha, Wakan Tanka (Great Spirit) from the Lakota tradition, or Baphomet from Western Mystery Tradition, among others. Again, any one of these campos can have its own divinities and attributions. It is up to the initiate to decide what works best for themselves; otherwise, if it does not resonate, it will not work at all.

The only time represented within the campo medio is the present, which is both now and infinity all at once. It truly encapsulates the idea that time is not linear but synchronic, forever infinite and cyclical, and it is all happening in the eternal now.

CAMPO GANADERO	CAMPO MEDIO	CAMPO JUSTICIERO
Field of the Magician	Field of Equilibrium	Field of the Mystic
Energy: Magic	Energy: Medicine	Energy: Mysticism
Gender: Feminine	Gender: Androgynous	Gender: Masculine
Healing: Dispatching, Protection	Healing: Balance, Transmission	Healing: Raising, Uplifting
Patron Saint: San Cyprian/Santa Justina	Patron Saint: Jesu Cristo, San Pedro	Patron Saint: San Martin de Porres, Madre María
Time: The Past	Time: The Present	Time: The Future

Figure 19. The campos and their attributes

Practicum 10: Building a Mesa

Although there are certain steps to building a mesa, the process is also a very personal experience. First, you will want to acquire a sacred blanket or cloth to act as the base of your altar. In curanderismo, Andean textiles are normally used due to their thick and durable fibers. A thick textile provides a steady and protective palette for your ritual objects to be placed on. More important than that is to use something important to you, a cloth that resonates with your spiritual path or one that you are aesthetically or artistically drawn to. Many mesas are of Andean origin, but I have seen others with Shipibo (Amazonian), Celtic, Native American, and Tibetan designs. Others use cloths that are sentimental or meaningful to them for personal reasons. The mesa is your "control panel" that you will be using to navigate the unseen powers of the universe, so it is important to find something that resonates with you.

Next, if you have the capability, locate a space within your home that can be reserved specifically for sacred ceremony. You can use a separate room, a basement or attic, or even an entire outbuilding, such as a refurbished shed or guest house. If you do not have much space available to you—such as in an apartment or a dorm with roommates—then make do with what you have: a coffee table or corner space in your bedroom. It is fine to be creative and innovative. You can choose to have your mesa set up permanently or just for ceremony. Because my wife and I have such giant altars, we leave our mesas out all the time. However, I know some individuals with smaller altars who bundle them when they're not being used. This may be more convenient for those who may have limited space in which to operate. If so, it is important to follow the consecration process every time one sets up the mesa for ceremony.

Some people choose to have their mesas and altars pointing north; others choose to have them facing east to the rising sun. There is no right or wrong way. Choose the facing direction that feels good to you or that your space allows. Regardless of where it is, this is a space you will use for your shamanic work, so it is up to you what direction aligns most with your spiritual path, if any.

When your space is chosen, you will then want to consecrate the space before setting up your mesa. Consecration is a declaration of your intention to the universe—and to the land you reside on, along with the spirits which occupy it—that you are creating a space for ritual work. This is not only a declaration of intent, but it is also an offering to satiate the unseen powers of the earth around you, a ritual feeding that will begin a rapport between you and forces of creation. This process can seem like ceremonial protocol, though it is more of a meditation to prepare yourself for the shamanic work ahead. Consecration is a reminder of one's place in the greater universe, connecting with the powers of the shamanic realms and their healing potential. Allow consecration itself to be a shamanic process, a healing endeavor allowing the energy of each action to flow into your consciousness and envelop your mindfield, your poq'po.

The burning of incense is a good way to cleanse any dense or negative energy from the area. Some of the more popular options for this include sage and palo santo. It should be noted that mass demand for white sage and palo santo have caused a strain on the ecosystems of those plants, so other alternatives, such as frankincense, copal, and mugwort, can be more eco-friendly options. The smoke of these essences is known in folk and indigenous traditions to ward off any unwanted influences and open a new space for growth and rejuvenation. Then, follow these simple steps to consecrate your ground. These were transmitted by don Daniel to me and are also practiced in the Pachakuti Mesa Tradition. The steps assume your altar is facing north, but, again, it does not have to. Adjust the directions according to your needs.

1. First, offer a few drops of *agua de florida* to the ground on which you will be placing your mesa. Agua de florida is floral water used often in Peru for cleansing the energetic body as well as for offerings for Pachamama. There is a story that the original shamans of Peru journeyed to heaven and returned. Upon their return, they recreated the scent of heaven, which came to be known as agua de florida. This offering to your ceremonial ground is a libation meant to satisfy Pachamama's thirst and should be offered in gratitude for the life she has given us. You can normally find agua de florida in most Hispanic markets in your community or online. A word of caution: agua de florida is alcohol based. Practitioners of curanderismo, as well as Voodoo, normally spray the water forth by imbibing the liquid, and then spraying it out of their mouths in a cloud of mist. This is called a *phukuy*, a powerful (yet graceful) outbreath meant to establish an energetic connection between the shaman and the ritual process, whether it be for a blessing, healing, or some other ceremonial endeavor. It also creates a beneficial ionization in the energy body and space around wherever it is sprayed in this way. Putting agua

de florida in the mouth can sting for the new practitioner, so be cautious and do not be afraid to just use a spray bottle instead. Performing a phukuy with agua de florida is not mandatory for shamanic practice. Also, if you have allergies, be sure to check the ingredients on the label of whatever agua de florida you use to avoid any possible side effects.

2. Next, offer some cornmeal, taking a few pinches with your fingers and drawing a circle around that central point where you offered the agua de florida. Corn is a sacred plant to the indigenous peoples of South, Central, and North America, a continual source of nourishment for the people. Start in the south and draw the circle clockwise. Traditionally, drawing a circle clockwise is the direction of creation, whereas drawing counterclockwise is a direction of undoing. This circle represents the sacred hoop of life, that all things are connected in an infinite cycle of time and space.

3. Now you will offer some tobacco, another sacred plant of the indigenous peoples of the Americas and throughout the world, often used to carry prayers and to heal. Taking a few pinches of the tobacco, draw a line from the northern tip of your cornmeal circle to the south, then from the east to the west. This is to symbolize that the infinity of the circle becomes squared within our human understanding of space-time. Spirit comes down to earth (north to south), the sun rises and sets from our microcosmic perspective (east to west), and life has a finite beginning and end. We honor this limited existence just as much as we honor the infinite landscape of soul and universe.

4. Finally, acquire three bay or rose leaves (in Peru, coca is typically used) to offer a *k'intu* (KEEN-too), a ritual offering marrying the spiritual power of a plant with the breath of the practitioner. This marriage generates a union between the

human and the power of prayer (or intention). The number three is a vital number in curanderismo. For our purposes—as will become apparent as you read along—the three leaves of the k'intu represent the three shamanic worlds of existence (upper, middle, and lower worlds, which we will discuss later), the three campos of the mesa, or the three attributes of Andean shamanic service: love, wisdom, and hard work. Gently blow your intention to embody the campos and these three attributes, then place the k'intu in the center of the circled cross. This brings all your intention for this shamanic work to the center of your ground, which is a mirror for bringing it to the center of your attention and awareness.

5. Snap your fingers or clap your hands over the k'intu, symbolizing your completion of the consecration ceremony. This is a common action in many magical traditions to denote the completion of a spell or ritual or sealing a magical power in place.

6. Now, delicately place your chosen cloth over the consecration so that the circle of the consecration is centered in the middle of your cloth. Bless this sacred ground with your gratitude and appreciation for the good which you will complete together. If you want, burn some more sage or palo santo or spray some aqua de florida for an extra benediction. The better your mesa smells, the higher the vibration.

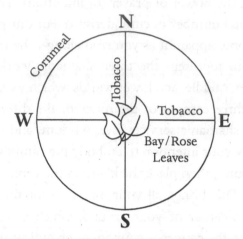

Figure 20. Consecration

You might notice this consecration looks a lot like a Native American medicine wheel in form. In fact, this symbol is prevalent in many cultures across the world. Closely related to the cross, it unites all the directions, all the different aspects of being alive and human, into a single entity. Also, you do not need to follow all these steps if you feel like you are just following a recipe and it is not creative or resonating with you. Maybe just try one or a combination thereof; you can also come up with your own. The goal of consecration is that you have use of some sort of ritual process meaningful to you, establishing your intention for laying down the mesa to begin your shamanic work.

Artes

In shamanism, everything is alive. To explain, in anthropology there is a term called "animism," coming from the root Latin word *anima*, which means "breath" or "life." This concept implies that all things in the world have life, have a consciousness. Typically, this suggests plants and animals each have a spirit or soul. In shamanism, *everything* has a consciousness of some sort. Everything! Every plant, every animal, every rock, and yes, even this book in your hand, the carpet in your house, and your cell phone. Now, one level of consciousness may be denser than others, some lighter and more interactive. Yet, everything has a vibration, a frequency with which you can connect.

You ever go to a place (either in the wilderness or at a chapel) and just feel a certain resonance to it, like it's alive? Ever feel a strong connection to a certain plant or animal? Ever hear a fortune-teller or occultist say their tarot deck has a life of its own? It's because these things do have life, and all things in life can participate with one another in some shape or form, depending on how willing you are to do so.

This is a primary concept behind artes—the ritual objects placed on a mesa—and the mesa itself. For an arte to exercise the shaman's power, or its own, there needs to be an inherent belief in the soul of the object. There is a saying attributed to the great Renaissance artist Michelangelo that every block of stone has a statue inside of it, and it is the task of the sculptor to discover it. This is no different from a painter and their canvas, a musician with their instrument, or a shaman with their artes and mesa. It is up to you to find the life and purpose in the ritual objects you decide to use. This recognition of the story of the arte is traditionally called its *cuenta*, its account. The accounting of an arte is vital to harnessing its power. The account of an arte can include its name, its healing or spiritual intention, its history, and even its personality. Knowing the account of your artes is vital to harnessing their true potential and power.

Selecting the right artes for your mesa should not be a frivolous endeavor. Take your time and acquire them based upon your intuition, your inner guidance of what feels in alignment with your mind, heart, and body. Take a walk out in nature. Ask the universe to send these artes your way. Clear your senses and allow these items to come to you as naturally as possible, rather than forcing the process. Whether they can be found in the wilderness, a metaphysical book shop, or even a flea market (my personal favorite), the universe will deliver what we need as long as we stay open to receive. Keep your mind and heart open.

You will want to select artes whose accounts align with the specific campo in which they will be placed. Start with acquiring one arte per campo at first, and then build from there. A good place to start is to be conscious of the healing energy of each campo as we discussed before. Here is a breakdown of that energy and some suggestions for your first arte acquisition:

Arte de Defensa: Campo Ganadero. Though many of the artes in this campo tend to be for cleansing and dispatching unwanted energies, a good starting arte would be an *arte de defensa* (artifact of defense). You can use this arte to shield your ceremonial space and individual person in ceremony or otherwise. Curanderismo is a typically superstitious culture, so these artes have traditionally been used to shield against sorcery. However, you can use this arte to shield from taking on any unwanted energy or thought forms that may be causing you stress or exhaustion. Typical artes of defense can be a dense or dark stone, a shell, or maybe a statue of a protective deity. There is no wrong choice, but make sure the object you choose somehow aligns with the ceremonial purpose.

Arte de Levantada: Campo Justiciero. In traditional curanderismo culture, the prospects of attaining good luck—or reversing bad luck (*mala suerte*)—in one's life are viable reasons to visit a curandero. Typically, this field is filled with such good luck charms to steer one's life toward good fortune. Artes such as the *arte de levantada* (artifact of raising) can assist in raising your life upward to the direction you desire. It can be a source of inspiration or give you an uplift of energy when you feel depleted. This item can be a candle, a feather, a necklace, or another stone or statue. Again, the choice is yours as long as it represents the accounting (power and meaning) for which you are acquiring it.

Nuna Khuya: Campo Medio. As stated in the pillar of light exercise (practicum 8), *nunay* is the Quechua word for living soul. The root word of nunay is *nuna*, which means, generally, "soul." A *khuya* is an arte that is an expression of deep love for the practitioner. The nuna khuya is an arte that represents the highest qualities of medicine you can imagine. It should be a point of balance, an arte that (despite whatever day you may be having) will return you to the centering of your soul's purpose. In some lineages of curanderismo (Andean Paqokuna and the Pachakuti Mesa Tradition), this arte is called a *mesarumi* and is three objects laid on top of each other: a scallop shell on the bottom (representing the lower world), a *sepka*—flat stone—in the middle (to represent the middle world), and a cross on top (the upper world). Not only do most curanderos utilize a cross in the campo medio to recognize their faith in Christ, but there are also ancient connections to indigenous versions of the cross (such as the *chakana*, the Andean cross in figure 21) recognizing the qualities of the four directions, a uniting of opposites to create unity in the soul. I personally use the traditional mesarumi, but I know many practitioners who use a single object for this khuya as the central axis of their mesa.

Figure 21. The chakana, the Andean cross

Be sure to cleanse and bless all your ritual objects by bathing them in sage, palo santo, or even agua de florida before laying them on your mesa. Activating each arte before placing it on the designated space of your mesa is vital to accessing and securing the aim or account of each ritual object. In all magical work, your will and intention are above all else the canvas on which the imagination can manifest a new reality. As with anything placed on a sacred altar, take some time to activate each individual arte.

Practicum 11: Activating Artes

Sit at your mesa in a relaxed stance but with your back straight if possible. I recommend beginning with the breathing basics exercise before any ritual and then following with the kawsay activation and the pillar of light. After that, you will be in the perfect state to begin your ceremonial work. Choose an arte to activate and place it in your right hand. Open your left palm upward to the heavens. Close your eyes and relax your body, breathing comfortably in a steady rhythm. Clear your mind of all thought, opening yourself to the emptiness of a meditative state. When you feel sufficiently clear of all distraction, bring into focus this visualization using the pure power of your imagination:

1. Imagine a shaft of light (the same as from the pillar of light) coming down from the heavens and pouring over your body. Feel this light as the power of creation itself, seeding your intention with the backing of Creator.

2. Open your crown, allowing yourself to be filled completely with this essence. As stated before, you can imagine your crown to be a lotus flower blossoming to drink the light of the sun, its life-giving nourishment infusing your body.

3. Receiving this light also in your left palm, feel the light rush through your left arm, into your heart space, and then down through your right arm into the arte in your right hand. Through this passageway, you will turn the life-giving light from the heavens into a specific intention to embody within the specific arte. For the protection talisman, you will of course call in the campo ganadero and all its attributes, including the patron saint or deity, to invoke the power of protection into

the stone or other object. Spend a few minutes drawing forth the fullest potential for the powers of this campo into the arte.

4. When you feel the transmission of that power is sufficient, ask for a name to come forward as a designation for that arte. Speak out loud the first name that comes to mind. This can be the name of the arte whose power you call forth from now on.

5. To finish, bring the arte to your lips and blow (phukuy) a final honoring of intention into it. Place it in its designated campo on the mesa and snap your fingers in completion.

6. Complete this process again for each arte in designation with its campo. You will of course change the healing powers for each campo based upon the attributes and patron saints or deities as explained earlier.

Over time you will collect more and more artes for your mesa, each with its own unique intention for your shamanic work. Incorporate your own understanding of these powers into your activation process. Without your personal flavor of spirituality, the mesa will become a stagnant tool without any life. Feel free to incorporate spiritual practices and interests that suit your alignment with Creator. Remember, mesa traditions have evolved through a history of synthesis, different cultures merging to create something new and unique. This is how shamanic and folk traditions have survived the tests of time.

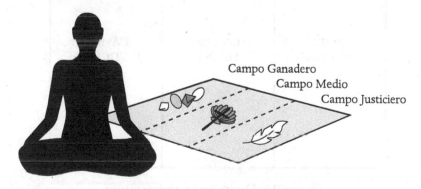

Campo Ganadero
Campo Medio
Campo Justiciero

Figure 22. Campos on the mesa

Practicum 12: Opening of the Account

It is understood that when not using the mesa and your artes that the energetic consciousness of your altar is "asleep," and the artes and the mesa are awoken to implement a ceremonial process. This is done by opening and closing the mesa for the time that you need it. Otherwise, the mesa's magic is still alive, but normally lying in wait for your use.

You may have noticed that when I have described the campos thus far, I have first noted the campo ganadero on the left of the mesa, then jumped to the right for the campo justiciero, and finally settled in the center for the campo medio. This has been purely for didactic purposes to best explain the inner workings of the energetic qualities of the mesa. However, when activating the mesa for ceremony, traditionally, there is a special flow one can follow to generate an efficient result of energetic circulation in the mesa.

The first circuit of this circulation is known as the *apertura de la cuenta*, the "opening of the account." In this process, you will awaken the powers of the mesa to begin your ceremonial work. The sequence of this flow normally starts with the campo justiciero as the decree for your intention of the ritual. Because this is the campo of mysticism, starting here ensures your ceremonial intention starts with honoring and invoking your understanding of the Divine.

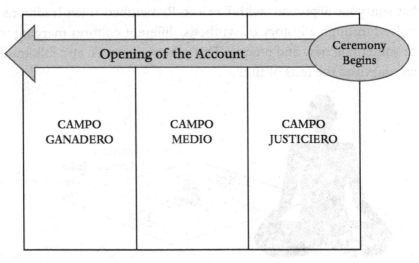

Figure 23. Opening of the account

Here are some suggestions for protocol in opening your mesa, the opening of the account.

1. Burn some copal or frankincense, both wonderful incenses for connecting with the soul realms. Breathe it in and allow the smoke to flow over the area of your mesa and artes with blessings and gratitude. It is helpful to do this entire exercise while standing, but you can do it while sitting if needed.

2. Perform breathing basics, kawsay activation, and the pillar of light (see appendix A for ceremonial routine). For the rest of the opening, keep the visualization and feeling of the pillar of light ritual going. This is why it is important to practice some of these rituals repeatedly, to gain a level of skill where it becomes more like breathing than something you have to try to remember and refer to. I have found that allowing the pillar of light to be infused within my being for the duration of any ritual increases the effectiveness of that ritual.

3. With the pillar of light ongoing, use your imagination and intent to draw down another pillar of light from the Source of Creation to your mesa. Just allow that light for now to shine over the top of the mesa, illuminating whichever artes you have collected so far.

4. Exercising your imaginative visualization further, bring your attention to the qosqo chunpi (the navel belt/chakra) in your stomach. Extend a cord of light from your qosqo to the campo medio of your mesa, most specifically connecting to your nuna khuya, your most prized sacred item. Allow that cord to harmonize the relationship between your soul body and the soul of the entire mesa itself, like an umbilical cord connecting mother and child, though in this case you are the architect, the mother of the artes, which are your children.

5. After a few minutes of establishing that connection, you may call out to any, then bring your focus first to the campo

justiciero. Imagine the pillar of light especially beginning to illuminate that particular campo much more brightly than the others, infusing that light into the artes of that field. Call to mind the account of those artes, their histories, powers, and connection to you. If you have more than one arte, it is helpful to bring forth that account for each one. Then, vocally call out the account of that field into full awakening. You may do this in your own way, but an example of this call, which I personally use, is "I call the powers of the campo justiciero into account. I call forth the power of San Martin de Porres (my personal governor of that field) to fill me with your essence, to guide my mind, heart, and hands on the field of the mystic. Teach me humility and devotion to all creation. I call forth the power of (insert name of arte here) and your ability to (insert healing power of arte here). Thank you for your service and for guiding my mind, heart, and hands." You may call out each arte in that campo.

6. Spray agua de florida three times over the campo as a blessing and flowering, fully activating the powers of that campo and its artes into being.

7. Now move to the campo medio and do the same, changing the verbiage of the account to match the governor and artes for that particular campo, spraying agua de florida three times afterward. Repeat for the campo ganadero.

8. When finished, retract the cord of light from the mesa and return it to your qosqo chunpi. Take a deep breath in and hold it for three seconds while you contemplate the beauty of your creation in the mesa, then exhale a strong phukuy back into the mesa itself as blessing of gratitude. The opening of the account is complete.

9. Consider creating and using your own ritual process to call forth the powers of your mesa and each campo, as well as the arte's medicine.

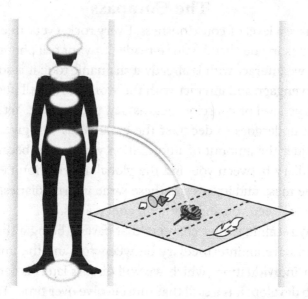

Figure 24. Opening of the account with the pillar of light

It is often typical for a curandero to be rattling, drumming, or using bells throughout the duration of this exercise. It is up to you whether or not you would like to perform some type of music to enhance the activation of your artes on the mesa. In a way, this is like an alarm, waking them up from the slumber. Other examples I have seen used are flutes, singing bowls, and even a guitar. You can also just speak or sing if you like. Sing a medicine song you know to bring a blessing to the mesa. If you do not know any medicine songs, just sing what comes into your heart, but also don't feel awkward about singing a song you love from the radio or pop culture. If that song is important to you, it carries medicine, regardless of its social or cultural background. If you do not like to sing or play music, find another way to awaken and enliven the mesa. I have seen some use dance and others use breathing techniques, yoga, or even poetry. Personally, as a visual artist, I like to draw a picture and place it on the mesa. The magic and intention are still there, despite the vehicle in which it is being delivered. Be creative. Be you.

The Compass

All things have a level of consciousness. Every rock, every tree, everything. Even this book in your hand, your e-reader, or your cell phone. Therefore, everything we interact with is already a shamanic tool: it is something we are using to engage and interact with the world. Your cell phone may not have the same level of consciousness as, say, your pet cat. Yet consider the processes it undergoes to decipher the commands you give it on a daily basis. Consider the amount of information you receive because it acts as an intermediary between you and the global information network. Now consider the mesa and its artes as these same intermediaries, channels of connection between you and shamanic soul realms.

You may recall in earlier chapters that part of being a shamanic initiate is not to have an intermediary between you and the universe. Well, that sort of individuation (which we will discuss later) is something you will have to develop; it is a skill that must evolve over time. The mesa and artes are only intermediaries in the sense that they are the compass, not the direction. They are tools only, not the broker arranging the shaman's relationship with the universe. You are the broker, the liaison between seen and unseen. You decide how you want this arrangement to be by making your mesa and artes on it personal to you and not adhering to any one tradition or standard. Follow your intuition and create an altar that works only for you and no one else.

CHAPTER FIVE
Shamanic Magic(k)

This chapter is a very brief note on magic and the implementation thereof.

I have stated earlier that magic plus mysticism equals medicine. But what of magic? How do you define it? Some will designate magic with a *K* to distinguish magic (the Houdini-style illusory stage theatrics) from magick (the art of causing change in accordance with one's will). I think it's fine to use either one, but for this chapter specifically we will quickly examine magick in theory and practice.

My favorite definition of magick comes writer and magician Alan Chapman in his book *Advanced Magick for Beginners*. In the first lines of his book, he poses the question "What is magick?" and then answers himself: "There isn't a man, woman or child on this planet that does not know what magick is. Don't ask silly questions."[29] Although that answer is facetious, Chapman has a point. Most everyone understands that magick involves ceremony and spellwork in order to make something happen that wouldn't ordinarily happen. Causing change in accordance with one's will does not involve shooting fireballs out of one's hands as the stories of fantasy and Hollywood films would have you believe. However, one can change aspects of one's world around them to better their life. The shaman, most definitely, is a master of the magickal arts.

Magick is as basic and essential as breathing. We cause magick all the time and don't even realize it. Magick is the art of creating reality—not

---

29 Alan Chapman, *Advanced Magick for Beginners* (London: Aeon Books, 2008), 15.

necessarily creating the reality you desire, but the reality in alignment with your soul. But basically, you're still doing it all the time. You're creating magick while reading this, when you are going to work, when you are interacting with your family.

What kind of magick, then, are you creating? How are your thoughts and actions contributing to the conditions in your environment?

Whatever you do will determine the result you get from your magick. Your magick will suck if you are inattentive and don't put a lot of effort into what you're doing. Your magick will rock if you are determined, disciplined, and focused. Anyone you can think of at the top of their game—the best athletes, musicians, doctors, teachers, artists—are excellent magicians in their particular field. If someone claims to be good at magick, but they don't have much going for them and are unhappy, I would venture to say they haven't quite mastered the art.

Magick is often referred to as an art. As an artist, I will tell you, art requires skill, it requires practice, it requires discipline. Many artists (and I include all the arts) will brush off the compliment "You're so talented!" Why? Because it takes a lot of practice to become successful. Mozart may have started composing symphonies when he was eight years old, but that doesn't mean they were that great, and they definitely weren't the works he is known for. Plus, he grew up in a situation where his circumstances allowed him to make such an achievement: in an affluent family in which musical education was not just encouraged but a requirement. These are just some of the considerations when thinking about magick and how it works.

Here is a little anecdote about how magick changed my life, which manifested through intention and effort.

Daimonic Thought Forms

There is a common assumption out there that every shaman has a specific spirit animal they relate to as a primary symbol or astral ally in their shamanic endeavors. This could be true for many of you, but it does not have to be. Personally, I have a strong relationship with the jaguar, but I also have deep connections with the elephant, goose, manta ray, and coyote. These just happened to be animals that have come across my radar and were a part of experiences that contributed to my own shamanic training.

There are others. There are beings—both humanoid and otherwise—who have come to me in dreams or other visionary experiences to teach me things, as evidenced by my vision in the previous chapter. Some people refer to these beings as ascended masters, angels, or even star beings. Call them imaginary friends, if you will, which I often do. Regardless of how they are termed, there are entities existing outside the common range of perception that tend to enjoy interacting with us two-leggeds. These entities can manifest in a variety of ways, such as journeying, which we will do in future exercises.

One such entity, it just so happened, came to me in the form of a fictional character. As a writer and artist, I am often coming up with different stories and characters within my imagination. One character idea came to mind during a crisis point in my life. In early 2011, my marriage was in a rocky decline and I didn't know what to do. I was concerned about how this marital distress was affecting my son and distraught over losing a relationship I was hoping would have been sustainable. However, my wife at the time disliked my shamanic activities. She couldn't understand my commitment to shamanism, despite seeing the results I was receiving in healing my fractured psyche. My individuality was feeling more and more secure, but—coming from a conservative Christian background—my wife disapproved of my training and ceremonial practices. During this time, I spent many countless nights away from bed, writing and doodling, communing with my mesa in creative ways.

Being a fan of occult fiction, I concocted a sort of occult detective character whom I named Simon Myth. The name was a derivative of the legend Simon Magus, a religious figure who first was featured in the Holy Bible but later showed up in stories across Gnostic and even Druidic lore. Also, I included the term "myth" as an homage to Joseph Campbell's monomyth work and recognizing the wisdom of stories inherent in all cultures. There was a resonance with Simon that gripped me. In a way, he took the guise of a modern-day Gandalf, with magic, the occult, and all kinds of supernatural hubbub taking center stage in his adventures.

Now, since that time, I have written approximately twenty different short stories and three different prose novels starring this character Simon Myth, all of which have never seen the publishing light of day. I have just never been able to get the character "right." He has taken many incarnations since his initial inception; no longer an occult detective, Simon has gone from being a wily professor to even a magical assassin-for-hire.

Simon Myth has clung to my consciousness, never letting go. He shows up in dreams, in shamanic journeys. I even have an arte on my mesa that represents Simon. He has taught me a lot about magick, especially making use of whatever materials I have in the moment, seeing the potential of the sacred in every situation and location (even if it's a run-down diner in the middle of the desert). However, I was still never able to get Simon's representation on paper in such a way that made sense, that felt, again, "right."

I have since happily remarried and my current wife, Autumn, has endured every script for a Simon Myth story that has spilled out of my brain. Most every time after reading, her feedback is "It's really great, honey, but I think it needs to be a comic." Simon himself has prodded me with many such hints over the years.

Now, a little background. Since I was a child, I always—from when I can first remember—wanted to be a comic book artist. That was my dream. From my earliest days, I was inspired by the Sunday strip greats such as Charles Schulz and Berke Breathed. You could catch me daily redrawing comic book art from the masters of the Silver Age like Jack Kirby, John Buscema, or Herb Trimpe. Growing into adolescence, I spent countless days and nights mimicking the styles of Jim Lee, Rob Liefeld, and Erik Larsen. I was obsessed; it's what I always wanted to do. Even more, it's what I always knew I was *meant* to do. Everyone in my family and at school knew me as "Danny the Artist." It was my destiny, and I embraced it fully!

Then, I went to college, focusing on art along with writing. Somehow through that experience, art began to panic me. Due to the critiques and competitive culture, my fears and insecurities got the best of me. By the time I graduated, I had a degree in English (as well as one in studio art, but that was perceived as a side note). My now-preferred mode of creative expression was creative writing. For some reason, prose just seemed less vulnerable; it was easier to hide behind words and grammar than through your brush strokes or pen marks on a page to be scrutinized. I was using writing as a mask to hide my fear of rejection. After college, I never pursued art again. I doodled here and there, but I never went after my dream of being a cartoonist.

It is probably no surprise to you when I say my creative life was unsatisfactory to me this whole time. I do receive joy from writing. However, for decades, instead of doing what I know I was meant to do in this world, I compromised. This compromise of my true desire led to consistent bitterness toward myself and the world, which I constantly projected outward to others.

Many synchronistic moments, including Simon and his adventures, can be traced in my journals for years, leading me eventually to the conclusion that both Simon and my wife had been nudging me toward. Even in Peru during a very special *mesada*—a wedding ceremony between Autumn and me—a powerful curandero working with us told me that I needed to be working creatively with my hands again, doing more artwork. Both Autumn and Simon would keep dropping those hints: "Do comics! Do it!" Eventually, Autumn surprised me with a full set of correspondence courses from the Joe Kubert School of Cartoon and Graphic Art (the school I had always wanted to attend but never allowed myself to) and that was it: I dove in!

From that moment, I started drawing comics and have never looked back. Two things have happened as a result: (1) I have never been happier with myself in my whole life, and (2) Simon Myth is finally coming to fruition. By following this imaginary ally's poking and prodding (along with my wife's and others'), I have come into a sense of wholeness I never truly thought existed, except as concepts in books on psychology and mysticism. If only I had listened to those daimonic notions earlier instead of suffering for years.

By "daimonic" I do not mean anything "demonic." In fact, the word "demon" comes from the Greek *daemon*, which was originally defined as a being acting as an intermediary between the gods and humanity.

The Christian tradition later took this word and bastardized it over time, painting anything other than what was attributed to the one God as "demonic," the word becoming synonymous with evil. However, daemons have a long-standing lineage in Gnosticism and Neoplatonism. It is said that Socrates himself had a daemon who frequently warned him against making wrong decisions or times of trouble. The daimonic realm exists within us and as a medium for the *anima mundi*, the Greek term for the "World Soul," which we will cover more in depth in chapter 10.

Patrick Harpur has done a lot of great work surrounding daimonic beings and their nature. In his book, *Daimonic Reality*, he states that "the daimons are archetypal images which, in the process of individuation, conduct us towards the archetypes (gods) themselves. They did not have to convey messages; they were themselves the message."[30] The daimonic realm is dream, it is the three pachas, it is the astral, and more. The daimonic realm cannot be pinned down. All daimonic phenomena dodge the opportunity to become a literal reality in which we can measure or test: ghosts, UFOs, the Loch Ness monster, Bigfoot, and so on. They all show up just so we can catch a glimpse, but we can never really get that verifiable evidence needed to have empirical proof. The picture is always hazy. The film is grainy. The daimonic realm is amorphous, and that is its true power. We can never truly grasp it with our hands, but it lures us with an inner yearning to have more, to lift the veil and uncover the mystery.

But that's the thing about the daimonic realm: it is the mystery itself. Without mystery, there is no daimon. Without the daimon, there is no connection to the World Soul, which—as stated in the previous chapter—is the storehouse of all imagination. "Personal daimons are not fixed," Harpur says, "but can develop or unfold according to our spiritual development."[31] Watching Simon change and evolve over time—in a way matching my own life path—I have been able to see the strong link to

---

30 Patrick Harpur, *Daimonic Reality: A Field Guide to the Otherworld* (London: Viking Arcana, 1994), 38.

31 Harpur, *Daimonic Reality*, 42.

the daimonic realm and imagination more clearly. In fact, imagination is the key!

This is why visualization and shamanic journeying are so important. Our imagination is that bridging point between our minds and the universe. It is what fuels innovation and creativity, ultimately generating the very reality we live in: roads, buildings, songs, sports, politics, TV, hotdogs—it all comes from a result of imagination spawning something into being. Why then wouldn't this being in my imagination set me down a better path in my life? Is the fact that he *comes* from my imagination any different from receiving guidance or wisdom from another human being? In Tibetan Buddhism, there is a concept called a *tulpa*, which is a being or creature generated as a thought form through extreme concentration. In Judaism, there is the golem, a creature built of clay but infused with consciousness by the breath of the rabbi. We also have the concept of the *egregore*, a non-physical entity created by a collective group all concentrating on a single idea. When the mind is focused and repeatedly hits on the same idea over and over, that idea has power. The more energy you put into that idea, the more it grows, evolves, eventually having a life of its own. In effect, these ideas can develop their own autonomous sense of consciousness.

A Magickal Formula

Whether the result of a magickal working comes as a daimonic entity, as a spirit animal, or through just your own will and tenacity, the point of my story remains true: when you change your actions to align with your will and sense of purpose, life gets better. That is the essence of the magickal act.

Anything can be a magickal act. If you are changing reality based upon your intention, then you are practicing magick. Yet, this does not mean that anytime you have an intention, and it comes true, that you are practicing magick. Magick tends to make some people crazy because sometimes they believe they are creating everything. They aren't—they're just crazy. One of the most important aspects of magickal practice is *discernment*.

To know you are practicing discernment, here is a basic formula you can follow when performing any magickal ritual, especially in concert with the shamanic practices throughout this book:

1. **What do you want to create?** Establish a statement of intent. What do you want to create in your experience of life?

2. **Consider if this creation can actually manifest.** Not everything is possible, actually. I'm not going to have a billion dollars land in my lap just because I want it. I have to earn it. Plus, that's not necessarily in alignment with my soul's purpose. But maybe if I make a product or host a bake sale, I can make some money, eh?

3. **Imitate the experience you want.** This is where ritual comes in, which is nothing more than a dramatization of what you want to come true. Go to your mesa, or set up some other type of ceremonial space, and create a ceremony replicating the reality you want. Put on a play, draw a picture, sing a song, write an essay, beat a drum—whatever. Make sure whatever you do, in your consciousness, symbolically represents what you want to have happen.

4. **Forget about it.** The way magick works, for some reason, is that you have to let go of the desire for whatever you're asking for. I think magicians through the centuries have tried to figure out why; I don't think anybody knows. It's just the way the universe works. In my experience, when I hold on to the desire for something, it will never manifest. As soon as I let it go and no longer care if I want it or not, it lands in my lap. Release your expectations.

If you follow these steps and what you wanted comes true, then you could be practicing magick. The only way you will find out is to just do it. Experiment. Have fun. If you're not having fun, it won't be worth it and the magick won't work.

Every ritual or ceremony you do, you are doing magick. Even if that ceremonial intent is just to connect with the universe spiritually, that is a magickal act, because you are changing your consciousness. At the end of the day, that is what magick is about: changing consciousness. It is not about whether or not you can conjure lightning or teleport across the country, although I have seen miraculous things like this happen. It all starts with the root of changing your own consciousness and how you interact with reality.

According to the great chaos magician and author Phil Hine, "Consciousness arises from perception, which arises from our direct engagement with the environment."[32] The true miracle is you changing your own life, shifting your course (whether through shamanic means or not) so that you achieve what you came here to do. End of story.

Your thoughts are magick. Your words are magick. Your actions are magick. All these things create reality.

Now, let's create some magick.

---

32 Phil Hine, *Condensed Chaos: An Introduction to Chaos Magic* (Tempe, AZ: New Falcon Publications, 1995), 78.

Shamanic Cosmos and Consciousness

My training in northern coastal curanderismo continued for years, consisting of both solo and group settings. One particular evening early in my training, it was just don Daniel and I, sitting in his lodge in the country plains. It was dark, as the sun was slowly dipping past the horizon line. Besides the deep purple haze of twilight, only the candles on his mesa provided what little luminescence permeated the room.

"You are fragmented, mixed up. You need to become whole," don Daniel said while flitting a condor feather over his mesa, guiding it through the smoke of burning copal. "To do this you must get in touch with your own soul."

"How do I do that?" I asked, a question that would never directly get answered.

"The first shaman was known as *Mallku*," he told me, candlelight flickering on his leathery face, "which comes from *mallki*, the word for 'tree' in Quechua. The first shaman was called this because trees are the only living beings on Pachamama to be able to live in the three worlds at once, which is the true function of the curandero."

"Three worlds?"

"Yes, Mallku was the first human to have roots in the lower world, with a strong trunk in middle world, and his branches reaching up high into the upper world. Mallku was the perfect representation of 'as above, so below; as below, so above.' This is the motto of the curandero. It is said that long ago these three worlds were one, but then they were fractured. Some people refer to this as the Fall from the Garden of Eden. Either way, we now live in a fractured reality, but the shaman's role is to unite the worlds into one reality."

"Unite them?" I could not fathom exactly how that would be. Three worlds uniting into one sounded something a little too much like science fiction or from a movie like *The Dark Crystal*. It sounded pretty out there.

"Follow me." Don Daniel walked out of the lodge, covering himself in his bright white poncho, and I followed suit. We stepped outside to the expanse of acres on his property. A forest of oaks and persimmons stretched around the perimeter. There was one tree at the front of the woods that stuck out among all the others: a gargantuan hedge (Osage orange) tree, fully matured, its branches stretching like an octopus about three stories high, its roots plowing through the soil in all sorts of crests and troughs. It was a magnificent site, something that could very well be the portal to some other dimension from a fairy tale, like the wardrobe in C. S. Lewis's *Chronicles of Narnia*.

Don Daniel motioned for me to sit in a nook at the base of the tree, cradled by two giant roots, each larger than my whole body put together. I crouched and settled into it, very soon getting comfortable despite the furrowed bark sticking into my back.

"Now close your eyes and allow yourself to be fully enveloped by the tree. Breathe, and allow this great mallki to take you over. You and the mallki are one!"

I practiced the breathing I had been taught, as well as the basics of shamanic journeying (which we will discuss later this chapter). Eventually, my poq'po bonded with the tree, melting together into a seamless whole. Finding myself within the darkness of mallki, I felt my form descending through the trunk, past its arachnid roots, and into the soil below.

In the cavernous vistas of the underworld, the wisdom of the mallki held up a mirror to me, one I first rejected, disliking what I saw staring back at me. It was an ugly, neglected form, an aspect of myself I didn't want to admit existed. It contained my fear, my shame, my anger, and all the other things limiting me, preventing me from achieving the happiness and success I so desired.

However, it occurred to me that this shadowy form of myself existed deep in the earth, a part of the soil from which the mallki itself received the nutrients that fed its roots. It was then the mallki showed me that this aspect of myself was nothing to suppress or discard. In fact, the mallki needed it just as much as the trunk or the branches, one part of a holistic system operating in unity as a singular organism.

The Three Pachas

This is not the first book on shamanism—and it won't be the last—that references the idea of three worlds that exist in the shamanic cosmos. Academically, it is very easy to examine most indigenous cosmological frameworks and conclude that there are three distinct realms or worlds of being in which the universe operates. Colloquially—thanks to the work of anthropologist Michael Harner, as popularized in his book *The Way of the Shaman*—they are called the lower world, middle world, and upper (or higher) world.

Though there are strong correlations among the many disparate cultures around the planet, each culture's system is also unique. It's true that complexities exist in their distinct cosmological systems, but the goal of our shamanic work in this book is not to conduct an academic study into cultural anthropology. Rather, it is about understanding what it is we need to know in order to practice the art of shamanism.

Similar to Harner's three-world concept, the indigenous Peruvian cosmology exists in a comparable structure. In the Quechua language, these worlds are called *pachas* (PAH-chahs). As referenced earlier in the pillar of light exercise (practicum 8), a pacha can mean a world, but it also has a deeper meaning of a location among time and space, a dimension, or even a bardo of Buddhist spiritual understanding. In truth, they are not so much specific locations in the universe, but they more so represent an experience of existence. Here is a basic breakdown of the three worlds, or pachas, as understood by most shamanic traditions, using the Peruvian Quechua phraseology.

Hanaqpacha (hah-NAHK-pah-chah): *Hanaq* means upper or higher, so this is a designation for the upper world. Generally, one could take this to mean the heavens, the place where Creator and all the angelic beings of a more refined energy of existence reside. In Peru, the Hanaqpacha is often related to the tops of the mountains (called *apus*), the roof of the world.

Kaypacha (KAI-pah-chah): *Kay* is a reference to the here and now, the current thing in front of you; therefore, the Kaypacha is the middle world. This is the world in which we are currently incarnated, where we exist to live and do our work.

Ukhupacha (OOK-hoo-pah-chah): Though this term normally indicates the lower world, the word *ukhu* is more of a reference to the interior spaces of the world and even within oneself. The Ukhupacha can normally be understood as the place of heavy or dense energies and the darker things of existence.

It is easy, especially having a Western frame of mind, to relate the Hanaqpacha to the idea of heaven and the Ukhupacha to hell. However, these are literal concepts, and if there is one thing to remember about shamanism and learning to navigate the mysteries of the universe, it is that you should never take anything literally. Personally, I have learned over time that these pachas are modes of consciousness that exist here and now; it's just that the Kaypacha realm is the more immediate state of awareness for us. The Hanaqpacha and Ukhupacha are within reach at all times. In fact, there are myths from the *paqos* (shamanic priests of the Quechua) that the three worlds used to be united, but at some point in time a great division happened and they became three instead of one.

To illustrate this point, I want to revisit the tree, the mallki, from my experience on don Daniel's land.

Trees are important symbols in many spiritual traditions across the planet, especially shamanic cultures. During the Sundance ceremony of the Native American Lakota, the people cut down a tree together and carry it to the dance, to replant it in the ground as the ritual center of their annual celebration of life and community. In Haitian Vodou, the *potomitan* is a central pillar—often a wooden post—which acts as the bridge between the earth and the loa (the spiritual pantheon of Vodou religion). The indigenous Makuna of the Colombian Amazon even bring this tree symbolism into their daily lives, with the posts supporting the roof of their homes representing ancestors who bridge the sky and the land. Like the Norse Tree of Life, called Yggdrasil, and the Tree of Life of the mystical system of Qabalah (discussed in my previous book, *Shamanic Qabalah*), the anatomy of a tree can easily be likened to a model of the cosmos.

I believe the mallki is the perfect symbol for the three worlds because a tree does have separate parts, but they are not actually *disparate* parts: they are all part of the same organism.

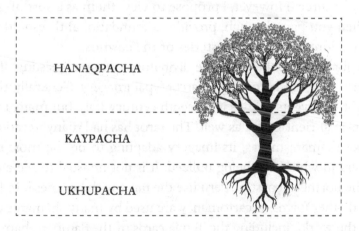

HANAQPACHA

KAYPACHA

UKHUPACHA

Figure 25. Mallki and the three pachas

Stand with your feet firmly on the ground. Reach your arms into the sky. Your feet and legs are the roots of the tree, extending into the ground and drawing the kawsay from the earth. Your body is the trunk, the primary pole of your physical form. Your arms and crown are the branches, extending upward to the sky, to the spiritual realms of existence. The tree is the perfect symbol of this balance because it does not separate its parts; they all work together—seamlessly—to make the thing we know of as a tree. The three worlds are no different. Shamanic cosmology resides in the notion that the universe is whole but has various parts that are meant to act in unison. If they do not, it is up to the shamanic initiate to draw them together.

The Pachas on the Mesa

The job of the shaman is to be a mediator of these three worlds. This can be accomplished through the vehicle of the mesa and, thus, unite them once again.

There are many ways to view reality, just as there is a multitude of dimensions for the shaman to psychonautically travel and to acquire the information needed to cure. Among these varied realities, there are three basic dimensions or worlds in which the universe as we know it is contained. I encourage you to understand these three worlds not as the only way in which these realities can be experienced, nor is reality limited only to three. However, I propose to view them as a sort of gateway that, when you pass through, provides a foundational threshold for you to then explore the deeper mysteries of the cosmos.

Take for instance the tarot, the divinatory system consisting of a deck of seventy-eight cards containing archetypal imagery. Generally, the tarot is thought to have its origins in fifteenth-century Italy, but many believe it has roots in ancient Egypt as well. The tarot has had many iterations over time, like shamanism has, its imagery adapting to be the most efficient for the era in which it is being utilized. It is not unusual to see a curandero in the northern coast of Peru use the tarot with her mesa. In fact, the tarot and other forms of cartomancy are used by many shamanic cultures around the world, including the Teuila cards of the Samoan shamans, the Lenormand cards of French fortune-telling fame, or the Tikar spider cards (originally plum leaves) of West Africa. These cards are not just used to perform traditional divination practices, but they act as gateways to the invisible forces and realities in action around us at all times.

The tarot is divided into two groups, the major arcana and minor arcana. Consisting of twenty-two cards, the major arcana represent prime archetypal forms of the universe, whereas the rest of the cards contain the minor arcana, which symbolize specific life activities. One of the most prominent cards of the tarot is the major arcana card called the High Priestess. This card portrays a woman who is seated on a throne and crowned with the crescent moon, a symbol of magic and mystery. She holds the Torah in her hands as well as a set of keys to unlock that mystery of the holy text. Behind her stand two pillars labeled *J* and *B*, which stand for Jachin and Boaz, with a veil stretched between. This veil is said to hide the mystery of life, the unseen realms of magic and mysticism. To lift this veil, one must unlock the mystery symbolism of the High Priestess herself. She is the gateway to the great originating mystery of the universe.

Figure 26. The High Priestess

The imagery of this card is important to meditate upon, for each description in itself is a vital symbol leading to a deeper understanding of shamanic practice. Most specifically, I would like you to focus on the pillars in the High Priestess card. These pillars also symbolize the two pillars in the entrance to King Solomon's temple—Jachim and Boaz—a holy icon of Judaic mysticism (normally displayed as one being black, the other white, as adopted by the Masonic temples, as well). Behind her, the veil covers the entrance to the temple containing the Great Mystery for the initiate to uncover themselves, through her.

Similarly, and quite astonishingly, the entrance of Chavín de Huántar, the temple of the pre-Columbian Peruvian culture heralding the origins of northern coastal curanderismo, is framed by two pillars: also one white, one black. Like the High Priestess, the initiate enters Chavín de Huántar in the darkness, their eyes veiled, housing the force (*El Lanzón*) contained within. Although the coloring of the pillars is not as prevalent today due to age and erosion, analysis and models show they were clearly painted in those distinct colors. Similar intimations of the duality embodied by these pillars is revealed in other imagery at Chavín de Huántar, including the ingeniously carved Raimondi Stele: another fearsome Lanzón-like deity holding two pillar-like stalks of the huachuma cactus, another symbol of the balancing act between one force and another.

Figure 27. Chavín de Huántar

This is a prime example of how ancient the imagery of the tarot truly is as well as how its symbols can be found in multiple cultures around the world.

One way to understand the three worlds is prevalent in this imagery of the pillars, including both how and why they were used as the entrances to these sacred spaces. In my book *Shamanic Qabalah*, I went to great lengths describing the polarized relationship of these pillars in accordance with the Tree of Life (the Judaic symbol of creation), and how they represent the concepts of Force and Form, the Middle Pillar (the initiate) being the stabilizing entity of equilibrium between them.[33]

Let's view the pachas not as a tiered structure of these three worlds, like some sort of hierarchy (above or below one another), but through the lens of the mesa itself. This helps in better understanding pachas because a vital concept in shamanic practice is that the pachas, the worlds, are not something separate from you—they are within and a part of you.

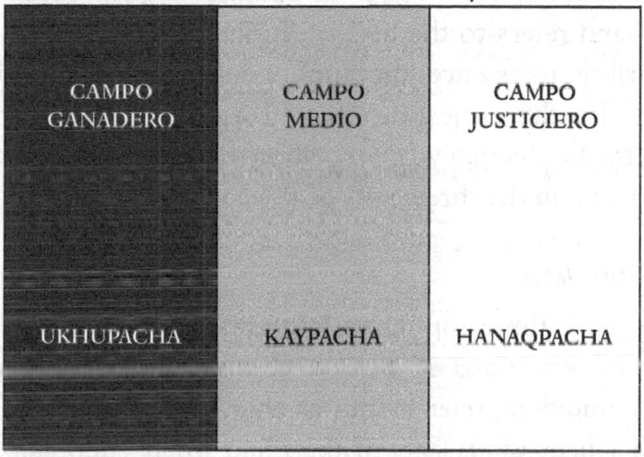

CAMPO GANADERO	CAMPO MEDIO	CAMPO JUSTICIERO
UKHUPACHA	KAYPACHA	HANAQPACHA

Figure 28. The campos and the pachas

This verticality of the three campos rids the three worlds of a sense of hierarchy and more closely resembles the columns in the High Priestess card of the entrance to Chavín de Huántar. There is no one greater than another; they all serve their purpose in an interconnected network of experience. Anthropologist and shamanic expert Dr. Roger Walsh states that "the shaman's worlds and levels are more than interconnected; they also interact with one another. Shamans believe that these

---

33 Daniel Moler, *Shamanic Qabalah: A Mystical Path to Uniting the Tree of Life & the Great Work* (Woodbury, MN: Llewellyn Publications, 2018), 89–100.

interactions can be perceived and affected by one who knows how to do so and that the shaman, like a spider at the center of a cosmic web, can feel and influence distant realms."[34] The correlation of the Kaypacha with the campo medio provides for us that template of interconnectivity, while the other two polarities of the universe interact to create the holism of reality.

Sombras

How do we interact with these three worlds? We live in the Kaypacha; we are the campo medio. It is through us these worlds engage and, in fact, exist. Each of these pachas relates to aspects of ourselves, for we are the tree, the mallki. These parts that make up the self are known in curanderismo as the *sombra*. In Spanish, *sombra* means "shadow" or "shade" and refers to the idea of an image—our image—cast upon another surface. In essence, the sombra is not only a reflection of your psyche but also the projection of your astral self. The sombra is the image cast by the shaman when traveling through pachas of the cosmos. Let's walk through the three parts of the sombra.

Sombra Ganadera

Correlating with the campo ganadero and the Ukhupacha, the *sombra ganadera* is the apparatus of the soul that remembers and reacts to the past. Other traditions refer to this as the lower self, and most often it resides in a subconscious state of the mind where suppressed memories are stored. This is why the sombra ganadera often manifests when we are hurt or triggered: our instincts kick in to protect us from past trauma and we end up saying and doing things we wish we hadn't later on. For this reason, some curanderos call this aspect of the sombra *contrario* ("contrary"): the sombra ganadera will sabotage our lives, when all it is really trying to do is protect itself. In many Western circles, this sombra is normally just referred to as "the shadow." Regardless of the terminology, the sombra ganadera makes everything about "me, me, me!"

---

34 Walsh, *The World of Shamanism*, 126.

In our society, most sombras ganaderas are out of control because we do not have the institutions in place to care for that part of who we are. In fact, we often repress it and try to pretend it doesn't exist. The sombra ganadera is not bad or evil—it just is. Like an ill-tempered child, it just needs attention and care. In fact, one of the first major endeavors of the shamanic initiate is to turn the sombra ganadera into an ally, to embrace it and find a way to engage in such a relationship that it becomes a source of wisdom rather than an agent of chaos. For curanderismo, this is paramount. All curanderos face a trial period in their training, faced with the decision of whether or not to be ruled by the sombra ganadera.

My sombra ganadera has become my greatest teacher. This does not mean it still doesn't get out of control sometimes, but I have developed (through my own shamanic training) a relationship with the sombra ganadera so that I can better mitigate any outbursts or sneaky ways it might manifest in my life. It is important to note that I am my sombra, even though I am speaking of it as if it were separate. You are your sombra. It is not separate. Like the roots of the tree, the Ukhupacha, or the campo ganadero, it is all part of the same whole of the self, the mallki, the three pachas, or the mesa.

Sombra Primera

Whereas the sombra ganadera is a very personal sombra, the *sombra primera* ("prime shade" or "first shade") is an interpersonal one. Housed in the Kaypacha, this is the part of yourself concerned with relationships and being in this world. In psychology it may be known as the ego, which, like the sombra ganadera (or subconscious), can get out of control. However, the sombra primera reminds us that it is this world in which we live and operate, regardless of the ability to travel to other realities. The ability to be grounded, to honor the schedules of society and the boundaries of community, is the principal aim of the sombra primera's function.

As many of us know, the ego can become a source of rigidity, controlling its environment. It is important to note the sombra primera has its inverse ways as well.

Residing in the campo medio, the sombra primera acts as the mediator between all realms. The Hanaqpacha and the Ukhupacha can only exist through the medium of the Kaypacha. Likewise, the sombra primera is the reconciler between the other two aspects of the self. The sombra primera is concerned only with the present. "Here, right now, always," the great Ram Dass said. "Nobody is going anywhere. Nobody is coming from anywhere. We're all here in eternal time & space."[35] This is the chief mantra of the sombra primera (Ram Dass's book I just referenced, *Be Here Now*, is an excellent resource for this). The key to the sombra primera's role is balance.

Sombra Criandera

Criandera is the Spanish word for "wet nurse" or "nursemaid." Therefore, the *sombra criandera* is the aspect of the self which nurtures the curandero upon their path of shamanic practice, encouraging them toward evolution. Other traditions call this the higher self, that which is concerned with transcendent reality. Residing within the campo justiciero, the sombra criandera reminds you that you are Creator made manifest as this human incarnation; you are divine and whole just as you are. This is why the sombra criandera is often associated with the Hanaqpacha.

However, in curanderismo there is no one thing that is "good" or "bad." Like the tarot, in which all cards can be reversed, all aspects of soul have their inverse. The elevated aspirations of the sombra criandera can lead to an inflated ego. In fact, in Peru the Hanaqpacha itself can be a source of illness via a psychic instability of overexposure to the energies of the higher realms. This is an important lesson that, again, the sombra primera is the beginning and end state of the shaman's reality. No matter what journeys you take into the heavens, you should always be grounded and attentive to the "mundane" world (where we all live and interact). Trees do not float; they are rooted in the soil of Pachamama always.

---

35 Ram Dass, *Be Here Now* (New York: Crown Publishing, 1978), 80–81.

CAMPO GANADERO	CAMPO MEDIO	CAMPO JUSTICIERO
Field of the Magician	Field of Equilibrium	Field of the Mystic
Energy: Magic	Energy: Medicine	Energy: Mysticism
Gender: Feminine	Gender: Androgynous	Gender: Masculine
Healing: Dispatching, Protection	Healing: Balance, Transmission	Healing: Raising, Uplifting
Patron Saint: San Cyprian / Santa Justina	Patron Saint: Jesu Cristo, San Pedro	Patron Saint: San Martin de Porres, Madre María
Time: The Past	Time: The Present	Time: The Future
World: Ukhupacha	World: Kaypacha	World: Hanaqpacha
Self: Sombra Ganadera	Self: Sombra Primera	Self: Sombra Criandera
Mallki: Roots	Mallki: Trunk	Mallki: Branches

Figure 29. Campos with additional attributes

Individuation

Psychoanalyst Carl Jung was a seminal influence in the analysis of dreams. Later in life, with his fascination with dreamwork mixed with a love of alchemy, he developed methods very much like those of shamanic initiatory practices. In fact, many scholars have, in countless studies, related Jung's work to a modern form of shamanism. In his autobiography, he discusses how this type of work, related to the aspects of self, led him to one of his greatest contributions to mapping the psyche:

> I became aware that the unconscious undergoes or produces change. Only after I had familiarized myself with alchemy did I realize that the unconscious is a process, and that the psyche is transformed or developed by the relationship of the ego to the contents of the unconscious. ... Through the study of these collective transformation processes and through understanding of alchemical symbolism I arrived at the central concept of my psychology: the process of individuation.[36]

36 Carl G. Jung, *Memories, Dreams, Reflections* (New York: Vintage Books, 1989), 209. Jung's emphasis.

Individuation is essentially taking the disparate parts of the psyche and integrating them, making them whole. Carl Jung did this primarily through working with mandalas through trance and dreamwork, all intrinsically shamanic practices. For the shamanic initiate, individuation is not just a process, but a way of life. The curandero works continually to be aware of and keep all three sombras integrated and working harmoniously. The goal of shamanic practice is not to rise to the higher self (sombra criandera) but to integrate all aspects of the sombra, of the self, into a harmonious mechanism in order to operate in all three worlds.

For me, it took years of working with don Daniel before I came to a place where my suffering eased. I still suffer, because I am human. I am not enlightened nor will I ever claim to be. However, before my shamanic training I was so consumed with fear and trauma that I could not walk into a room with more than one person without having a panic attack. I couldn't hug another person or even shake hands without getting dizzy or nauseous. You can only imagine how my personal relationships were: my sombra ganadera often exploded into fits of rage when I thought I was under attack, verbally or emotionally. I was controlled by my fear.

Now this is not the case. I can breathe easily every day. I can teach a room full of two hundred people and not even break a sweat. I hug most everyone I meet. I may still get angry, but my rage is controlled, and my family feels safe around me. These are all considerable gains, and I owe most all of it to the shamanic way of life.

The following exercises in this chapter and the next two will focus on various practices that assisted me in this process of individuation.

Practicum 13: Shamanic Journeying 101

Shamanic journeying is all about focus, visualization, and imagination. Quick exercise: Focus your will on your favorite fruit. Visualize this piece of fruit, its texture, its color, even bring forth its smell. Use your imagination to create a scenario in your mind in which you eat this fruit, imagining how it tastes, how it feels in your belly. Feel its nutritive qualities fill your belly and satisfy your hunger.

There you go—you just went on a shamanic journey. Journeying is using your will to create a scenario within the space of imagination.

I have already discussed at length in chapter 2 how reality is the result of dreamtime. Imagination is our access point into this dreamtime, into the true shamanic reality, which is why children are typically more adept in the shamanic arts from the get-go. Their imaginations have not been hindered by years of conditioning in the mundane world (yet). Just imagining something doesn't necessarily qualify as a shamanic journey; it takes a lot of time and practice in order to refine qualities of the unseen to begin feeling tangible results of the journeying process.

How will you know you have achieved these results? Signs. Jung calls them *synchronicities*, meaningful coincidences that hold a significant meaning to your spiritual work, tying together what once seemed like disparate fragments of your reality into a holistic framework that makes sense to you (and only you). This will help distinguish between mere fantasy and true shamanic imaginative work.

We have already practiced a form of journeying, but let's run through a more sophisticated scenario to help you fine-tune your journeying prowess, especially in conjunction with the mesa as your guide and control panel for navigating the unseen realms of consciousness. For the following guided journeys, you may want to either read through them first and allow your memory to guide you through, or you can read them aloud into a recording device and play them back as a guide. Also, I have recordings available on my website with Autumn reading the journey out loud (a much more soothing voice than mine, I assure you), linked in appendix C.

Establishing Your Temple

Sit comfortably in front of your mesa. I recommend not lying down for journeying, as it is too easy to fall asleep. Although dreaming is an important aspect of shamanic practice, for journeying you will want to be awake as we are seeking to achieve a specific result in assimilating the pachas within the self.

Practice your breathing basics and then continue with the kawsay activation and pillar of light (appendix A) so that you have aligned your body with the work to be done.

Then, open the account of your mesa.

Next, close your eyes and continue a steady rhythm of breathing using your breathing basics.

With your will, visualize the kulli chunpi (purple belt) at your crown glowing brighter than before, pulsing and enlivening. A cord of light extends from the kulli chunpi, flowing up and away from your body, stretching out toward your mesa. This cord of light lands in the center of your mesa, directly into the arte you have chosen as your nuna khuya. This cord acts as an umbilical connection between you and your mesa, a doorway between you and the unseen realms of consciousness (specifically, in this case, the pachas that reside within your mesa). Settle into this visualization for a few moments, breathing and being aware of your connection with your mesa as a mirror of your own soul.

Once you feel that connection is stabilized, now use your imagination to visualize an image of your self—your sombra—begining to lift out of your physical body and travel along or inside the cord of light, to your mesa. Some people imagine themselves as smaller and traveling within the cord as a sort of tunnel; others visualize themselves as normal size but traveling along the cord as a sort of tether. There is no wrong way to do this, as long as that cord is your connection between your physical body (which is being left behind) and your mesa.

When you arrive at your mesa, drawing ever closer to your nuna khuya, imagine that arte as a portal through which you can travel.

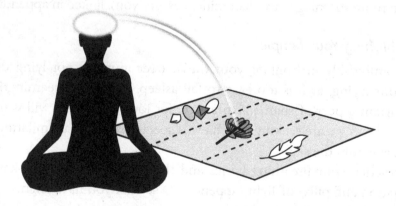

Figure 30. Journeying with the mesa

As you pass through the portal that is your nuna khuya, you will see nothing but complete darkness. It is a comfortable darkness, like being in the womb of your mother. After a while, indiscernible forms begin to manifest in the dark. Those forms will slowly morph into the interior of your own personal temple in the unseen.

This temple is yours and yours alone: it is your personal gateway into the many dimensions of the dreamtime and astral plane. You construct what this temple looks like to you. Is it a massive gothic cathedral? A cave in the wilderness? Maybe it more closely resembles your home or a place from a childhood memory or dream. Construct the temple to your liking, and be as detailed as you can. Are there pillars in the temple? Is there an altar or fireplace, possibly furniture? This temple should be a tribute to you, to your soul. You should feel perfectly comfortable and at home here, as well as inspired to continue the work of shamanic practice, for this temple will be your launching pad into the other realms available in shamanic consciousness.

Also, visualize your sombra. In this temple space, this image of yourself is the sombra primera. When you do any form of astral projection, any sort of journey work into other realms, the sombra primera is your "prime" image of your shamanic power. From this temple, your sombra primera can travel anywhere in the universe and has all the power it needs to cure and collect wisdom for your own individuation, as well as serving your community. The image of your sombra primera can stay the same, but it will likely shift over time into a form suitable to the task (where the concept of shape-shifting comes from). For now, just get to know your sombra primera as is, tracking all the details of your astral form.

Take some more time and get to know the space. How is your temple decorated? Do you see any symbols? How does the floor feel on your feet? What is the temperature of the room? Are there other beings and figures who reside in the temple? Is there an outdoors, and if so, what is it like outside? Are you in a jungle, the desert, or possibly the mountains?

It is important to gather as much detail as possible. Visualization is a key component of shamanic journeying, but do not limit your experience to visuals alone. Pay attention to any aromas that come to your senses. What sounds do you hear? This is all valuable information that will essentially provide a virtual reality of experience. You will want to be as connected to this imaginative world as much as possible. If anything from the outer world—including stray thoughts—pulls you away from the experience, just return to your temple. Don't judge yourself. It takes a lot of practice to fully trance into the visionary state and, even then, you don't want to be completely disconnected from the outer world anyway (you never know what you may need to attend to at a moment's notice).

When you feel you have spent a suitable amount of time in your temple (approximately twenty minutes is a good start) go back to the space in your temple where you first started. Have your sombra primera (your astral self) close its eyes. Return to the deep darkness of the womb again.

Within that darkness, you see a flash, and before you know it, you have been birthed back out of your nuna khuya, traveling through the cord of light above your mesa. Allow your sombra to travel across that cord and into your crown, your kulli chunpi. Guide the form of your sombra to rest inside your physical form, allowing its arms and legs to align with your physical limbs, spines and torsos aligning, and finally the heads, all sliding into one another perfectly like fingers sliding into a glove.

Become fully aware of your breathing. Get in tune with its rhythm. Visually imagine the cord retracting from your nuna khuya and return it to your crown, fully phasing into the kulli chunpi. Stay aware of your breathing and know you are whole, all parts of yourself together, intact, and in perfect unity. When you feel ready, begin to slowly move your limbs and open your eyes to the waking world around you.

As the anchor of your experience, the mesa is that entry point to your temple and all the experiences of the unseen. Therefore, give an offering of gratitude to your mesa for providing safety and being the vehicle of your shamanic work. You can spray some agua de florida on the mesa or blow some sage or tobacco smoke. Some curanderos make offerings by spraying waters from a nearby river or lake that is sacred to them, some bring flowers to lay on the mesa, and others sing songs of thanksgiving. It is up to you how you want to make your offering, but it is vital that you do so after each ritual.

After your offering, immediately go to your journal and record as much of your experience as you can. You can write down or draw, or both, the experience of your temple. I recommend visiting your temple at least once a week for a few weeks, possibly even a month or longer, before continuing on to the next exercise. Your goal is to be intimately familiar with your temple, almost like a second home. If your temple changes and shifts upon you revisiting it, that is fine. If you want to meditate in your temple or experiment with walking around and exploring, do so. There is no wrong thing that can happen in your temple; you will just need to make sure it retains the familiarity of being your space alone.

I also highly recommend visiting your temple as you lie down to sleep, as an entry point into dreamtime. You do not have to have your mesa next to you for this, for the cord of light can extend across your entire home (or town) if necessary. A suggestion can be to retrieve the nuna khuya from your mesa and put it on your bedside table for the night, connecting your cord of light to your khuya from there. Your khuya can act as a temporary connector to your mesa as a whole. When you wake in the morning, you can visualize your sombra returning and realigning with your physical body. You can then return your khuya to the mesa and give your offering of gratitude.

Another suggestion is to create or designate another arte specifically for dream and/or journey work to act as that anchor if you do not want to use the nuna khuya. To do this, just follow the same protocol in the activating artes exercise (practicum 11), but just set the intention for this particular tool to work specifically with journey work into the pachas and beyond.

As a side note, I have created a list of music you may want to play to accompany you on your journeying in appendix C.

Practicum 14: Journey to the Ukhupacha

The sombra ganadera is a part of us and always will be. Again, also commonly referred to as the shadow, the sombra ganadera represents the aspects of ourselves that we put to the side and do not attend to. In shamanic practice, one must become whole. As author Robert Bly (who wrote extensively on the human shadow of the psyche) once said,

"Every part of our personality that we do not love will become hostile to us. We could add that it may move to a distant place and revolt against us as well."[37]

That "place" Robert Bly is referring to is indeed the Ukhupacha. The purpose of journeying into the Ukhupacha is to manage those aspects of ourselves that are repressed, to uncover habits and tendencies rooted deep in the subconscious whose effects we are unaware of in the material world (the Kaypacha). For the record, this is not meant to be used as psychoanalysis, and, in fact, I strongly advise you to seek professional assistance if you require psychological help. This journey is to be used as an initiatory tool for yourself and no one else, for the purposes of shamanic training only.

Be sure to block off a good chunk of time for this process. I recommend an entire evening in which you will not be disturbed, a good three to four hours. A week or two in advance, set your intention for this work that you will be traveling to the Ukhupacha to interact with the sombra ganadera for the purposes of spiritual growth. It is important you do not rush this. If you are in a frame of mind where you are not ready or comfortable enough to perform this journey, then don't do it. There is no shame in waiting or delaying. Shamanism is not a race, and there are no medals to be won. What's important is that you are ready and feel safe to continue forward.

Before you begin, write down these questions on a piece of paper and answer them:

1. How do I sabotage myself in my life's choices?

2. In what ways do I react instead of respond?

3. At what moments do I become the most triggered?

4. What is it I want to change most about my life?

Put this piece of paper on your mesa, in the campo ganadero. When the time you have blocked off arrives, begin to set your space. Follow the guidance as it is laid out in the previous practicum, shamanic

---

37 Robert Bly, *A Little Book on the Human Shadow* (San Francisco: Harper & Row, 1988), 20.

journeying 101. For music, I highly recommend *Dream Tracker* by Byron Metcalf, Dashmesh Khalsa, and Steve Roach; *Medicine Work* by Byron Metcalf and Rob Thomas; or *Helpers, Guides, and Allies* by Byron Metcalf.

Start your ceremony again with breathing basics, kawsay activation, the pillar of light, and the opening of the account, as referenced in appendix A. Burn some sage or incense (copal recommended) to cleanse the space and tune your consciousness to the ritual at hand. Take a moment to review the questions you wrote down and your answers. Make sure the issue you are hoping to resolve in these questions is clear in your mind. We will now do a journey to initiate you to the Ukhupacha and sombra ganadera.

Close your eyes and begin your journeying process by connecting a cord of light from your kulli chunpi to the center of your mesa at the nuna khuya. Now, further extend the cord from your nuna khuya to your arte de defensa in the campo ganadero. Settle into this visualization for a few moments, breathing and being aware of the connection with your mesa as a mirror of your own soul.

Once you feel that connection is stabilized, use your imagination to visualize your sombra lifting out of your physical body and traveling along the cord of light, to your mesa. When you arrive at your mesa, drawing ever closer to your nuna khuya, imagine that arte as a portal through which you can travel. With the nuna khuya connected to the arte de defensa, the campo medio will mediate your experience with the campo ganadero (Ukhupacha).

As you pass through the portal that is your nuna khuya, you will see nothing but complete darkness. It is a comfortable darkness, like being in the womb of your mother. After a while, indiscernible forms begin to manifest in the dark. Those forms will slowly morph into the interior of your own personal temple in the unseen. You are back in your temple. Take a few moments to settle into your temple; observe any aspects or changes to your temple and/or sombra.

Exit your temple to the wilderness outside. Take a moment to observe the particular ecosystem outside your temple space. Feel the temperature of the weather on your skin and the texture of the ground underneath your feet. Walk around. Listen to the sounds of nature. Walk deeply into the wilderness, to the point where your temple is no longer in view.

Soon, you come upon an opening in the ground. It can be a cave, a hole in a tree, or any other opening, as long as it leads into the interior of the earth. Enter the opening. As you do, it becomes dark, damp, and chilly like a cave. You are in a small tunnel or canal. You cannot see but know that you move forward through the tunnel, which leads down beneath the surface of the planet. The journey is long; at times the tunnel becomes almost too low or too narrow to maneuver, but you crawl through in complete darkness. Soon, you see a faint light up ahead, almost ultraviolet. As you move onward, the light becomes slightly brighter, but not blinding. It is coming through another opening ahead. The tunnel shimmers as if a black light is shining on you and you can see the ridges of the tunnel walls in that ultraviolet haze.

Finally, you come through the opening and step into a cavern so massive you cannot see the ceiling or the far walls. In fact, an entire jungle-like wilderness exists in this cavern, all prevalent of the soft glow of that ultraviolet light. Remnants of amethyst can be seen protruding from the ground, which emanate this glow of ultraviolet luminescence. You can hear crickets and other wildlife in the wilderness, though it is like listening to the sounds of animals at night. In a way, this space seems almost more alive than the world above, even though it is the Ukhupacha itself.

From out of the Ukhupacha wilderness, you see a figure approach. In a way, this being resembles a mirroring image of you, but younger. In fact, it resembles a version of you from a specific moment in your past. This younger version of you is one who at one time was hurt and broken, a version of you that you have shut away or repressed. It was a defining moment that caused great pain, maybe even trauma. This figure is one of many versions of your sombra ganadera.

As the sombra ganadera approaches, they ask you to follow. This is what you came here to do. You can trust this figure is an aspect of you from your past. Your sombra ganadera may seem like it is a broken image of you, but in actuality, it is wise, a great teacher, here to show you the medicine you need to heal your wounded self. Follow your sombra ganadera and trust that the answers you need to the questions you wrote down for the medicine of this experience will be revealed, even though they may not be immediately apparent: How can you prevent yourself from sabotaging your life's choices? In what ways can you respond instead of react? How can you better care for yourself when you are triggered? What steps can you take to make the change you want for your life?

Spend a few minutes on a journey with your sombra ganadera and receive the medicine they have for you. When the medicine feels complete, end the journey and return to your physical body. See your sombra ganadera returning to the tunnel leading upward out of the Ukhupacha. Take this time to thank your sombra ganadera for their wisdom and exit the realm through the tunnel. The corridor is dark and damp, much as it was going down. Soon, you will see a light from above: the exit into the natural world.

After you have exited the tunnel, go back to your temple to the exact space where you first started the journey. Have your sombra primera close its eyes. Return to the deep darkness of the womb again.

Within that darkness, you see a flash, and before you know it, you have birthed back out of your nuna khuya, traveling through the cord of light above your mesa. Allow your sombra to travel across that cord and into your crown, your kulli chunpi. Guide the form of your sombra to rest inside your physical form, allowing its arms and legs to align with your physical limbs, spines and torsos aligning, and finally the heads, all sliding into one another perfectly like fingers sliding into a glove.

Become fully aware of your breathing. Get in tune with its rhythm. Visually imagine the cord retracting from your nuna khuya and returning to your crown, fully phasing into the kulli chunpi. Stay aware of your breathing and know you are whole, all parts of yourself together, intact, and in perfect unity. When you feel ready, begin to slowly move your limbs and open your eyes to the waking world around you.

Practicum 15: Journey to the Hanaqpacha

Like the sombra ganadera, the sombra criandera is a part of us and always will be. It is an aspect of our soul moving us toward higher dimensions. Some even say it may be a future aspect of yourself, goading you to a better tomorrow. The purpose of journeying into the Hanaqpacha is to tune in to these higher aspirations of our soul's growth, to gain inspiration on the actions we will soon take in our life's walk. The goal of the Hanaqpacha journey is to get in tune with the higher realms, which the sombra criandera aims to reign, and be of higher service to Pachamama and all humanity. Again, this is not to be used in lieu of psychotherapy and is an initiatory tool for yourself and no one else, for the purposes of shamanic training only.

Be sure to block off a good chunk of time for this process. I recommend an entire evening in which you will not be disturbed, a good three to four hours. A week or two in advance, set your intention for this work that you will be traveling to the Hanaqpacha to interact with the sombra criandera for the purposes of spiritual growth. It is important you do not rush this. If you are in a frame of mind where you are not ready or comfortable enough to perform this journey, then don't do it. There is no shame in waiting or delaying. What's important is that you are ready and feel safe to continue forward.

Before you begin, write down these questions on a piece of paper and answer them:

1. What is my purpose for being alive on planet Earth?

2. What is my medicine that I provide to those around me?

3. What is the medicine that feeds me?

4. What are the next steps to take to evolve myself?

Put this piece of paper on your mesa, in the campo justiciero. When the time you have blocked off arrives, begin to set your space. Follow the guidance as it is laid out in the shamanic journeying 101 practicum. For music, I highly recommend *Buddha Nature* by Deuter or *Canyon Trilogy* by R. Carlos Nakai.

As always, start your ceremony with breathing basics, kawsay activation, the pillar of light, and the opening of the account (see appendix A). Burn some sage or incense (copal recommended) to cleanse the space and tune your consciousness to the ritual at hand. Take a moment to review the questions you wrote down and your answers. Make sure the issue you are hoping to resolve in these questions is clear in your mind. We will now do a journey to initiate you to the Hanaqpacha and sombra criandera.

Close your eyes and begin your journeying process by connecting a cord of light from your kulli chunpi to the center of your mesa at the nuna khuya. Now, further extend the cord from your nuna khuya to your arte de levantada in the campo justiciero. Settle into this visualization for a few moments, breathing and being aware of the connection with your mesa as a mirror of your own soul.

Once you feel that connection is stabilized, use your imagination to visualize your sombra lifting out of your physical body and traveling along the cord of light to your mesa. When you arrive at your mesa, drawing ever closer to your nuna khuya, imagine that arte as a portal through which you can travel. Your nuna khuya in the campo medio will mediate your experience with the campo justiciero (Hanaqpacha).

As you pass through the portal that is your nuna khuya, you will see nothing but complete darkness. It is a comfortable darkness, like being in the womb of your mother. After a while, indiscernible forms begin to manifest in the dark. Those forms will slowly morph into the interior of your own personal temple in the unseen. You are back in your temple. Take a few moments to settle into your temple; observe any new aspects or changes to your temple or sombra.

Exit your temple to the wilderness outside. Take a moment to observe the particular ecosystem outside your temple space. Feel the temperature of the weather on your skin and the texture of the ground underneath your feet. Walk around. Listen to the sounds of nature.

Look above you into the sky. Feel the expanse and the magnificence of the higher world above you, the Hanaqpacha. Watch the wind blow the clouds and the birds soar. Feel yourself become light as a feather; it soon feels as if you are floating above the ground. A great gust of wind comes out of nowhere, and you are lifted far above the earth until you are floating among the clouds.

You continue your ascent, past the clouds and through the very atmosphere of the planet. Soon, you find yourself beyond the orbit of Earth and in the cosmos itself. While before you were flying among the birds and clouds, you now soar among the stars and nebulae. This is the Hanaqpacha, the transcendental origin of creation.

From out of a cluster of stars, you see a figure approach. In a way, this being resembles a mirroring image of you, but far more evolved and advanced in spiritual growth. In fact, it resembles a version of you far in your future. This evolved version of you is one in your highest potential. This figure is one of many versions of your sombra criandera.

As the sombra criandera approaches, they ask you to follow. This is what you came here to do. You can trust this figure is an aspect of you from your future. Your sombra criandera is wise, a great teacher, here to show you the medicine you need to evolve to the level of your shamanic practice. Follow your sombra criandera and trust that the answers you need to the questions you wrote down for the medicine of this experience will be revealed to you, even if they are not immediately apparent: What is your purpose for being alive on planet Earth? What is your medicine that you provide those around you? What is the medicine that feeds you? What are the next steps to take to evolve yourself?

Spend a few minutes on a journey with your sombra criandera and receive the medicine they have for you. When the medicine feels complete, end the journey and return to your physical body. See your sombra criandera returning to the world, to the spot where you first ascended up into the stars. Take this time to thank your sombra criandera before they return to the Hanaqpacha.

Go back to your temple, to the exact space where you first started the journey. Have your sombra primera close its eyes. Return to the deep darkness of the womb again.

Within that darkness, you see a flash, and before you know it, you have birthed back out of your nuna khuya, traveling through the cord of light above your mesa. Allow your sombra to travel across that cord and into your crown, your kulli chunpi. Guide the form of your sombra to rest inside your physical form, allowing its arms and legs to align with your physical limbs, spines and torsos aligning, and finally the heads, all sliding into one another perfectly like fingers sliding into a glove.

Become fully aware of your breathing. Get in tune with its rhythm. Visually imagine the cord retracting from your nuna khuya and return it to your crown, fully phasing into the kulli chunpi. Stay aware of your breathing and know you are whole, all parts of yourself together, intact, and in perfect unity. When you feel ready, begin to slowly move your limbs and open your eyes to the waking world around you.

Getting to Know Yourself

Shamanic journeying is not about tripping out or having some amazing visual experience. Shamanic journeying is about getting to know yourself deeply. The three aspects of your sombras mirror the three pachas, and thus the three campos of the mesa (all "smoke and mirrors," they say). Be patient and do not overdo journeying to the Ukhupacha or Hanaqpacha. I have experienced numerous initiates getting lost in the addiction of escaping everyday life by visiting these other realms. Always remember that true shamanic practice happens here in the Kaypacha. We only visit these other realms when we need to, not because it is a recreational diversion. The shamanic initiate should always remember that they are the mallki, the tree that integrates these three realms into a singular whole.

CHAPTER SEVEN
Shamanic Individuality

In northern coastal curanderismo, there is a night-long ceremony called a *mesada* (Spanish for "allowance"), which takes place in complete darkness. There are no lights, not even candles. Only moonlight, if there is any, is allowed to illuminate the proceedings. The mesada is a curing ceremony, wherein the curandero and participant(s) imbibe the liquid sacrament huachuma, which is the visionary medicine derived from the San Pedro cactus. The effects of the huachuma heighten the shamanic power of the curandero, providing an amplified vista that allows them to diagnose and cure illness within the participant. This ceremony is a centuries-old tradition for the northern coastal curanderismo lineage, possibly even dating back to the Chavín culture.

From my first mesada, I could tell the difference between huachuma and other psychedelic plant medicines: despite its mind-altering affects, I felt completely rooted in my body. For instance, the late author and psychedelic researcher Ross Heaven has compared huachuma (San Pedro) to the more well-known ayahuasca found in the Amazon rainforest: "Ayahuasca takes us *out* of our bodies and into the unseen world, where we may be taught by spirit and return to reflect upon what we have learned. San Pedro, meanwhile, is of *this world*. It teaches us to see the spirit and beauty already around us and apply its lessons to the business of living."[38]

---

38 Ross Heaven, *The Hummingbird's Journey to God: Perspectives on San Pedro, the Cactus of Vision & Andean Soul Healing Methods* (Winchester, UK: O Books, 2009), 43.

My experience was the same. Whereas my previous experiences with other psychedelics completely incapacitated my ability to operate in the world, huachuma provided me with an acute awareness of the world around me. In the dark, I could clearly see the curandero—maestro Daniel—and the other participants. I could also clearly see myself, my fears, my inhibitions, my beauty, and my power. I could see it all: the way Pachamama hummed beneath us, the way the air vibrated with the song of our souls. I was immediately able to see that this awareness is available to us all the time; we just don't allow ourselves the freedom to see it. This is why this ceremony is called a *mesada*: it is an allowance for one's True Self to shine through the dark.

There are many reasons given by curanderos all through Peru why the mesada ceremony takes place at night and in complete darkness. Some stories tell that the curanderos of the past chose this venue in order to avoid persecution from the Spanish conquistadores. However, there are plenty of reasons to suggest otherwise, that the purpose of darkness resides more in symbolical mechanisms.

Dating back through the centuries—via the pre-Incan civilizations of the Chavín and Moche, in which San Pedro use was highly prevalent— there is still some pottery and other archeological evidence that survived colonialism and provides glimpses into these wonderous rituals within the curanderismo lineage. For instance, many of the pots uncovered from these eras include elaborate figurine sculptures, many of which represent female healers (curanderas) working on patients or holding slices of the huachuma cactus stalk, which anthropologist Douglas Sharon intimates could be evidence of "an ancient grass-roots sisterhood of wise women persisting under a variety of sociopolitical structures from formative to colonial times."[39] A large portion of these sculptural curanderas have their eyes closed, their perceptions attuned to darkness. One possible reason for this closing of the eyes is to represent that the divine essence of the spiritual powers conjured by these curanderas could not be perceived by human eyes.

---

39 Douglas Sharon, *Shamanism & the Sacred Cactus: Ethnoarchaeological Evidence for San Pedro Use in Northern Peru* (San Diego, CA: San Diego Museum of Man, 2000) 10–11.

The ancient temple of Chavín de Huántar—referred to in chapter 6—provides further clues to the ceremonial darkness so important to curanderismo rituals. The interior of the temple contains a series of low and narrow subterranean passageways. There is no source for natural lighting to come through; although there is evidence that torches were sometimes used in the tunnels, it is generally believed these passages were utilized in shamanic ceremonies in which the initiate was to make their way through in complete darkness. There are vents carved within the walls, leading to the outer complex, which would have generated a cacophony of echoing sounds due to the winds of the area (including the blowing of conch shells from the priests outside). According to archeologist Richard Burger, "The intention seems to have been to create a sense of confusion and disorientation in which the individual is severed from the outside world."[40] This observation from Burger is key: the mesada and other curandero ceremonies revolve around severing the self from the world.

Speaking again to Jung's process of individuation, this is a primary component of the uniting of the various aspects of the self as represented in curanderismo: the sombra ganadera, the sombra criandera, and the sombra primera. All too often these parts of the self are in a battle to remain in charge. I would venture to say that it is this battle itself that most mystics refer to as the ego. The ego is not a negative thing per se, for it has its usefulness in the psychological constructs of being human in this world. Yet, when ego is allowed to exert its influence over one's life, imbalances occur. The ego does not want a harmonious conjunction of the sombra: it survives off the conflict inside of the individual.

This is why shamanic initiation ceremonies often remove the individual from the known world and place them into an unknown setting. Darkness. Disorientation. When the ego has no sure footing to exert its influence, it becomes unstable and unable to overpower the individuation process.

Don Daniel had at one point in my training put me through a series of mesadas that ended up being some of the most trying experiences of my life (some of which are represented in my comic series Psychonaut

---

40 Richard Burger, *Chavin and the Origins of Andean Civilization* (London: Thames and Hudson, 1992), 135.

Presents). At the end of this run of ceremonies, I was brought to his lodge for a night-long mesada in which I was wrapped, mummified in death shrouds, until dawn. After I imbibed multiple cups of the huachuma medicine, his *auxilios* (assistants) laid me on the floor and covered me in oils as they would prepare a dead body. They bound me in cloth wraps so that I could not move for the entire night, whispering into my ear that I was dead and decomposing. Being naturally claustrophobic, the containment at the time was unbearable!

In this space there was no light. The sound of rattles snaked through me. My limbs were bound. Up, down, and other directional notions had long passed away. My identity was lost completely.

My mind raced between fight and flight throughout the first half of the evening. There were moments I wanted to scream, cry out, and even just leave all of this behind. It was too much to bear! Don Daniel's rattling pulsed through me, becoming the only sensory framework available to me. At times I felt like a snake, bound with no limbs, squirming on the ground. Other moments I wanted to lash out like a jaguar and tear the wraps off my body with my claws.

Yet, as time went on, my ego waned, tired from the battle it was putting my mind through. Eventually, the effects of the huachuma medicine, the complete darkness, and the mummification all worked together to wear me down. I was left with nothing but my isolation. Just me and the dark. There was nothing. It was, undoubtedly, the closest I had felt to my truest self, alone and quiet without thought. It was in this space—which was more like a void—that I felt a chrysalis build around me, containing this (for lack of an appropriate English word) pacha.

The wraps had become the outer coating of a cocoon, and inside I had become an alchemical brew. I wasn't just changing; I was *transfiguring*: a profound psychic metamorphosis. After an expanse of time that had no time—feeling both eternal and instantaneous—the amorphous light of the sun began to show. I was unwrapped from my shrouds, from the cocoon, and rebirthed into something new and glorious, with great wings both intricate and delicate spanning from my back. I had become a being not unlike a butterfly, yet humanoid. My eyes were insectoid, sharp, and the sun's early morning rays struck them in shimmering gold bands.

The Shape-Shifter

It was years later from this point that I began my studies into the Chavín culture. I was not surprised to find that within the temple complex of Chavín de Huántar reside numerous sculptures and reliefs, most of which include figures and faces that resemble a shape-shifting mix of various animals. One of the more striking images to come out of the Chavín de Huántar galleries is a stone frieze at the ceremonial center of the temple. The frieze depicts a mythical anthropomorphic being holding a stalk of the San Pedro cactus in its hand. The figure has the fangs and claws of a jaguar, hair made of snakes, and the wings of a condor or harpy eagle stretching out from its back. I have heard this being referred to by many names: the Jaguar God, the Huachuma God, *Ángel-Atigrado*, and more.

Figure 31. Huachuma God frieze, drawn by the author

Outside of Douglas Sharon, another noteworthy anthropologist who has uncovered the mysteries of northern coastal curanderismo from Peru is Mario Polia. Studying Andean folk healing since the early seventies, Polia has examined the symbolic nature of the animal forms of Chavín de Huántar, of which there are many. He has organized these symbols into the primary groupings of bird (condor or harpy eagle),

147

jaguar, and serpent. In reference to the three pachas of the Andean cos-movision, Polia remarks,

> *The iconographic symbolism alludes to the three cosmic zones*
> *or worlds represented by the three animals: the upper cos-*
> *mic zone is represented by the bird of prey (harpy eagle); the*
> *intermediate cosmic zone, the world of men, is represented*
> *by the jaguar whose symbolism also extends to the chthonic*
> *zone, where the emblematic animal is the snake. ... The*
> *three zones of the world—i.e., the totality of existence rep-*
> *resented by the associated animals—express the prestige of*
> *the priest-shaman in the cult of Chavín de Huántar and the*
> *range and effectiveness of his power.*[41]

Polia is not the only one who attributes these animals with the asso-ciated zones, or pachas, of the Andean worldview. You can find these iconographic associations all over Peru in statues, reliefs, paintings, and even T-shirts. Therefore, the animal figures are clear symbolic represen-tations of the three worlds:

Ukhupacha: Snake (campo ganadero)

Kaypacha: Jaguar (campo medio)

Hanaqpacha: Condor (campo justiciero)

It is a popular motif in modern shamanism to have what some call an "animal ally" or "spirit animal," a being from the animal kingdom that acts as an astral guide or influence while navigating one's shamanic path. In my experience, a shaman doesn't so much have a single spirit animal ascribed to them inasmuch as they have the ability to call upon the sym-bolic attributes of the animal kingdom to assist them in their endeav-ors. One of the shaman's many skills is the ability to shape-shift. What this means is the shaman can allow their identity to be relinquished in order to take on the role and necessary attributes of any animal, spirit, or other identity.

---

41 Mario Polia, "Andean Cosmology and Cosmography in the North-Peruvian Shamanic Mesa," in *Mesas & Cosmologies in the Central Andes,* ed. Douglas Sharon (San Diego, CA: San Diego Museum of Man, 2006), 36.

The reason I call the being in this frieze the Huachuma God is because, to me, it represents the ultimate shape-shifting tactic of the shamanic initiate: to be a complete unification of all three pachas of consciousness. In the Chavín culture, this was achieved through the auspices of the huachuma (San Pedro cactus), which is why the figure holds this cactus stalk as a staff. Yet, imbibing a hallucinogen is not needed. Think of the wizards Merlin or Gandalf carrying their staffs, or maybe Moses and his magical staff used against the pharaoh of Egypt. The staff is a common motif that represents that energy of the mallki, like a lightning rod conducting the charge of all three realms into a single unit that the individual can harness for magical power.

A true shape-shifter is one who is able to harness the attributes of these three worlds and incorporate them into their daily life. These attributes host a considerable amount of medicine, not just as symbols of the pachas themselves, but they contain a wisdom that one can learn from them each individually and as a whole.

Snake: The snake is a symbol of the Ukhupacha, the lower world. Known as *amaru* in Quechua, the snake teaches us to be close to the earth. Whenever I see amaru in nature or in my dreams, it is a reminder to shed any extraneous energy in my life (like a snake sheds its skin) that may not serve my better self. Whatever is separating me from nature, from being grounded and rooted as a child of Pachamama, I will examine it and consider ways to change it or dispense of it entirely. The snake has no limbs; therefore, its belly is always on the soil or is burrowed into the earth. When amaru makes itself known in my life, I will often spend a considerable amount of time lying directly on the soil of the earth, lying completely on my back or belly, to see and feel what Pachamama may have to tell me. This is a good time to nap and see what dreamtime has to say. This is a personal experience, so the snake is a teacher reminding us we may need "me time."

Jaguar: The jaguar is representation of the Kaypacha, the middle world. Known as *otorongo* in Quechua, the jaguar is the intermediary between the upper and lower worlds. The jaguar is a symbol of balance and precision, for the way a great cat stalks its prey requires a delicate pacing and discernment in how it walks. Its eyes are sharp and can pinpoint exactly where it wants to go and what it wants. When I encounter any cat (even my house cat) either in real life or dreams, I remember otorongo and get in touch with that inner feline. I may even get on all fours and prowl around in the dirt. I most especially will play like a cat with my own cat, for play is also a big lesson from the jaguar: life is a game and we cannot take it too seriously. Play requires others, so cat energy allows me to reconsider my interpersonal interactions with the world around me and reflect on the health of my relationships.

Condor: The condor is a symbol of the Hanapacha, the upper world. Any winged bird will remind me of the upper world, which really is just a reminder of the creative Source of the Universe that we all have access to. The winged ones teach us to recall that we are Creator made manifest here on the earth. Also, a condor or eagle can soar to such great heights—think of the expanse of vista they have of the world below. They do not see or abide by the borders we create. They do not see our small-minded reality tunnels. They see the bigger picture, the world as a single organism. When I encounter the condor or any large bird soaring high above, I remember to take myself outside of my narrow point of view and look at the wider picture, which encompasses a more transpersonal experience of being. This can often take the form of a hike to the highest spot I can find or a drive into the countryside.

The Individuality

To harness the snake is to remember your journey(s) into the Ukhupa-cha and embody its teachings of going within, into the interior wisdom places of Pachamama. To harness the jaguar is to remember life within the Kaypacha, to live in the moment and know the value of the life we have. To harness the condor is to remember your journey(s) in the Han-aqpacha and invoke the inspiration of the creative universe into one's actions. Uniting these three animal forces—each representing one of the three worlds—is vital to the shamanic path. There is a concept like this in mystical Judaism called Adam Kadmon. Referring to Adam as the first man, Adam Kadmon also represents the perfected human, a human who is purified of the polarities of reality so that a true alignment with the Divine can be achieved.

In the Qabalistic tradition, specifically that of the Western Mystery Tradition, the great mystic and author Dion Fortune referred to this aspect of the self that is truly integrated as the Individuality. Our mundane consciousness, ruled by the ego, is made up of what Fortune calls the personality. According to her, the aim of initiation is that "the personality must be tuned to the same key as the Individuality."[42] Similar to the aim of Jung's individuation, the shamanic initiate must tune all aspects of their self (in all three pachas) to the construct of the Individuality, or what I prefer to call the True Self.

The True Self is who you are at your core, what you came into this life to be and do. This is you as a shamanic individual, one who is not swayed by base fears or future aspirations, but empowered by the strength of it all coalesced into a seamless whole. This is why, of all the practices in this book, I believe the pillar of light may be the most important. It is a reminder that you are not only a manifestation of Creator on the earth but also an extension of Creator: you are Creator experiencing itself through you.

In practicum 6, thought tracking, I referred to the mystic Franz Bardon. In his works, he lucidly communicates the concept of the Individuality and the importance of truly remembering, not just as a concept

---

42 Dion Fortune, *The Training & Work of an Initiate* (San Francisco: Weiser Books, 2000), 36.

but as a life experience: "The true image of God is the human being, who has been created in the image of the universe. Everything that can be found in the universe on a large scale is reflected in a human being on a small scale. That is why a human being is called the microcosm, in contrast to the universe, the macrocosm. In reality the whole course of nature takes place in a human being, and it is the task of ... the student to learn, to observe, to know and to master this."[43]

Unfortunately, there is no exact formula for this mastery into the True Self. What worked for me will not work for you or anyone else. All I know is that I was stripped of my identity in that cocoon, the disparate aspects of my personality unable to function as normal. This allowed my True Self to blossom, to spring forth.

Since I emerged from that cocoon resembling a being not unlike the Huachuma God (bearing wings and other animalistic qualities), the panic attacks I had endured for years lessened considerably. My rages became minimal. I was able to better manage my emotional state, and thus my physical and mental health returned. My relationships with loved ones healed. Finally, I was more clearly able to see the opportunities before me in life that better fit my Individuality, choosing life circumstances that aligned with my True Self rather than an aspect of my shadow.

Practicum 16: Staff of Individuation

Staffs are a great way to harness all powers and attributes of the pachas into a singular whole, and they make a great addition as an arte to a shaman's mesa. According to maestro curandero don Eduardo Calderon, "staffs are like antennae that pull and emit and transmit radiations."[44] Most artes—which sit directly on a mesa—represent various places within universal consciousness (e.g., the pachas). Known in curanderismo as *varas*, staffs act spatially on a mesa as transmitters to tune in to and harness particular powers. Therefore, varas are normally positioned at the head of the mesa, directly across from the curandero, and stood upright to act as that transitive "antennae" that don Eduardo spoke of.

---

43 Bardon, *Initiation into Hermetics*, 31.

44 Sharon, *Wizard of the Four Winds*, 72.

In northern coastal curanderismo, most varas are made of special holy wood called *chonta* and may have particular symbols or animal figures carved into the head. Other varas include swords, canes, and any other rod-type artifact (even a branch from a tree). Some are wand-size; others as large as a walking staff. Each has its own distinct purpose and power, being placed at the head of the campo it is designed to emulate and harness.

For this practice, we are going to create and initiate a new arte onto our altar spaces, a vara that I call the Staff of Individuation. To do this, I invite you to first sit at your mesa and practice breathing basics, kawsay activation, the pillar of light, and then the opening of the account (see appendix A). When your mesa is open and activated, make the declaration that you are seeking a Staff of Individuation, a vara that will assist in uniting all aspects of the three worlds into your True Self. You may drum or rattle as a part of the declaration, in order to enhance the efficacy of your statement. You may also sing your statement if you wish. Regardless, make your statement clear. Here is an example:

> *I call upon the universe to bring to me a staff that I may wield as a symbol of my True Self. I will use this staff as a reminder of my connection to Spirit as a human being. This staff will unite my sombra ganadera, my sombra primera, and my sombra erlandera as a single Individuality. This staff will unite the Hanaqpacha, the Kaypacha, and the Ukhupacha, so that I may be able to harness the attributes of the condor, the jaguar, and the serpent at all times. I ask that this staff become revealed to me at the right time. So it is!*

Feel free to use this statement or modify it to your purposes. When you have made the statement, seal the words with a clap of your hands or snap of your fingers. You may also use your breath to blow the prayer out into the universe. Make an offering of some tobacco or incense in gratitude to the universe being in this dance of life with you. Then, close the ceremony and wait.

Do not rush the process of how this staff may appear to you. I would suggest to not actively seek it out. Allow it to come in its own timing. Remember, like artes, all things are conscious and varas are no different. This staff could be revealed to you as a stick you find while walking in the woods. Or maybe it's a cane you discover tucked away in the corner of a flea market. Maybe it is a walking stick you already own that calls to you. It could even be something you stumble upon while browsing the internet. Regardless of how you find it, you will know it is the right vara for this work because it will call to you.

I knew my Staff of Individuation was the right one for me upon first sight. It is only about a foot and a half in length, made of chonta, which came from a shaman's market in Peru. On the head of the vara is sculpted a stalk of the San Pedro cactus, obviously a strong connector for me, as that is the primary medicine used in the northern coastal curanderismo lineage in which I was trained. Below the head was carved a hexagram (sometimes known as the Star of David), which is a perfect symbol representing the microcosm and macrocosm (two triangles, one inverted) uniting as one. Also, that is a prime symbol of Qabalah, another mystical lineage very important to my life path.

Once that staff is revealed to you, bring it to your sacred space. Start your ceremony again with breathing basics, kawsay activation, the pillar of light, and the opening of the account (see appendix A). Burn some sage and run the smoke across the length of the vara. This is to ritually cleanse the staff of any extraneous energy that may be attached to it from when you acquired it. When you feel that cleansing is sufficient, hold the staff in both hands in front of your mesa. You will now do a journey to initiate this vara onto your mesa as your Staff of Individuation. For this journey, I recommend the music *Tree of Life* by Loren Nerell and Mark Seelig.

Close your eyes and begin your journeying process by connecting a cord of light from your kulli chunpi to the center of your mesa at the nuna khuya. Settle into this visualization for a few moments, breathing and being aware of the connection with your mesa as a mirror of your own soul.

Once you feel that connection is stabilized, use your imagination to visualize your sombra lifting out of your physical body and traveling along the cord of light to your mesa. Your sombra will not have the staff with you at this time. When you arrive at your mesa, drawing ever closer to your nuna khuya, imagine that arte as a portal through which you can travel.

As you pass through the portal that is your nuna khuya, you will see nothing but complete darkness. It is a comfortable darkness, like being in the womb of your mother. After a while, indiscernible forms begin to manifest in the dark. Those forms will slowly morph into the interior of your own personal temple in the unseen. You are back in your temple. Take a few moments to settle into your temple; observe any new aspects or changes to your temple or sombra.

As you come to the center of your temple, you will see a pool of water. If you have not seen such a pool of water before, you notice one now. Walk to the pool and examine its shape and construction. The water in it is perfectly clear, pristine. There is no movement, its surface like glass. As you approach, you note your reflection on the surface of the water. Observe how clearly how your features are being reflected to you. Allow yourself to relax into your own gaze. Bring to mind the three pachas and their attributes, as well as the animal representations of those worlds. Remember that you are the true image of the Creator as a human being. You are the center of the universe, just like everyone else, part of a greater whole that is both infinite and singular at the same time.

When you are ready, recite these magical words:

> *As above, so below.*
> *As below, so above.*
> *I am the condor, the jaguar, and the serpent.*
> *I am the Hanaqpacha, the Kaypacha, and the Ukhupacha.*
> *I am the Individual; this is my True Self.*
> *I am One! I am!*

You are a reflection of these three worlds, a mallki, able to contain all aspects of the universe into a single form. You are the representative power of the Huachuma God, the Staff of Individuation itself.

Blow into the water, into your reflection. Watch as your breath ripples out over the surface of the water. As you do this, your Staff of Individuation rises from the water before you. The staff may or may not look like the one you picked out to use in the waking world; it doesn't matter. What you are now seeing is the *soul* of the Staff of Individuation, its sombra. With the utmost care and reverence, retrieve the staff from the pool of water.

Spend a few moments holding the staff in your temple. Ask for it to speak to you. Ask it its name. Ask how best to carry it, hold it, or use it. Interact with it as you would a person. When the interaction and initial meeting with the Staff of Individuation feels complete, go back to the space in your temple where you first started. Have your sombra close its eyes. Return to the deep darkness of the womb again.

Within that darkness, you see a flash and before you know it, you have birthed back out of your nuna khuya, traveling through the cord of light above your mesa. Allow your sombra to travel across that cord and into your crown, your kulli chunpi. Guide the form of your sombra to rest inside your physical form, allowing its arms and legs to align with your physical limbs, spines and torsos aligning, and finally the heads, all sliding into one another perfectly like fingers sliding into a glove.

Become fully aware of your breathing. Get in tune with its rhythm. Visually imagine the cord retracting from your nuna khuya and return it to your crown, fully phasing into the kulli chunpi. Stay aware of your breathing and know you are whole, all parts of yourself together, intact, and in perfect unity. When you feel ready, begin to slowly move your limbs and open your eyes to the waking world around you.

Become aware of the vara you are holding physically in your hands. Bring it up to your lips and, conjuring the entire journey you just experienced in your mind, including the image of the soul of the Staff of Individuation you retrieved from the pool of water, blow the soul of the Staff of Individuation from your journey into the vara in your hands, sealing its essence. If a name came to you for the Staff of Individuation, speak it out loud and into the vara. When you are ready, place the Staff of Individuation at the head of your mesa, directly in the center of the campo medio.

This is the prime place for individuation to take place, for you to recall your shamanic Individuality. This vara is your reminder of your divinity, of your inherent godhood as a human being on Pachamama. Use it as a reminder for yourself or to assist others in that remembering. This staff will fuse all aspects of the self together into the True Self.

To get the vara to stand up, it is typically inserted into the ground if you are outside. For our indoor altars, my wife and I filled a planter with sand. The staffs can then be placed into the stand upright. I have seen others use small pebbles in individual containers for each staff. Others lean the staff against the wall, if the mesa comes up against a wall in your sacred space. There is no wrong method, but do find a way to have your staff situated upright as that antenna to harness the powers of the universe into your mesa.

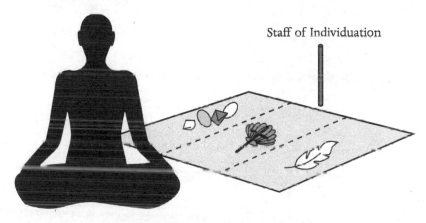

Figure 32. Staff of Individuation

Your True Self

Individuation is the driving force of shamanic practice. Use your vara as a source of power, to help you remember that your True Self is the three pachas combined: you are whole! Become a shape-shifter. Expand your awareness even beyond the snake, the jaguar, and the condor to other animals in the animal kingdom. How do the characteristics of these animals relate to you and your shamanic path? How can you adopt them to help further get to know yourself? These are all questions that must be answered only by the individual, and answers cannot be given to them. Be open to all information and possibilities contributing to your own individuation. As this self-awareness expands, a resonance builds with the outer world. With this transpersonal awareness comes a need for the shamanic initiate to develop a fellowship with the powers of nature, which will now be discussed.

CHAPTER EIGHT
Shamanic Rapport

We were in heaven. A few clouds danced around us, but otherwise the sky was open and vast. Autumn and I sat on the gleaming green slopes and pristine ruins of Machu Picchu. After years of being trained in Peruvian shamanism, we had finally made it to one of the origin points of the teachings of curanderismo, as don Daniel had suggested we do as a ceremonial pilgrimage to get in touch with the roots of the tradition.

During the Incan Empire, the ceremonial complex of Machu Picchu was once the center of spiritual learning for the surrounding communities (*ayllus*) and beyond. People traveled for thousands of miles to learn astrology and magic from the great shaman priests of Machu Picchu, residing atop the most picturesque tropical mountain-scape to ever grace any postcard. Truly, it looks just like the pictures, so much so it felt like a surreal dream stepping through the intricately carved stones of the ruin walls. Though the elevation is quite low compared to most sacred peaks in the Andes, you feel as though you are sauntering through the heavens with the gods themselves.

There are numerous features of Machu Picchu, as well as the many other ceremonial sites in Peru, that show a distinct emulation of the natural world. These wonders are a true testament to the pre-Columbian peoples of Latin America and their innovative capacities in architecture. The jigsaw formulation of the stone walls was (and still is) an efficient reinforcement against the earthquakes that typically ravage the region.

Further, the Inca were known for the great gardening terraces that look almost like staircases for giants carved into the mountainside. With the right eye, one can also find gigantic figurines of totem animals sculpted into the peaks the size of the mountain itself. In essence, Machu Picchu truly deserves its place as one of the Seven Wonders of the World.

Yet, there are other feats in the complex that hint at a deep reverence and respect for the sacred language of the natural world. For instance, in various rooms of the complex there are pristine pools of water carved into the bedrock, so as to reflect the heavenly ambiance of the nightly stars for divinatory purposes and astrological observation. There is also the Intihuatana Stone, which points directly at the sun during the winter solstice and is believed to be the sacred stone, which was tethered to the sun as it ran its course across the heavens throughout the year. You will also find numerous stones throughout the complex carved to mimic the surrounding apus, almost as if Machu Picchu were a mirror of the outside world, as if the ceremonial site were a mesa or altar itself.

Figure 33. Carved apu stones of Machu Picchu

This tendency to reflect the natural world within the architecture is seen all across the Sacred Valley of Peru. It is a reminder that the people of this area are highly agrarian; as farmers and herders, they depend on the natural world in the most intimate of ways. They connect with nature not because it is a luxury but because it is practical. It is truly a way of life.

Also, this imitation of the raw power of the natural world infuses the infrastructure of the society with that of the World Soul. According to anthropologist R. Donald Skillman, this type of power is called *encantos*: "Encantos are the forces of nature that exist independent of and uncontrolled by other powers. It is the role of the curer to call forth and dominate the encantos."[45] Now, "dominate" is a strong word, but I encourage you to think of it as commanding or managing the influence of encantos, rather than as a form of tyranny. This is precisely what the mesa of the curandero is designed to do. The curandero's job is to channel these encantos and manage them within the artes of the mesa.

This is an important aspect to remember before beginning healing practices: that the artes on the shamanic mesa should indeed reflect the powers of the natural world. Brought together, filtered, and homed in, these encantos together form the *calicanto*, the framework of power that comprises the mesa and thus the curandero. What this means is that the process of shamanic healing, using the mesa, is a joint effort on the part of the curandero and nature. The curer is not in this work alone, nor would they want to be—the shamanic path is at times taxing and requires a great deal of effort.

When we arrived in Cuzco, we were excited to visit the Qoricancha. Cuzco used to be the capital of the Inca Empire, one of the largest and most advanced societies to grace Latin America before the Spanish invasion. Traces of the pre-Columbian society can be seen all over as many of the foundation stones of the great Inca city still stand firm, with the colonial architecture of the Spanish laid right over it. A perfect example of this is the Qoricancha itself: the Convent of Santo Domingo resides directly on top of the foundations of the Incan temple.

It was from this temple that the Sapa Inca (Inca Emperor) governed as both the political and spiritual head of his mighty empire. The Qoricancha was of course a great ceremonial center rife with astrological

---

45 R. Donald Skillman, *Huachumero* (San Diego, CA: San Diego Museum of Man, 1990), 10.

observing tools built within its framework, including separate temples for the sun, the moon, and other celestial phenomena.

The temple was said to be a marvel. Of course, the Quechua term for gold is *qori-*, with the term *-cancha* referencing a dome or shell. Spanish chroniclers describe the complex as having a gold-covered crest lining the primary walls circling the Qoricancha. The terraced gardens were filled with opulent gold statues. Inside, many of the temple rooms were completely covered in gold walls and furnishings. One can imagine the thirst of greed that burned in the hearts of conquistador Francisco Pizarro and his men upon gazing at the wonderous and shimmering edifice. Unfortunately, Pizarro and his entourage would eventually get their wish, decimating the Inca Empire and melting down almost all the Inca's gold into coins for their own colonial prosperity.

It is depressing how so many beautiful and ceremonial artifacts are lost to history. However, within the Qoricancha, there currently resides on display a great golden plate that many historians believe was situated above the main altar of the Temple of the Sun. Evidently, this plate depicts an engraving that is regarded as the most accurate diagram of the Inca cosmos.

Figure 34. Inca cosmogram

Upon first notice, one can see the entire plate, a representation of the cosmos itself, is in the shape of a mountain. We have already discussed how the mountains, the apus, are the primary connection to the supreme divinities of the Hanaqpacha. Ultimately, the etchings tell the story of the *runa* (the people) in the form of Incan constellations and portrays the Incan pantheon with the creator god Wiracocha, an androgynous being, at the peak of the plate and then the sun (Intitayta) and the moon (Mamakilla) extending to the right and left as iconic expressions of the masculine and feminine polarities of the universe.

In the seventeenth century, native chronicler Juan de Santa Cruz Pachacuti Yamqui Salcamaygua created a drawing of this plate (which has come to be known as "Pachacuti's Drawing") that has since been analyzed and refined by anthropologists and historians over time. In this drawing, we can more clearly see the story being told of humanity's role in the greater scheme of the cosmos.

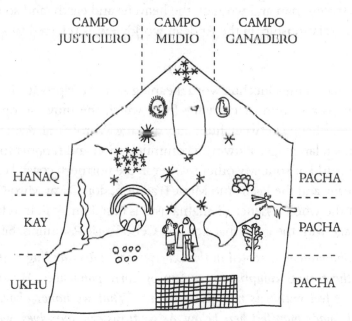

Figure 35. Author's depiction of Pachacuti's Drawing

As you can see, there are clear lines of demarcation on the illustration. It should be noted that right and left verticals are represented from the point of view of the actors (the deities of the cosmogram). Therefore, the more masculine icons are depicted on the right and the feminine on the left, much like the mesa itself. One can also observe horizontal lines of demarcation that represent a layered depiction of the three pachas, thus establishing a nine-panel grid over the diagram. Within each compartment of this grid, we can observe a relationship woven among Wiracocha, Intitayta, and Mamakilla through the icons of the runa couple, the feline creature, and the depictions of a lake, a rainbow, the granary storehouse, lightning, and stars.

According to anthropologist Douglas Sharon, "From this we can see that the Inca cosmogram depicted the diurnal, seasonal, and stellar rhythms of nature and the elements, along with their negative and positive effects on the interdependent network of life shared on this earth by human beings, plants, and animals."[46] The important lesson that can be learned from this is the reciprocal relationship and participation inherent in life between man and woman, the heavens and earth, and so on. This reciprocal relationship, in the Andean worldview, is referred to as *ayni*.

Ayni

Ayni (AI-nee) is the Quechua word meaning sacred reciprocity. In essence, I see ayni as a system of currency from which the universe operates, a means of exchange between humanity and the World Soul. Ayni is a form of unspoken language, allowing a communication and rapport to be built with the world of soul. My other teacher in the northern coastal curanderismo lineage and the Pachakuti Mesa Tradition, don Oscar Miro-Quesada, says that the whole essence of shamanism is based on ayni. In referencing his tutelage with the great maestro don Celso Rojas Palomino, he states,

> *Shamanism is rooted in the experiential understanding that the cosmos comprises a system of correspondences. What we feel within is manifest without. What we honor above is made manifest here below. As we transform ourselves, we transform others. ...*

---

46 Sharon, *Wizard of the Four Winds*, 131.

> *... Don Celso knew that participation in these graceful ritu-*
> *als [of ayni] has the power to restore relationship with sen-*
> *tient allies that do not walk on two legs. And once this right*
> *relationship is restored, we enter into a dialogue with their*
> *soul-power. For, as our awakened souls are manifestations*
> *of Divinity, so are the souls of our Earth mother, the moon*
> *and sun, the sacred rainbow, the stones and trees, all plants*
> *and animals, all world teachers, our star relatives, angels,*
> *Shining Ones, and all our ancestors. And, as we reclaim*
> *our rightful place at their side as co-creators, we gain*
> *access once again to that crack between the worlds where*
> *miracles abound.*[47]

The aim of ayni is rooted in a perspective of gratitude, giving thanks for the life that is given to us and for having the opportunity to partici-pate in reality. It is the shamanic worldview that we are not just spiritually but literally the children of the earth. Ayni is expressing thanksgiving to Pachamama and the other denizens of the cosmos. The authenticity of this expression is where a true shamanic healer's power resides. Instead of the usual human paradigm of taking resources from our Mother, we should establish a routine of giving in return. As don Oscar says, this opens a dialogue of interconnectivity with the World Soul, which opens the true power inherent in shamanic magick, which is ultimately one of cocreation with the cosmos, remembering, again, that we are extensions of Creator.

Ayni is usually expressed in the form of *haywas* (offerings), which can come in a variety of ways. For instance, we have already established in our practices the offering of sage, incense, or agua de florida as a means of clearing a ceremonial space. These offerings can also be used, with intention, to express gratitude to Pachamama, the encantos, and any other powers you wish to draw from nature into your mesa. As stated before, the offerings of thanksgiving at the end of ceremony in the form of a song or dance can be another meaningful expression of ayni.

---

47 Bonnie Glass-Coffin and Oscar Miro-Quesada, *Lessons in Courage: Peruvian Shamanic Wisdom for Everyday Life* (Faber, VA: Rainbow Ridge Books, 2013), 14–15.

The descendants of the Inca still participate in annual festivals of ayni, filled with dancing and music, such as the annual Inti Raymi'rata (Festival of the Sun).

One of the more beautiful ceremonies of ayni in which I have the honor of participating manifests in the form of a ceremony in the spiritual community of my hometown, the Kansas City metro. Facilitated by another great teacher of mine—the medicine man named Lee Stumbling Deer—the Stone People's Dance is an annual dance not unlike other ceremonial dances of the indigenous peoples across the United States. Stumbling Deer refers to this ceremony as a "giveaway," where the very act of dancing, singing, and drumming is a prayer offered to encourage a relationship of healing between the earth and the people. Dancers come forward throughout the year to offer themselves to the dance occurring on Memorial Day weekend. The dance itself takes place within a massive medicine wheel, itself a beautiful depiction of the cosmos as a series of stones lining the ground in the formation of an encircled cross of the four directions.

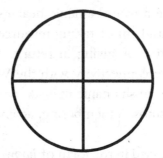

Figure 36. Medicine wheel

Like the Incan cosmogram, the directions of the medicine wheel represent facets of an aspect of life: seasons on the calendar, totemic animals, spiritual attributes, and so on. Together, encircled, we can experience the interconnectivity of the world and our place within it. According to Stumbling Deer, there is no right or wrong direction—they are all equal. What I learned from him is that we are always standing in the center of these directions and thus in the center of the universe; we are never *not* in the center.

At the beginning of this dance a tree is selected by Stumbling Deer and the elders to be offered as the central post of the medicine wheel of the dance, the axis mundi. Rather, the tree offers itself! Stumbling Deer spends a significant amount of time with the land in sacred reciprocity, providing offerings of sage, tobacco, sweetgrass, and other herbs to commune with the encantos. A tree will come to him or one of the other elders in offering. More tobacco is given. When the community gathers to chop down the tree, not a single strike of the hatchet is made without an offering of tobacco and gratitude. When the tree falls, it is carried by the community as if, as Stumbling Deer says, it is "a wounded warrior we are taking home." On the way to the medicine wheel, the community is regularly ordered to pause and hold their march so that the tree may be abundantly saged in thanksgiving.

Upon entering the wheel, the tree is stood in the center and decorated with a cornucopia of prayer flags and prayer ties. A prayer tie is a simple way to make an offering: a pinch of tobacco infused with prayer and intention, wrapped in a cloth and then tied to string that can be hung around the neck or in a tree or bush. The dancers themselves must create 405 prayer ties (100 for each direction and then an extra five for Creator). When the prayer ties are strung up in a stunning array, Stumbling Deer will facilitate an *inipi* (sweat lodge ceremony) and share a *chanupa* (sacred pipe) with the dancers to set the intention of dance. Then, with the accompaniment of a mother drum, the dancers dance for two days, every step a giveaway to the Mother Earth. The dancers give of themselves completely, consistently providing offerings of sage and tobacco throughout the weekend in a visionary ritual that soon lifts the veils of separation between the mundane world and the World Soul. By the first day, the dancers have given so much of themselves in sacred reciprocity that they become shimmering beings of pure light, pristine shamanic examples of ayni.

Again, there are numerous ways to participate in sacred reciprocity. In the end, you will have to find your way of participating in this mutual exchange of rapport with the soul realm. However, let's look at one of the more well-known offerings of ayni in Peruvian curanderismo: the *despacho*.

Practicum 17: Despacho Creation

A despacho is an offering of gratitude and reciprocity made to Pacham-ama and the spirit guardians of the natural world. This practice originates from the indigenous Quechua people of Peru, and it is one of the healing artforms don Oscar desired to incorporate into his own practice when seeking tutelage from the great paqo don Benito Corihuaman Vargas. The despacho is indeed a ritual craft that can take many shapes and styles within the tradition. When visiting the markets in Peru, one can find a despacho for almost any ceremonial occasion: for healing, for acquiring love or wealth, and even for assisting the transition of a soul into death. According to writer and ceremonialist Matthew Magee, the despacho is "a type of ritual offering that uses focused, reverent intention to return the gifts we have received back to the source they originated from."[48] It is a clear way of participating in the system of ayni, which the denizens of the natural world understand and respond to.

The ceremony for creating a despacho is often a community event. However, it can also be done individually as well. You also do not need a despacho kit from a Peruvian market in order to make one. Anyone can build a despacho with the items they have at home or directly from nature. Crafting a despacho is truly a simple practice, although with focus and intent it can become an extremely advanced art. Take for instance the *pampomesayoqs* (shaman healer-priests) of the Quechua like don Benito, whose medicine of the despacho is so potent that sickness is healed in the community and sacred trust is repaired with the natural world. Truly, this is the goal of the despacho ritual: to build a rapport of sacred reciprocity between human and nature.

Ingredients of the Despacho

Here is a list of recommended ingredients to start the foundation of your despacho craft:

Piece of White Paper: The crafting of a despacho is normally done on white paper. You will need to make sure it is large

---

48 Magee, *Peruvian Shamanism*, 71.

enough to do your work of laying out your offerings. My wife and I normally use wrapping paper because it is large and we can adjust the size as needed. The reason the paper is traditionally white is because symbolically the color white represents the apus, the sacred mountain spirits who are the emissaries of Hanaqpacha.

Red Ribbon, String, or Yarn: White and red are primary colors in the Quechua tradition to represent two of the three primary worlds. White for the Hanaqpacha (as noted above) and red for the Ukhupacha, the blood of Pachamama, the source of all planetary life. Marrying these two colors represents the union of the above and below. You will use the red string eventually to tie the bundle of your despacho together when it is complete and ready to offer to the natural world.

Flowers: Flowers of all kinds are a traditional gift brought to ceremony, just as you would bring flowers to a dinner party or your mother or a spouse. It is a celebration of beauty shared between Pachamama and her children. Traditionally, red and white carnations or roses are used, but you can use any combination of floral arrangements that calls to you. Very often only the petals are used for the despacho ingredients, but sometimes whole flowerheads are used as well.

Sugar, Candies, Sprinkles, and Cookies: Just as you would bring flowers to a loved one for a gift, you might bring candies as well. All these things represent the sweetness of life, a sweetness we try to nurture with Pachamama as a part of this ritual.

Seeds of All Kinds: Seeds are a vital component to any magickal act, as they represent renewal and new growth. The Quechua are an agricultural society, so seeds are a crucial ingredient to planting the seeds of your intention for the despacho ceremony.

Incense: When your despacho burns (if that is how you choose to offer it, as will be discussed later), the smoke of the incense assists in carrying the prayers of your intention. You may choose to use whatever incense is calls to you, though copal and palo santo are often used.

The Choice Is Yours: You can add any other ingredients to your despacho as well. Find what calls to you to add to the artful palette you are creating: spices, raisins, beads, glitter, cotton, coca or bay leaves, rice, cornmeal, tobacco, perfumes, and other herbs. Be sure that whatever you use can be burned or is environmentally friendly and can be safely incorporated back into the earth (if buried). Your items should be biodegradable, so no plastics or metals.

Building the Despacho

As with any magickal act, establish a clear intention for your ceremony. Follow the magickal formula guidelines in chapter 6. When initiating a ceremony, I find it helpful to write down a statement of intent so that it is clear in my mind, and I will even speak it out loud. What is your intention for the despacho? Are you asking for healing for yourself? Are you asking for physical, emotional, or spiritual healing? Are you trying to assist another in need? Or maybe you are creating a despacho to just express gratitude, to deepen your relationship with Pachamama and the natural world. Whatever your intention, be clear and focused.

Then, lay out the paper flat in your ritual space. If you are doing ceremony outside, you will want to anchor your paper from any potential winds using rocks or some other type of paper weight. Arrange your items outside of the paper first, directly surrounding its perimeter, ensuring that each offering is in view for others (if you are in a group). You will want to clarify for yourself and others the ritual intention of each offering so that when that offering is made, the ceremonial act is clear.

Next, in quiet alignment with your intention and the intention of each ingredient, begin the process of picking an ingredient and adding it to the paper. Personally, my wife and I usually start with building a consecration configuration as described in practicum 10 in chapter 4. That is a good way to start with a foundational design for you to build from. Then use the petals from the flowers, the cornmeal, the sugars, and all the ingredients you chose with the objective of creating a design on the paper that matches your end intention for the ceremony. In essence, you are creating a mandala, a geometric design to align your prayer with the balance of universe. This mandala represents the holism of the cosmos, the microcosm and macrocosm joining in harmony through your hands and onto the two-dimensional paper before you.

It is important to pace yourself throughout this ritual act. Traditionally, a despacho ceremony can take hours, maybe even a full day. Time does not matter; in fact, the goal is for time to stop entirely so that the only thing within your focus is the mandala you are creating. The paqos in Peru operate a despacho ceremony with the utmost reverence, as priestesses and priests of the Pachamama. Move slowly and carefully with that level of reverence and awareness. Imagine you are like the Buddhist monks who create their ornate sand mandalas, intricate and methodical diagrams of perfection that they will inevitably sweep away, caught up only in the beauty of the present moment. That beauty, they know, is finite, as is the beauty you are creating with the despacho. Your task is to take your time to build an astonishing design that is meditative, trancelike, and a gift to yourself and the invisible pachas that support you. The building of the despacho is itself a meditation. Every action you make is a prayer.

You do not have to use all the items you have gathered. Only use what you feel is right for the moment and stop adding ingredients when you feel the design is complete and in alignment with your intention. You will only know this within your heart; it is not a thing that can be taught or instructed. Follow your instinct for when you feel balance arise from your creation and pause before you add too much. You do not want to clutter the design. Some practitioners—such as Autumn, a master despacho creator—have a stockpile of ritual items they use from ceremony to ceremony. In the spirit of conservation, you will want to keep your leftover items to reuse for future ceremonies.

Here are some examples of despacho mandalas created by Autumn:

Figure 36. Despacho examples

Offering the Despacho

When you feel complete, take a moment to pause. Reflect upon the beauty of what you have created. How does this beauty relate to your own life, to your original intention?

After your reflection, gently fold the paper of the despacho—with the offerings inside—into a bundle. Like the sand mandala of the Buddhist monks, this will inevitably wipe your beautiful creation, and that is okay. That is precisely as it should be. There is life and then there is death. Nothing is permanent. Start with the top third of the paper and fold down. Next, fold the bottom third up, then the left third, and finally the right third, inserting the right side into the left like a sleeve. Tie the bundle with the red string or yarn.

There are many ways to offer a despacho. One way is to bury the despacho in the soil of the earth. This is a good way to plant your intention as you would a seed in the soil. If you bury a despacho, you will again want to make sure all items in the despacho are natural and biodegradable. Burying a despacho can be tricky, especially if you add sweets, because animals are likely to smell it and dig it up. If you do bury a despacho, it is good to dig a deep enough hole to prevent any wildlife intrusion and causing a mess (a hole about two feet minimum usually works fine). When filling the hole with dirt, you can also cover the area with a large stone to further secure the burial.

One of the more common ways of offering a despacho is burning through fire. This method is great for purging and releasing old things, as fire is an element of purification. Burning allows a clearing of the old so new things have room for growth. Fire is also a source for focus and creation; the discovery of fire changed the trajectory of human destiny, providing us with the capability of being able to operate in the dark. When a despacho is burned, the smoke of the offering will carry the prayers into the upper realms and on the land you reside. This offering becomes a propitiation to the natural world around us. The ashes will return to Pachamama to become new soil for growth and renewal.

You can use a fire pit outside or a fireplace inside if weather does not permit an outdoor ceremony. When creating your fire, you will want to continue the ceremonial focus engaged in the despacho creation process with reverence and sacred awareness. When your fire is lit, call forth the spirits of the land, making some music and heightening the energy of the ceremony. Using sacred sound makers such as drums or rattles, engross yourself in ecstatic dance and singing. Build up your own spiritual energy (and the energy of the group, if you are in community) as the fire blazes. When you feel the fire has burned sufficiently so that the coals are burning hot, carefully use a tool to safely make a space within the coals for easy distribution of the despacho bundle. Forming the remaining logs into a U-shape is a common practice, so that the open space of the U is facing your access point to the fire. You will want to make sure the coals are in that open U space.

Before releasing the despacho into the fire, you will want to engage in a final blessing of the offering you have created. If you are in a group, give everyone and yourself a final blessing by touching the despacho to your brow (your kulli chunpi), your heart (the sonqo chunpi), and your stomach (the qosqo chunpi) as a way to receive a final transmission of medicine from your creation. Traditionally, the youngest of the group will perform this blessing and bring the despacho to the fire, provided they are old enough to be safe and assisted by an adult if necessary. If you are not in a group, offer the despacho yourself. The despacho should be gently placed (or lightly tossed if the fire is too hot) onto the coals of the open U shape.

When the bundle is offered, quiet should settle throughout the group and within yourself. This is another time of meditation. All focus should be on the act of burning. The burning of a despacho is itself a practice of divination. Do you see things in the smoke, in the flames? Do you hear anything? What is the despacho trying to say? Do you see any shapes or faces in the embers that provide answers for the despacho's purpose? Do the scents of the burning bring anything to mind? How does the smoke trail into the heavens? You will receive further guidance on divination with smoke in the next chapter, but for now just remain open to what comes. They key is to have your mind open to all possibilities. Bring yourself back to your own childhood and what it was like watching a fire. Allow your imagination to guide you. Do not concern yourself with anything other than what the fire has to say.

Sacred Communion

Creating and offering a despacho is an ancient ritual that has evolved over centuries. There is no need to concern yourself with whether you are building a despacho according to the correct protocol or not. This craft is a sacred communion between you and Pachamama. Nobody else can tell you how to develop that relationship. Create your own practice and experiment based upon your own intuition. Fire is often depicted in the modern world as a tool of destruction, but in ancient times, it was a tool of creation and inspiration. By engaging in a despacho ritual, you can establish a rapport with Pachamama and the world around you. Through regular practice, you will begin to develop a renewed communion with the unseen realms that greatly contributes to your vista and shamanic journey work for the future.

CHAPTER NINE
Shamanic Healing

A primary component of the shamanic path, and specifically curanderismo, is curing. Shamans, after all, were the first doctors. In Peru, curing exists in a very superstitious culture; specifically, a client will typically seek a curandero to cure bad luck or sorcery. In the Western world, we do not normally ascribe illness to these causes. In the modern world, health is associated with either physical or psychological well-being. However, the shamanic paradigm rests in the knowledge that all things are rooted in actuality.

I would never suggest anyone rely only on shamanism when sick, yet I do believe shamanic healing can augment the healing experience. There are many experts in the modern world who recognize more ancient and indigenous methods of healing as a holistic approach to wellness. Acupuncture, craniosacral therapy, meditation, yoga, and aroma therapy are just some of these ancient practices being accepted as common therapeutic techniques.

A close friend of mine, Dr. Jill Strom, runs just such a clinic in the Kansas City area. Her clinic, Cura Integrative Healthcare, offers a variety of services focused not just on physical healing, but also on the mind and spirit as well. Their modalities are numerous and even include shamanic healing (facilitated by my wife, Autumn) as a vital supplement to the healing experience. In her book, *The Cura Convergence*, Dr. Strom expresses the main ambition of her approach: "For genuine healing to occur, hearts and minds must be open to a self-awareness of the cause and effect of our lives and lifestyles on our health. Healing can occur on different levels, but true healing occurs when it happens in an integrated fashion, holistically—on all levels: energetically, biologically, and spiritually."[49]

For this reason, shamanism focuses upon all elements of consciousness from the healing perspective. Shamanic healing is the curing of mind, heart, and body, reintegrating them in alignment with spirit and soul. There is a quote from the Christian Bible that I appreciate, which states, "Do you not know that your body is a temple of the Holy Spirit within you?"[50] As stated in chapter 1, I was raised a Christian. Though my spiritual ideas and proclivities tend to scare the average Christian bystander, I have never discarded my early spiritual learning. I can separate the teachings from the people. And, frankly, Yeshua (the true, Aramaic name of Jesus) was the ultimate shaman! There is a lot to learn from our traditional upbringings, even if we have negative associations with the traditions in which we were raised. Uncovering the shaman within yourself involves turning those negative associations into something positive for yourself.

My intention with the quote from Corinthians is to show that "you are the temple of God." According to the Bible, Yeshua's only interaction with the actual, physical temples was to turn the tables of the money changers, to disrupt the corruption that had become of the orthodoxy. The way Yeshua communed with God was through isolation (in the desert, in the Garden of Gethsemane, etc.). He did not go to church or rely on a priestly class, and he taught his disciples to do the same. Further, numerous mystical texts from other traditions throughout history state that the true temple of God resides in the self: the human body, mind, and soul.

In the Vedic hymns of the Hindus, the body is referred to as the chariot of the soul, as well as the container for the entire universe, including Brahma (God). For the African Dogon, the Creator Amma's body was cut into many pieces which eventually became the stars, plants, animals, and eventually people. Although the Buddhist tradition usually reviles the desires of the physical body, it does put forward that a healthy body is essential to paving the way toward enlightenment. I can go on and on, but

---

49 Jill Strom, *The Cura Convergence: Healing Through Science and Spirit* (Bloomington, IN: Balboa Press, 2017), 8.

50 1 Corinthians 6:19 (NIV).

the point is most all spiritual traditions regard the body as some sort of seat, or gateway, to soul evolution.

Shamanic practice is no different. Not only your physical body but also your emotional, mental, and spiritual makeup collectively create the foundation for your shamanic path. If your foundation is not stable, your temple will not stand. Like your astral temple, your body is the temple within which Creator and the universe reside.

Hucha

Shamanic healing provides techniques to assist with keeping our body, our temple, clean. Recall our discussion about the poq'po in chapter 3 and ways to purify the body and mind. We went over the concept of a trigger, which is a puncture into the poq'po, a traumatic event that sends an energetic charge that disrupts the harmony of the poq'po's energetic flow. Not only does that trigger induce an illusory state in which one operates in an alternate reality (cue the sombra ganadera) but also the poq'po becomes infiltrated with what curanderos call *hucha* (HOO-cha). Hucha is heavy, dense, disorderly energy that disrupts the natural flow of the poq'po's ability to produce an alternating (rather than direct) current, preventing an authentic participation with life around you.

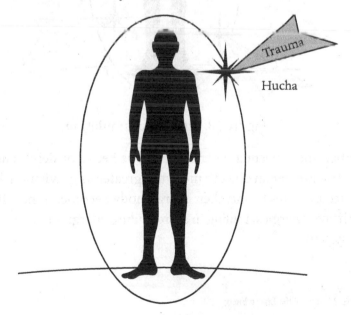

Figure 37. Hucha and trauma

Author and shamanic practitioner Joan Parisi Wilcox has worked extensively with the Quechua of Peru. She states, in her book *Masters of the Living Energy*, "If we do not cleanse the heavy energy from the surface of our poq'po, then hucha can accumulate, building up and seeping in more and more deeply. As this incompatible energy penetrates our energy field, it affects our physical, emotional, mental, and spiritual states."[51] Each time you receive a trigger, the energy body is punctured, and a blotch of hucha is left in its wake, sort of like a wound or bruise after being hit. If you do nothing about that wound, these bruises of hucha can certainly stockpile.

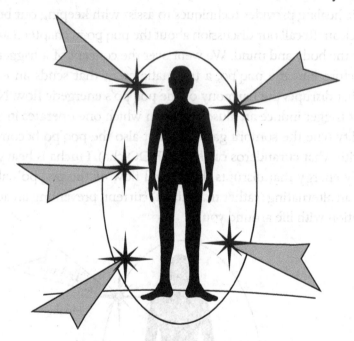

Figure 38. Hucha accumulation

Further, the Quechua describe hucha as heavy or dense energy for a reason. The greater an object's mass, the greater its gravitational pull. As a person accumulates hucha, their energy body becomes almost like a magnet for heavy energies, pulling in surrounding energies that are unhealthy for the system.

---

51 Wilcox, *Masters of the Living Energy*, 50.

Figure 39. Hucha attracting hucha

As this hucha accumulates, it becomes more difficult to be able to see the true form of the individual. This is indicative of the way a person interacts with the world around them. As hucha accumulates, it becomes more difficult for them to see the world in front of them, like too many fly splotches on a windshield.

Ever notice that when you are down, it is much easier for you to slip into depressive states and you are unable to see a positive outcome for your situation? This is likely due to a vast accumulation of hucha that needs cleansing from the poq'po. Instead of being able to participate with the world in a healthy way, a person is stuck in an alternate reality, only seeing their hurts from the past, reinforced by accrued hucha. This is the plight of the individual unaware of their misguided behavior (e.g., one who is ruled by the sombra ganadera).

When one is reacting from the sombra ganadera state, they are normally filled with so much hucha that it is difficult for them to maneuver their own emotional state. According to J. E. Williams in *The Andean Codex*, "Hucha darkens mood, decreases resistance to disease, and causes sluggishness and poor health."[52] This is a primary reason my own health failed for so many years. The hucha amassed, stockpiled within my poq'po and affected all aspects of my soul: spiritual, mental, emotional, and physical.

Curing Ceremony

We have discussed before how the opening of the account will normally follow the flow of the mesa from right to left. In curing, that flow of the mesa runs full circle by flowing left to right during the healing process. This is one reason why the shamanic journey started with the campo ganadero, then moved to the campo medio and finally the campo justiciero. In this sequence, the curing of the mind, body, and spirit will move first to a cleansing (*limpia*), an alignment (*alineación*), and then a flowering (*florecimiento*) for the individual (also known as a raising, or *levantada*). These are the primary stages of curing for the person, and as you can see in the following graphic, they create a circular flow of energy in the entire ritual process of the mesa.

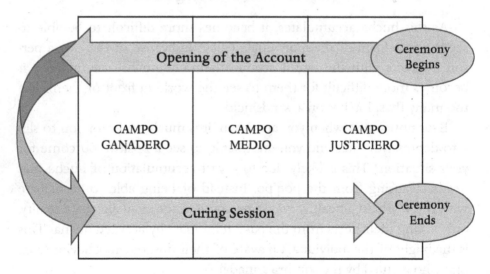

Figure 40. Curing on the mesa

---

52 J. E. Williams, *The Andean Codex* (Charlottesville, VA: Hampton Roads Publishing, 2005), 122.

The rest of this chapter contains processes that were used on me and taught to me by don Daniel during my shamanic training in curanderismo. These practices will help cleanse the poq'po using one's artes on the mesa, as well as reinforcing the body with energies to help bring about the harmonization of individuation. However, I highly recommend using these processes on yourself only for the time being, until you are able to seek tutelage from an experienced practitioner and are ready to be of service to others. Working with another person's energetic field should be considered with care; you want to know exactly what you are doing and have plenty of experience and proper education behind acting as a practitioner for others.

Practicum 18: Divination

Divination is the art of gaining insight into an issue using mystical means. There are numerous ways to practice divination, no one better than another. The important thing is to find a divination practice that works for you.

Vista is your key to uncovering the hucha within one's body. Where is it located precisely? How large is the hucha? Exactly what chunpi is it blocking? What caused this issue? Is it a physical injury? An emotional one? It is caused by reinforced trauma or a recent, specific incident? And so on. You must use your vista to get all the information you can before proceeding with a cleansing (see limpias in practicum 19). Also, divination should be a process of uncovering which arte to use to address the specific issue.

Before practicing any divination, I would again return to the foundational practices of breathing basics, kawsay activation, the pillar of light, and then opening the account of your mesa (appendix A). This will prime your poq'po and attune it to a more precise outlook for your vista to discern the cause and solution of the issue at hand.

From there, there are numerous types of divination you could use to configure a diagnosis and prognosis for the issue at hand. Here are just a few you can use, either individually or in conjunction with your mesa.

Capnomancy

Capnomancy is divination using smoke. This is typically done using incense but can be done through a source of fire such as a burning cauldron or campfire. It is a common idea that smoke is a representation of the essence of spirit and can be a carrier of prayers into the heavens.

To use smoke as a divination tool, get an incense burner that can be placed in the campo medio of the mesa. You will want it as near to the center as possible. Be sure to have an incense burner that will not cause a fire hazard on your mesa cloth. You are welcome to use stick incense, but I personally prefer charcoal that I can put into a cauldron filled halfway with ash. I normally place the cauldron on a coaster of some sort for extra protection. A common incense to burn in curanderismo is copal, which is a good opening into the soul realms and cleanser of the environment. You are welcome to use any incense that resonates with you personally.

Before burning, hold the incense in your hand and state your inquiry out loud or whisper it directly into your hand. Be sure to have no draft in your space as this will affect the smoke of the incense; close any windows, turn off fans, and be sure the air conditioning or heating unit is off for the time being if you are near an air vent. Then, you can burn the incense.

Watch the flow of the smoke as it burns. While you do, it is good to sing or whisper to the smoke, asking it to reveal the issue at hand for you. Here are some indicators about the flow of the smoke and what it may mean:

- If the smoke is flowing upward in an unbroken stream, then this could mean all is well. There is balance in the situation or with the client.

- If the smoke is not centered, then what direction is it flowing in? This could indicate what work needs to be done and what artes to use. Is the smoke flowing from one side to the other? Is it flowing toward the campo ganadero or the campo justiciero, or is it centered in the medio?

- Is the smoke flowing toward one certain arte in particular? Maybe this is the arte that needs to be worked with for a while.

- Are there figures in the smoke? Sometimes the smoke can form into symbols, letters, or numbers. This could provide a sign of something to investigate further in one's life or may reveal a synchronicity of some kind. These signs will be up to you or the client to interpret, as most sign meanings in the shamanic realms are very specific to the individual and cannot be interpreted via a book of definitions.

Cartomancy

Tarot has already been discussed as a viable tool in the curandero arts. Tarot is definitely one of my favorite methods of divination as an artist. The tarot is a great tool for divining an issue and getting guidance on a potential outcome. However, it is important not to ascribe any static standards on the card meanings and how they are interpreted. For instance, tarot expert Jaymi Elford, in her book *Tarot Inspired Life*, emphasizes, "There is no single way to read the cards! They are as diverse as you are a person. The meaning you select at any given point in time will be the right message to say according to the conditions and factors surrounding the reading you perform."[53] This is true in any kind of divination, but especially for the tarot.

Tarot can actually take a lifetime's worth of study in some cases. There is so much to learn, despite how many years one has been reading the cards. If you are new to tarot, I recommend getting a few solid books to help guide your tarot-reading experience, Elford's included. You can also utilize cartomancy as a divination method without tarot, using decks such as Lenormand and oracle cards. I highly recommend *Andean Healing Energy Cards* by Eileen O'Hare or Stephanie Red Feather's *Empath Activation Cards*, if you are not using tarot. In terms of finding your own deck of divination cards—tarot or otherwise—it's not necessarily about finding the art that is the most appealing but what *speaks to you*.

---

53 Jaymi Elford, *Tarot Inspired Life: Use the Cards to Enhance Your Life* (Woodbury, MN: Llewellyn Publications, 2019), 40.

Anthropologist Bonnie Glass-Coffin has documented many instances of tarot use with the mesa in her book on female curanderismo, *The Gift of Life*. I especially enjoy reading the tarot with my own mesa in a spread I call the Campos Spread.

When you've selected a deck of cards to use, bless them using sage or incense. When you are ready to use them, shuffle the cards and ask your question during the shuffle. Tarot is not normally helpful for yes-or-no questions, so it is customary to inquire regarding seeking understanding and guidance in a situation. When you feel the deck is sufficiently shuffled, select the top three cards and place them on your mesa in this order:

1. **The Campo Ganadero:** This card will represent what has taken place in the past to contribute to the current situation. It may signify an opposing force at play in your situation, including obstacles of dark magick in the works. It could also represent the feminine aspect of your situation that needs to be looked at. Also, it could be identifying an aspect of your life that needs to be dispatched or released.

2. **The Camp Medio:** This card is a representation of your present situation. It will identify the unifying factor in your life that will help bring you into alignment with your Self, a path to balance.

3. **The Campo Justiciero:** This card represents a future state, a path of guidance, or uplifting force. It could represent the solution for moving forward or the masculine aspect of the situation to be looked at closely. It can also identify what it will take to lift one from the current situation.

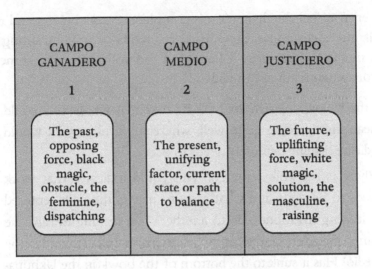

CAMPO GANADERO	CAMPO MEDIO	CAMPO JUSTICIERO
1	2	3
The past, opposing force, black magic, obstacle, the feminine, dispatching	The present, unifying factor, current state or path to balance	The future, uplifting force, white magic, solution, the masculine, raising

Figure 41. The Campos Spread

Most tarot spreads need to be read as a whole rather than each card read separately. This is a good lesson itself for the way the campos work. Regardless, this is just one way to use the cards in conjunction with the mesa; you are encouraged to experiment and find your own method, including the integration of spreads from other books and decks.

Oomancy

Oomancy is a folk practice of divining with an egg. Life is a strong source of power, and the egg of a chicken is a good container for harnessing kawsay for divination or limpias (see practicum 19).

Like anything else, select an egg and bless it before using it with some sage or agua de florida. Bring the egg up to your mouth and speak into it, asking the egg to assist with divining the particular issue. Then, carefully, roll the egg over the body. It is customary to start from the top of the head and work all the way down to the feet. Be sure to go over the arms, hands, and fingers; try to reach the backside as well. If there is a particular part of the body that is in pain or that comes to mind while doing the divination, this may be the area of focus for a healing. Speak out loud, sing, or whisper to your sombra (or the sombra of a participant) while doing this, asking them to reveal the condition to the egg you are using.

When you feel the divination is complete, crack the egg and release the yolk into a clear, glass bowl. It is preferred the bowl be sitting in the campo medio of the mesa. Then, read the yolk. Here are some basic indicators when reading egg yolk:

- Is the yellow yolk whole, or is it broken? A whole yolk could mean one is doing quite well, whereas a broken yolk would indicate healing definitely needs to occur.

- Where is the yolk centered? This could indicate what work needs to be done and what artes to use. Is the yolk centered or leaning from one side to another? Is it leaning toward the campo ganadero or the campo justiciero, or is it centered in the medio? Has it sunk to the bottom of the bowl (in the Ukhupacha), is it floating in the middle (the Kaypacha), or is it floating on top (the Hanaqpacha)?

- Is the white (albumen) clear, or is it cloudy or clumpy? If the white is clear, that is good sign of a clean energy body. If the white is cloudy, it could indicate there may be something preventing one from being able to see a situation clearly. If it is clumpy, that could mean there is some density and hucha that needs to be removed (especially if it was in the area of pain). If there is blood or black in the yolk or white, that will typically represent a great sickness (in this case, a very intense healing is needed, and I would possibly refer to another curandero and/ or medical doctor).

- Are there figures in the yolk? Like smoke, sometimes the yolk can form into symbols, letters, or numbers. Again, these signs will be up to you to interpret based upon your own life experience. If you are working with a participant, the signs you see may have a significant interpretation to them.

After inspecting the egg, release the egg yolk (along with the shell) at the base of a tree or flowing water to return it to Source. Perform some sort of blessing of gratitude, whether it be a prayer, song, or incense.

It is important to recognize that an egg is life, so show this life presence the respect it deserves.

Cleromancy

The art of casting. Likely, you've seen movies of shamans casting bones and reading the signs and portents within them. There are many types of casting—bones being one of them—and the most popular type is runes. However, in curanderismo, the more well-known type of cleromancy is the art of casting shells.

The most common shell to use is any type of small scallop, approximately an inch or less in size. The reason for this is you will want a shell that has the ability to land either on an open side (concave) or closed side (convex). Because of this, unlike other divination methods, shell casting can actually be conducive to yes-or-no answers for questions asked. Typically, a shell landing on the open side will mean yes, and the closed side will mean no.

It is common for a curandero to have up to seven shells for their casting. It is good to get these shells directly from the ocean or a large body of water if you can. If you do not have that ability, there are plenty of novelty and crafts shops where you can get some. Either way, bless the shells using the activating artes practice (practicum 11).

To cast, hold the shells in both hands and shake them like you would dice. Whatever your question is for the divination, state it out loud or whisper it into the shells. You can phukuy (a breath of prayer) a few times into the shells while you shake. Then, without directing the flow of the shells, cast them randomly over your mesa and examine where they landed.

Did the majority of them land in one campo versus another? How many are facing up (yes) versus down (no)? Does this give you an indication of what campo or pacha needs the most attention? Is there more than one shell touching a specific arte? Maybe that arte should be the one used for the healing.

Like any divination, there are many ways to interpret the shells, and ultimately, it is all based upon your own inner guidance.

Any one of these tools for divination can be stored on the mesa itself. In fact, I recommend it. You can place the divination tool in the campo or pacha where you feel it will draw the best source of power for its use. Feel free to switch the placement according to your intuition. Again, rarely should a mesa remain stagnant. These tools are artes in and of themselves and should be treated as such. Bless them before use and cleanse them afterward, with a final blessing of gratitude.

Practicum 19: Limpias

One of the primary goals of shamanic healing is to ensure that one does not live from a shadow state. A process to help facilitate this is to cleanse one's energy, extracting the dense energy associated with trauma or some other illness. As hucha leaves, the poq'po becomes clear and the individual is able to see and interact with actuality in clarity.

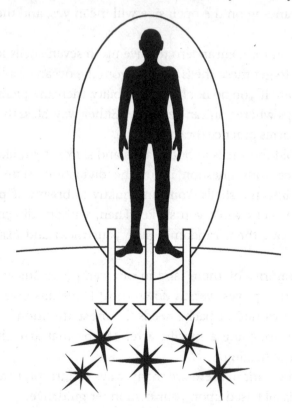

Figure 42. Clearing the poq'po

See how pristine the energy body looks now compared to the earlier images in the chapter? However, extracting hucha can be a tricky process, and every shamanic culture around the world has differing ways to approach this. Using the mesa and its artes has been well-proven over centuries as an effective method for this practice of clearing. When extracting hucha, in order to ensure the hucha does not infect them or wander off to infect others, the curandero can use the mesa as a medium to channel the hucha from the individual, as it can operate as a magnetic attractor. The mesa—because of its representation as a mirror of not only ourselves but nature itself—funnels the hucha straight into Pachamama, where it can no longer do any harm to the individual or others.

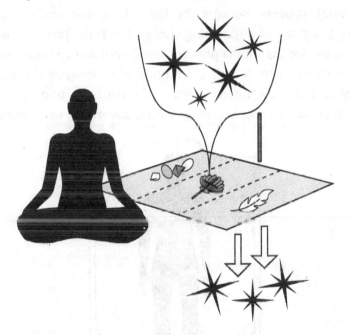

Figure 43. Hucha filtered through the mesa

Why return this hucha into Pachamama, our beloved mother? Well, in fact, all hucha should always be given to Pachamama. Trained in the energy healing ways of the Quechua, Joan Parisi Wilcox states, "Hucha empowers Pachamama; to her it is food, not waste."[54] Pachamama eats

---

54 Wilcox, *Masters of the Living Energy*, 52.

hucha: it is her food, which is composted, and later the energy can be turned into nutrients and then returned in life-giving ways back to the community, to the people. It is a sacred, reciprocal exchange, an ayni, which is the fundamental basis for maintaining balance in the world. Some shamans say it is because we do not honor this releasing of hucha to Pachamama that we have caused a collective sickness and malaise that is infecting modern society. If we were to rid ourselves of hucha and return it to Pachamama more regularly, we would not be facing the volume of issues we encounter today.

Limpias are ritual cleansings, the process of dispatching and ridding the body of hucha and returning it to Pachamama. This is the first stage of the curing process. Because the left side of the mesa—the campo medio—is the place of dispatching energy, this is the primary placement of artes to use for the limpia process. It is important to note that all limpias are performed by working the body in a downward motion. You will want to move the hucha down and out of the body, so whatever limpia you choose to do, perform it with a downward movement.

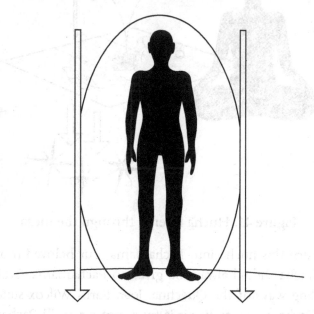

Figure 44. Limpias

There are almost infinite ways to execute a limpia in ritual, as many as you can creatively come up with. Yet, here are some of the funda-mental limpias in the curanderismo lineage.

Arte/Vara Limpia

You can use either an arte or a vara to perform a limpia. It is recom-mended to use an arte or vara located in the campo ganadero for this. If all you have acquired is the arte de defensa, then you may use that. How-ever, you may acquire artes over time that have specific uses for certain types of limpias, such as an arte to work specifically with hucha, trauma, dark magick, physical illness, or matters of the heart. It is up to you how you want the calicanto of your mesa to be structured. You decide how many artes you want and how specific their use should be.

Through divination you will have selected the arte you feel is right for the occasion of the limpia. If one did not come through divina-tion, simply ask the mesa which arte to use and select the first arte that either comes to mind or draws your eye. Next, follow these steps for a simple limpia:

1. Bless the arte and bring it to your lips. Call forth the name of the arte (if it has one) and ask for its permission and assis-tance in this task.

2. Bring the arte to the top of the head. Out loud, call forth the power of Creator and your mesa for assistance. Most spe-cifically, call out to the patron saints or deities of the campo ganadero for the limpia. In this case, the common saints of the campo ganadero are San Cyprian and Santa Justina, but again, you choose the deities that resonate the most for you. Ask for them to guide your hand and empower the chosen arte to cleanse the body of hucha so that the poq'po can be clear and clean.

3. Now, pass the arte down the front of the body, either rubbing directly over the physical body or hovering directly above it, based on your comfort and guidance. With your intention,

will the hucha in and around the body to be magnetically attracted to the arte, and visualize it leaving the body and sticking to the sacred artifact. It is common to be talking or whispering to the body, goading the hucha out of the poq'po and into the arte. If there is one area that is in pain or seems heavier with hucha, feel free to pass that area several times until you feel it clear. Pass the arte all the way to the feet. (If you are working with another person, it should go without saying to avoid any of the private areas of the body. A client should feel safe and secure with a curandero.)

4. Now, pass the arte down the back of the body, following the same protocol in step 3. Then, pass the arte down the left side of the body and finally the right. Again, feel free to go over any areas again with extra density or to experiment with the limpia based on your intuition. Some curanderos sing during the limpia to help draw out the hucha or calm the client.

5. When you feel the limpia is done (i.e., the poq'po feels cleansed of the hucha), point the arte to the mesa and blow (phukuy) the hucha toward the center of the mesa. Visualize the hucha flowing out of the arte and will it to be funneled down through the center of the mesa and into the earth. The strength of your will is imperative for this moment, as the hucha will require the full force of your intention to depart. If working with a participant, you may want them to blow the hucha away as well. It may be that you will have to phukuy the hucha into the mesa several times during the limpia, which is fine. Just be sure to have an awareness of hucha accumulation in the arte.

6. Finally, you will need to thoroughly cleanse the arte before returning it to your mesa. You can do this in several ways, most commonly by saturating it with agua de florida as well as passing it through sage or incense. If the hucha was

particularly heavy during the session, you may want to bury the arte in the earth for a full day and night to allow Pachamama to do the work for you. Only when the arte feels completely cleansed may you return it to the mesa. Be sure to give deep, heartfelt gratitude to the arte before putting it back in its original placement on the mesa.

Agua Limpia

Using waters to spray away (phukuy) hucha is another method of cleansing hucha from the body. There are a number of floral waters used in curanderismo for a variety of different purposes. The most common for clearing hucha in a limpia is called *kananga* water, a cologne with ylang-ylang and alcohol as its base mixed with citrus and other aromas. You can find kananga water at most metaphysical stores or any Hispanic markets in your area. Like agua de florida, kananga can be quite sharp, so if you are going to phukuy with your mouth, it would be beneficial to practice before performing a limpia. It is perfectly acceptable to use a spray bottle instead. Also, similar to artes for limpias, keep your kananga or other water stored in the campo ganadero so that it can resonate with the powers of that field. Be aware of any allergies with the waters you are using.

Here is a simple protocol for doing a limpia with waters:

1. Select the appropriate bottle of water for the limpia and bring it to your lips. Blow into the bottle three times. Blowing three times is a call for assistance from the three pachas.

2. Call upon your patron saints or deities of the campo ganadero to help cleanse hucha from the body and clear the mind and spirit of any obstacles obstructing one's path.

3. Just as with an arte or vara limpia, you will want to spray downward on the body of a participant. Phukuy the front first, then the back, then the left and right sides. If you do not have a spray bottle and are doing a limpia on yourself,

phukuy may not be an option (well, you can try, but good luck with that). Simply pour some of the water in your hands and brush it over your body, as if you were washing dirt from your body in a bath or shower.

4. When you are done, give a blessing of gratitude for the water and return it to its place in the campo ganadero.

If you do not have access to kananga, you may use another water of your choosing. Just be sure that, for you, it aligns with the attributes of the campo ganadero. I like to use moon water sometimes as a substitute, which is very simple to make. Gather some water from a clean stream and set the bottle outside during the night of the full moon. Perform a prayer or a blessing over the water, asking the light of Grandmother Moon to imbue the water with its magical power for the purposes of cleansing and purification. Leave the water out overnight, and when you retrieve it the next morning, leave behind some cornmeal, tobacco, or an offering of your choice in gratitude.

Another way to purify the body with water is simply to bathe in a natural stream. As the water rushes past, imagine the power of the current pulling the hucha away. Encourage the current's strength and ability to purify by singing a song or whispering blessings of gratitude. If you do not have access to a stream, take a bath. Pour some kananga from your mesa into the bathwater. Allow yourself to settle in the bath while the water and kananga act to pull the hucha from your body. Stay in the tub as the water drains and allow the hucha to flow away as the water empties from the tub.

Egg Limpia

An egg limpia is a simple process and is similar to egg divination. When you are ready to perform a limpia with an egg, place an egg on the campo ganadero before you begin to give it some time to acquire the attributes with the powers of that field. This would be a good time to do some drumming or rattling or sing a song to call forth the powers of the campo ganadero in the egg itelf.

Then, retrieve the egg and roll the egg down the body, calling forth the hucha much in the same way you would an arte limpia: first the front, then the back, the left, and finally the right side. Again, pay attention to the amount of hucha prevalent in a certain area and don't be afraid to roll the egg over it a few times, if needed. Be careful, though—the last thing you want is a cracked egg.

When the rolling is complete, do not crack open the egg as you do in a divination. Instead, take the egg outside and bury it, next to a tree if possible. Pachamama will take the hucha from there and reuse it however she sees fit.

Smoke Limpia

There are numerous ways to use smoke as a limpia to cleanse oneself. Smoke is associated with the spiritual essence of the universe, so it is a way to connect with a spiritual form of healing. Some of the primary ways of using smoke are burning a plant medicine inside a bowl or abalone shell and using a feather to waft the smoke over oneself or an individual. This is primarily done with sage in many cultures, although one can do that as well with incense or other appropriate herbs. When doing this for a limpia, you will want to follow the same protocol for an arte limpia as when trying to rid the body of hucha: waft the smoke over the front, back, left, and finally right side. Remember to work the smoke in a downward motion over the body. Using a feather, you can flick the hucha off the body and toward the mesa, rather than with phukuy.

Using tobacco is a common method as well. In Peru, *mapacho* cigarettes are very common, as well as using pipes. Just exhale the smoke over the body in a similar way to perform the limpia. Tobacco can be very strong and not healthy to smoke recreationally; if you are going to use it, please do so only in a ceremonial way and do not fully inhale. The goal is to use your will and breath, with the smoke of the plant as a tool, to cleanse the body of hucha.

Again, it is important that if you are going to use the plant medicines, use them in the same way you would any arte. Store them in the appropriate campo of the mesa, call in the powers of the mesa before use, and be sure to express gratitude with an offering or blessing after each use.

Practicum 20: Alineaciones

Following the flow of ceremony as seen in figure 40, you will now want to perform an *alineación* as aligned with the campo medio. Taking place after a limpia, alineación is an "alignment" of the person's well-being, a reorienting of mind, heart, and body into a holistic unity after being cleansed of whatever obstacles were obstructing the individual's path. It is a remembering of one's True Self, an Individuation.

For this reason, the healing of alineaciones is not performed with a motion downward, but by a centering of the energies within the poq'po. The goal is to bring the healing process inward, grounding the person into the Kaypacha realm. Oftentimes a limpia can leave a person disoriented; much like after surgery, a piece of them has been cut away. The alineaciónes will dutifully return a person's state of mind into one of clarity.

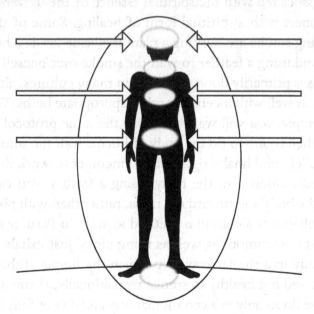

Figure 45. Alineaciones

Alineaciones are fairly uniform despite which tool you decide to use. The focus will be on activiating the three primary energy centers of the poq'po: the kulli chunpi (mind), sonqo chunpi (heart), and qosqo chunpi (soul).

These three combined will help enliven or awaken the physical body into awareness and allow it to become settled into the Kaypacha.

For these healings, I will normally intone a phrase for myself to help center my mind and heart. I will say, "My name is Daniel Moler. I call myself to myself. San Pedro help me thus!" San Pedro is my personal patron saint/deity for the campo medio, so that is whom I call to. You will want to call to your own patron saint or deity, or maybe just to the campo medio itself, or even just go to the big daddy or mama of them all: Creator. If I'm working with a client, I will have them intone the phrase for themselves.

Perform an alineación healing by working solely with artes from the campo medio. I recommend doing the pillar of light (practicum 8) ritual in preparation for alineaciónes; then keep the visual of the pillar of light in full force throughout the duration of the healing to better reinforce the alignment you are transmitting to the recipient.

Arte/Vara Alineaciónes

The Staff of Individuation is my favorite arte to use for this process, although you may use any vara or arte within the middle field of the mesa. Select the arte you feel will best align you or the participant into the Kaypacha realm. Ask the arte or vara for permission, then:

1. Perform the pillar of light ritual for yourself.

2. Bring the vara to the client's torso and make a declaration to the prospective saint or deity of the campo medio, asking for their assistance in bringing balance and wholeness to yourself or the individual. Call forth your or the participant's sombra primera to be aligned in balance within the body.

3. Put the bottom end of the vara to the participant's forehead and the top of the vara to your lips. Take a deep breath in, pulling in the power of the light from the pillar of light, then phukuy that power through the vara and into the forehead of the client. The intention is for your own pillar of light to activate the kulli chunpi.

4. Now take the vara to the heart and perform the same ritual of phukuy, activating the sonqo chunpi of the participant.

5. Then, bring the vara to the torso and phukuy through the staff, activating the qosqo chunpi.

6. Finally, give the participant your staff and have them hold it themselves, upright, at their torso. Have them intone: "My name is [full name]. I call myself to myself. [Saint/deity], help me thus!"

7. When complete, bless the vara with agua de florida or some other water you use for the campo medio (jasmine and sandalwood waters are often used as well).

You can use any arte in the campo medio for alineaciónes, not just a vara. For oneself, I recommend doing the pillar of light; then bringing the arte or vara to your own forehead, heart, and belly; breathing in; and exhaling a strong phukuy to reactivate each chunpi. End your ritual with the intonation to call yourself back to yourself.

Agua Alineaciones

As mentioned previously, some of the primary waters used in the campo medio are agua de florida, jasmine, or sandalwood. Again, you are free to create your own waters or find waters that resonate for you in the middle field. Truly, the ritual for agua alineaciónes is precisely the same as with a vara or artes, though you will just phukuy (or spray) the designated waters onto the forehead, heart, and belly of the participant instead. Be sure that you blow into the bottle three times before each phukuy, call in the respective saint or deity, and channel the pillar of light for each phukuy. For this process, you will want to be sure a participant's eyes are closed and covered so as not to get any of the waters in their eyes. For yourself, take a dab of the water in your hand and cleanse the forehead, heart, and belly with your hand. Be sure to give gratitude to the bottle of water as an arte itself and return it to the campo medio when complete.

Smoke Alineaciones

Smoke can be used in a similar way using the exact ritual prescribed for the arte alineación. Depending upon whether or not you use sage in a bowl or tobacco in a pipe or cigarette, you will waft or blow the smoke onto the forehead, heart, and belly. For oneself, you can blow or waft the smoke into your hand and apply to each area of the body. For the campo medio, tobacco and copal are my smoke medicines of choice, as sage is more for cleansing (in the campo ganadero), but you will decide which plant medicine works best for an alineación.

Practicum 21: Levantadas

A healing residing within the right field of the mesa, the campo justiciero, *levantadas* are ritual raising of the recipient's spirit. The campo justiciero is the field of good fortune and the path to the future. A levantada uplifts the recipient from their current situation and boots them into a forward momentum to live their life's purpose, to do what they came here to do. Because of this, a levantada works in the exact opposite motion of a limpia, with a motion upward toward the heavens.

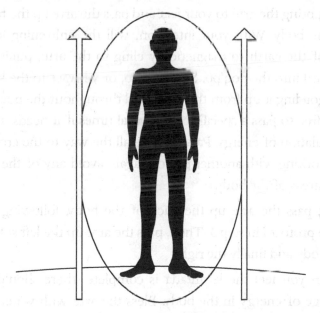

Figure 46. Levantada

The uplifting nature of a levantada cannot be understated: the goal is to direct to the recipient as much high energy as possible, so that they almost feel like they can float away. Have fun, laugh, raise the energy high! Levantada is about elevating the spirits!

Arte/Vara Levantada

Through divination, select the arte in the campo justiciero that you feel is right for the occasion of the levantada. Next, follow these steps:

1. Bless the arte and bring it to your lips. Call forth the name of the arte (if it has one) and ask for its permission and assistance in this task.

2. Bring the arte to the top of your head or the head of the recipient. Out loud, call forth the power of Creator and your mesa for assistance. Most specifically, call out to the patron saints or deities of the campo justiciero. Ask for them to guide your hand and empower the chosen arte to raise the energy of the poq'po.

3. Now, bring the arte to your feet and pass the arte up the front of the body. With your intention, will the enlivening kawsay of the earth to magnetically cling to the arte, pulling it upward into the poq'po. Sing, talk to, or whisper to the kawsay, goading it up from the earth and throughout the poq'po. Feel free to pass a specific area several times if it needs more stimulation of energy. Pass the arte all the way to the crown. (If working with another person, again avoid any of the private areas of the body.)

4. Now, pass the arte up the back of the body, following the same protocol in step 3. Then, pass the arte up the left side of the body and finally the right.

5. When you feel the levantada is complete, there should be a surge of energy in the body. Bless the arte with waters or

smoke with gratitude and return it lovingly to its place in the campo justiciero.

6. A good practice to complete the levantada is to then perform the kawsay activation ritual (practicum 7). This will provide a sufficient boost of energy in the poq'po to end the ceremonial healing.

Agua Levantada

For a levantada with waters, you will again perform the protocol for the arte/vara levantada but by exercising a phukuy with waters. In the campo justiciero, carnation, violet, and orange waters are often used for raisings. Be sure to spray upward, instead of down, for the levantada.

A common practice in Peru is to take a floral arrangement by hand and dip the flowers in a mixed bath of the floral waters above. With the flowers dripping with the sweet aromas, you can brush them across the body of the recipient or yourself in an upward fashion. This can be a sweet and satisfactory levantada for those who require a softer touch rather than their body being passed by an arte or vara. If you choose to do this, be sure to have the floral arrangement charge in the campo justiciero beforehand. Be aware of any allergies with the waters you are using.

Smoke Levantada

For the smoke levantada, the smoke is wafted or blown upward following the steps for the arte/vara levantada. Tobacco can be used, but most often the best smoke medicines are burning sweetgrass or using frankincense. You will need to make sure whatever smoke you use will actually be uplifting for yourself or the recipient, as some people can be sensitive to heavy scents. For this reason, it is very rare that I use smoke for a levantada, but again, that depends on the needs of the person.

Understand the Flow

It is not always called for to perform a limpia, alineación, and levantada for every healing. Sometimes you or a healing recipient may just need a healing from one campo over the other. Generally, I like to perform all three as a way to complete the continuum of flow in a healing session (as per figure 40) as a ceremonial whole. Remember to make these practices your own, improve, and experiment. Try something new. Shamanic healing only works if you understand the flow of what you are doing, rather than following a prescribed list of steps.

Also, you will notice that these healings align strongly into categories of earth (arte), water (agua), and air/fire (smoke). These healing practices utilize the full gamut of elemental power that resides in the natural world. Be aware and honor this as a way to channel the encantos of nature, as they make up the full calicanto of your mesa. Spend time outside of healings nurturing these artes, calling them into account, and drawing in the power of the encantos they represent. Shift your mesa as it needs shifting. Listen to it. Sing to the artes. Give them offerings. These artifacts are living, conscious beings that exist as a part of you, an extension of your own Individuality. They are representatives of soul.

CHAPTER TEN
Shamanic Soul

One of the most intense experiences in my life happened right before I met don Daniel and began my tutelage. Truly, this experience was one of the primary catalysts in my already-wounded state to seek out help from the shamanic perspective.

I had set out for myself, before ever learning the principles of curanderismo –including ayni—to create a ceremony to heal myself. I was long past exhausted from my physical ailments, which only exacerbated my mental and emotional state. Being taxed, I turned to using a plant medicine I had not used before at an incredibly high dose. In my hubris, I thought I could solve all my problems in one fell swoop without proper training and facilitation. What ensued was the most intense visionary experience I have ever had: I completely left my body. I felt my whole being slip through the floor, as if reality itself was a bathtub and someone unplugged the stopper; I became like ooze in the water slipping through the drain.

Although I felt as if my being was going downward, I know it wasn't *physically* down into the earth. In fact, the duct-like tunnel siphoned me underneath the entirety of the earth and the whole of the cosmos entirely. My sense of identity was chiseled away, moment by moment, the further out I was being pulled. I was no longer me; I was merely just observing this thing that was happening. There were no more planets, no more stars, no nebulas. There was only nothing. Pure, infinite nothingness.

Soon, within this visionary experience, I awoke. But I was not me: Daniel Moler. In fact, Daniel Moler wasn't real at all, merely a figment of the imagination of who I really was. I was "I am." I woke as my True Self, your True Self, the True Self of all of us, the One Being of all existence. I woke as this One Being in a single, square room. As this One Being, I was overwhelmed with a vast, lonely terror: Why did I wake up? I was asleep, dreaming. I was dreaming all of this! All reality! I was dreaming Daniel Moler, the wounded father whose marriage was falling apart. I was dreaming don Daniel Baxley teaching about the wisdom of San Pedro. I was San Pedro, being imbibed in ceremony. I was my wife, my son, the trees, the rivers. I was every living thing. I was you, reading this book. All of it, time and space, the entire cosmos, I was dreaming it all and it had all collapsed into nothingness when I, as the One Being, woke up. It was all gone now, and I was terrified.

The source of my dread became the most vivid and overwhelming sense of isolation. I perceived that all there truly was in existence—in all actuality—was this one room. Beyond this room lay that infinite void. There was nothing: a sheer nullification of all thought or form. The One Being was (is) completely, infinitely alone. In this isolation, the One Being dreams another world, dreams us, like a schizophrenic break, shattering its psyche into multiple disparate parts so that we don't remember the horror of the purest alienation. We are broken into many so that we can have something Other, other people and relationships. We are all One Being living in an amnesiac state inside our own dream.

From within the One Being, I became aware of the consciousness that was Daniel Moler and wanted to go back home. I didn't want to wake up; I just wanted to go back to sleep, back into the dream. If none of it was real, it didn't matter, because the alternative felt so much worse. I wanted to hold my son again, walk barefoot in grass again, feel the sun on my face again. The One Being went back to sleep and I returned to my body physically anchored in the world, quickly, almost as if I puked back into reality. My body was tremoring in a cold sweat.

After this experience, it took weeks to convince myself of the solidity of the reality around me. It took months before I could even truly process it and years before I could even talk about it without my body tremoring again. It also took years before I could even watch a movie like *The Matrix* or any other film or book that dealt with similar subject matter. The experience felt very much like that, as if we were living in a simulation, that the world was nothing but virtual reality. After a time, I began to find solace in such movies like *The Matrix* or books by Philip K. Dick, because it was a reminder that I wasn't alone in my trauma: others have had similar experiences as well.

I eventually came across the work of writer and researcher Michael Talbot. Referencing the contributions of one of the greatest quantum physicists of the twentieth century, David Bohm, Talbot says that "one of Bohm's most startling assertions is that the tangible reality of our every-day lives is really a kind of illusion, like a holographic image. Underlying it is a deeper order of existence, a vast and more primary level of reality that gives birth to all the objects and appearances of our physical world in much the same way that a piece of holographic film gives birth to a hologram."[55]

This notion can be found elsewhere in the spiritual traditions of the world. The Hindus refer to this virtual reality as *maya*, which is Sanskrit for "illusion." There are passages in the Upanishads that describe maya as the framework for the world, though all still part of the same one being, Brahman. Many others—the Dogon of Africa, the Lakota of North America, the Kabbalists of Judaism—have similar views.

Don Daniel spent a lot of time with me helping me process this experience and the information coming my way. In the shamanic worldview, it is understood that not only are all things in the world conscious (which is the central concept of animism), but there is an underlying essence tying them all together into a single fabric. Don Daniel introduced me to another Hindu concept called Indra's net, a metaphor about the Vedic deva Indra who holds a vast net that stretches into infinity. At each vertex of the cords there is a multifaceted jewel, and each jewel is reflected by all the others, thus revealing the holographic nature and interconnectedness of the universe. Don Daniel helped me understand that my experience did not have to be limited to just one vertex in Indra's net.

---

55 Michael Talbot, *The Holographic Universe* (New York: HarperCollins Publishers, 1991), 46.

I couldn't understand it at the time, because it was a very real experience for me. My body shook just thinking about it

"Just because it was a real experience," I remember don Daniel telling me, "doesn't mean it is the only experience available to you. Like every experience, what happens without is reflected by what is within."

This is a common adage in the Hermetic Tradition often cited as "as above, so below," implying that the macrocosm of all things (such as solar systems and galaxies) is merely a reflection of the microcosm (such as atoms) and vice versa. Like all things in the world being a part of Brahman, so then can Brahman be found in all things.

Don Daniel would often point me to the Gnostic Gospel of Thomas, a non-canonical text discovered in 1945 as part of the Nag Hammadi group of scriptures. It's sad to me that the Christian Church will not recognize these books as an addition to the Holy Bible, as I believe they contain great wisdom. In the Gospel of Thomas, Yeshua (the Christ) performs no miracles but instead focuses on mystical teachings akin to the Tao Te Ching. The saying don Daniel would often repeat to me came from the Gospel of Thomas, as Yeshua said: "If you bring forth what is within you, what you have will save you. If you have nothing within you, what you do not have within you will kill you."[56]

"What don't I have within me?" I would ask.

"That's the trick," don Daniel would answer. "You do not lack anything. You are already whole. You've just fooled yourself into thinking you aren't."

"How do I stop fooling myself then?"

"By growing soul."

Anima Mundi

The terms "spirit" and "soul" are often used interchangeably. In and out of spiritual circles, people will often use the terms "spirit world" or "Great Spirit" to denote the higher powers of divinity. I mean, we even refer to our communities as "spiritual circles" and our mystical paths as "spirituality." But what does "spirit" even mean?

---

56 Willis Barnstone and Marvin Meyer, ed., "The Gospel of Thomas," in *The Gnostic Bible: Gnostic Texts of Mystical Wisdom from the Ancient and Medieval Worlds* (Boston: Shambhala, 2003), 62.

"Spirit" comes from the word *spiritus*, which is Latin for "breath." This denotes the animated, living essence of all things. In many origin myths, God (or the Goddess, gods, etc.) breathes life into the world and human beings. Although we often refer to incorporeal things as "spiritual," the word actually refers to animating force of life (in Quechua terms, kawsay). Yet, the word "soul" actually comes from the Old English word *sāwol*, referring to the immortal essence within a human being.

If spirit is the essence of life that is a part of this physical reality, then soul is that aspect within us that transcends that physical reality. It is, as English philosopher Patrick Harpur says, "an intermediate world between the physical and spiritual, partaking of both."[57] What Harpur is referring to is soul as the medium between the above and below, within and without. He is referring to it in itself as a "world," often termed the World Soul, *anima mundi*. In Harpur's book, *The Philosopher's Secret Fire*, he states, "All Neoplatonists, Hermetic philosophers, alchemists and Kabbalists have asserted that the cosmos is annotated by a collective soul which manifests now spiritually, now physically, now...both at once; but which above all connects and holds all phenomena together."[58] This World Soul embodies the paradox within the Hermetic philosophy "as above, so below," because soul then implies that it is both the outer soul of the universe and the soul of the human at the same time. It is the underlying stuff of reality. Both macrocosm and microcosm, ambiguous.

The philosophers saw the soul as the storehouse of all imagination, which is the primary gateway into the World Soul. Indeed, this is the seat of power in the shamanic experience. As we have already practiced in our shamanic journeying, imagination is a key component to opening up the highways of the soul realm. In that case, it doesn't even matter if you are "imagining" an experience, because—as within, so without— the experience of the psyche is but a microcosmic reflection of the outer world. This is the lesson of Indra's Net, which is itself just a symbol for the World Soul.

---

57 Harpur, *Daimonic Reality*, 36.

58 Patrick Harpur, *The Philosopher's Secret Fire: A Secret History of the Imagination* (Chicago: Ivan R. Dee, 2002), 37.

As stated earlier, soul is ambiguous. It is non-static, like water or smoke, ever flowing. The purpose of walking the shamanic path is to grow soul within oneself. Don Oscar Miro-Quesada emphasizes this as a vital component of northern coastal curanderismo and the Pachakuti Mesa Tradition:

> *For, although we are born with it, our soul continues to develop with every life experience. Our sufferings are simply the secretions that add to its luster—like a pearl inside an oyster. Making soul is the process of a lifetime, or several lifetimes. Mystics, saints, and shamans of ages past and of today, from places far and near, refer to this eternal sojourn in many ways, yet whatever terms are used implies a conscious engagement with our true potential as divine partners in creation. This is what it means to 'grow a soul.'* [59]

My experience of the One Being certainly felt like an aspect of the World Soul. After all, I perceived all life in a single moment, in a single perception even. However, it wasn't until understanding the realities of soul and the passage from the Gospel of Thomas that I began to see how my personal perceptions at the time painted my experience of the anima mundi. At the time, I had felt in a place of lack, gripping onto the identity of my sufferings. By doing so, my victimization had filtered my experience of the World Soul. Therefore, my experience was terrifying: only amplifying what I was already feeling in the mundane world but on a macro scale. It was don Daniel's contention that, as I move through the initiations of my shamanic training, I would contribute to my soul growth; thus, my experience of the World Soul would grow as well, evolving to reflect my own personal growth.

This experience of soul growth continued and was amplified as don Daniel prepared me for the culmination of my shamanic training, my vision quest.

---

59 Glass-Coffin and Miro-Quesada, *Lessons in Courage,* 2.

The Vision Quest

"This is your pilgrimage," he had said. "Your rites of passage. Find yourself and leave yourself behind." As one of his seminal teachings, don Daniel had prepared me for a *paqowachu* (the Quechua word for "priest's walk" or "shaman's walk"), a quest into the wilderness alone to receive a vision and/or connection with Great Spirit, the creative source of the universe. The paqowachu is a pilgrimage, where one isolates oneself from the rest of the world to establish a deep connection with a specific *waka* (sacred site) or apu (sacred mountain).

For many cultures, this is the final rite of passage in which the initiate becomes a paqo, a curandero, a medicine woman, and so on. In the Lakota tradition it is called *Hanbleceya*, "Crying for a Vision." One should return from the vision quest anew, any semblance of the old self left behind.

My chosen spot for my pilgrimage was near the watershed of Blanca Peak, in the Sangre de Cristo mountain range of southern Colorado. That whole area had always been special to me. With the San Luis Valley below and Great Sand Dunes nearby, Blanca Peak is the highest fourteener in the region. Further, Blanca is known for being the east gate of the Dinétah (Navajo nation), known as *Sisnaajiní*. The region is known to have a high volume of UFO and other supernatural activity. Many synchronicities (meaningful coincidences) led me to Blanca. I felt drawn by my soul to make a pilgrimage to this place to go on my vision quest.

A vision quest is a very personal experience. The indigenous peoples of the plains (such as the Cheyenne and Crow) would paint a shield based upon their vision quest experience, which would become a symbol for their life's purpose. Others receive a "spirit name" or other such life-changing circumstance. The paqos of the Quechua, as I learned in the Pachakuti Mesa Tradition, connect with their *istrilla*, the star being acting as a guardian of the apu itself.

I encountered a physical manifestation that is burned in my mind to this day. After being on the mountain for a full day, I had made a despacho to honor the land (see chapter 8). I built a makeshift firepit on the mountain, and while the despacho burned, it shriveled into the shape of a heart. While on fire, it looked just like the iconography of the Sacred Heart of Jesus, which is most well known in Catholic devotions.

Giving prayers of gratitude, I turned to look out at the San Luis Valley stretched out before me.

The rays of the setting sun shot out across the wide expanse below. The valley is 122 miles long, so it was as if I could see the ends of the earth itself, multiple desert colors bouncing off the sunbeams in kaleidoscopic brilliance! A gathering of violet clouds moved in from the west, directly from the sun inching over the horizon. The clouds then formed into an exact image of Christ floating over the expanse of the valley, arms outstretched. The detail was all there, in the face, the beard, the muscles in the body. The phenomena resembled the painting *Christ of Saint John of the Cross* by Salvador Dalí. Except there was no cross. Just Christ floating, arms outstretched, and looking straight at me.

Figure 47. Author's vision

My heart leapt into my throat and I could hardly breathe. The only word I could think of to describe the feeling of exhilaration flowing over me was "glory"! It wasn't just an idea or a concept: the image of the Christ looked right at me, and I truly felt at one with the entirety of existence around me. The formation of Christ stayed, and his eyes locked into me for a few minutes until the image came over the mountain, directly over me, and dissipated. The sun went down. All was dark. And I went to sleep.

Time and space dissolved. My sombra floated out of my body. Normally, my sombra is an almost pure reflection of myself in the mundane world, pretty basic and practical; however, this time (and the only time I can remember) my sombra was made of smoky light. There were ribbons of pink, purple, and blue, but mostly I was composed of white light.

I found myself going through the center arte on the mesa I had built for my paqowachu. Going through it as a portal, I was then instantaneously transported to another realm entirely. I was in a landscape of green, lush rolling hills. Remnants of ancient ruins were splayed throughout the hills, some of temples, some of large sculptural heads like one would see on Easter Island. There was an overwhelming sense of peace, despite the crumbling age of the ruins spotting the landscape. I could feel the wind on my face, warm and inviting.

A massive sun took up most of the sky, so large I could barely see the sky. Even with the sun being so close, the temperature of this world was perfect, and what I could see of the sky was blue. The gargantuan size of this star seemed to have no impact on the climate or light spectrum of this world. In fact, the sun seemed to be composed of the same white light that I was, instead of a raging ball of hydrogen and helium. Somehow, I knew that this world was actually akin to the inside lining of the shell of an egg, surrounding this sun, which was the nucleus of that egg. I also had a great knowing that this was the world of the Ancient Ones, the Ascended Masters. This was the realm of those humans who have evolved to a level of the Hanaqpacha not quite at one with the Source of existence but relating to a level of bodhisattva service for the rest of the cosmos. In fact, the nucleus sun was the closest representation of the Source of All Creation that a human could get without losing their identity: the World Soul.

Without hesitation, I floated into the sun. In a dimension submerged in silky light, I was greeted by three figures: the first, my own personal istrilla, a star guide connected to the apu of my pilgrimage; the second,

Yeshua, who was holding hands with the third, Magdalene, Yeshua's wife. They all spoke to me, but not in words. It was not necessarily telepathic. They were able to convey meaning through ideas and concepts.

They explained to me that the further into this sun that I go, into its core, I will meet the One Being, the Source of Creation. The One Being, they said, came from another place, another universe or dimension entirely. We can only understand this realm by referring to it as the Unmanifest. In order to be here, in order to Manifest, the One had to separate into many, and that is what we are. We are many because that is the only way to manifest—to create more of ourselves into the ocean of consciousness. We are explorers of the One, pioneers of experience, which results in manifestation as separation, as disparate beings experiencing one another.

They ushered me to follow them to the core. As we floated inward, bits of ourselves began to chip away. What little semblance of our identities remained was burned away by the intensity of the light ahead. We all merged together into a single entity, and then eventually we faded away into the light itself.

Then, nothingness.

Though, this nothingness had no isolation or despair attached to it, as in my previous visionary experience. This nothingness was like an empty space of potential, rather than a void. Suddenly, space emerged. Stars speckled the darkness. And then I saw in the formation of these stars Magdalene, with Yeshua supporting her to the side, giving birth. A river of stars and nebulas were pouring out of her vagina. She was giving birth to Form, to Manifestation. I was watching creation in action! Soon, she morphed. A veil moved over her eyes and then her skin turned black as the blackest night, becoming the Primal Goddess of all goddesses, sometimes known as Isis. Yeshua morphed into a being that looked much like the depiction of Osiris in Egyptian mythology. Above them shone a single speck of light: the One.

I was pulled away into a vast spiral, going counterclockwise through the universe and back to our solar system, then spiraled down to Earth and Blanca Peak. I flowed into my body and woke, a seeming glow coming from my very skin.

This was my new experience. Soul changes, soul morphs. There is no one way to perceive reality, even within one's own consciousness. My experience of the One Being had changed because I had come to the work humbly, with reverence. I was in a space in my life where I was bettering myself and the results were paying off.

The universe was no longer something to be scared of; it was all just a matter of perspective and what I was willing to bring to it.

"The body is but a bringing together of goddesses and gods," says Daniel Odier, disciple of Kalu Rinpoche and responsible for one of the greatest commentaries of the *Spandakarika* ("Song of the Sacred Tremor").[60] The *Spandakarika* is one of the most essential holy texts of Kashmir Shaivism, written by Vasugupta in the ninth century while in a cave in Mount Kailash. *Spanda* is the Sacred Tremor, the vibration of consciousness expanding throughout the universe coming from the Source, the One Being, which the *Spandakarika* refers to as *Shakti*. The Sacred Tremor is the unitary movement of creation, the outpouring of the One making the universe manifest through us. In Zen, this is referred to as the Tao.

In curanderismo, this is known as *Kamasqa* (kah-MAH-skalı). Kamasqa is that flow of creation coming from Source, and it is our role as shamanic initiates to be open to it, to be channels of it. Kamasqa is the movement that makes us, as don Oscar says, "a divine partner in creation."

When I returned from the mountain, I shared my experience with don Daniel and don Oscar: both described to me various levels of consciousness in curanderismo (sometimes called Christ Consciousness) that connect to the creative source of all being, the One Being. In the Quechua worldview, the creator being is an androgynous presence called Wiracocha. There are many legends and myths of Wiracocha in Peru, some of which refer to both the creator god Wiracocha in the Hanaqpacha as well as to a human figure named Wiracocha who taught the people the ways of living with Pachamama. Either way, Wiracocha is both a presence and a pathway to connection with the World Soul, to being that partner in the creative act.

---

60 Daniel Odier, *Yoga Spandakarika: The Sacred Texts at the Origins of Tantra*, trans. Clare Frock (Rochester, VT: Inner Traditions, 2005), 48.

These levels of Wiracocha consciousness are as follows:

Taytanchis Wiracocha (tai-TAWN-chees WIHR-ah-KOH-chah): The ultimate center of all creation, the Source, the One. In Catholic terms, this being would be referred to as "the Father" in the Holy Trinity. Not meant to be taken as a literal male figure, the Father is a symbol for the seed of life, for which Pachamama is the womb. Taytanchis is a celestial spirit of creation, as located in the crown of the human body.

Taytacha Wiracocha (tai-TAW-chah WIHR-ah-KOH-chah): "The Son" in the Holy Trinity, the spawn of the Father who connects us to the wider heavens through the wisdom of the human heart. Taytacha is creative essence as it is expressed through physical form, like Yeshua himself. Yeshua is the lover of Magdalene, the bearer of Form; he is there to help usher in the outpouring of creation.

Nuna Wiracocha (NOO-nah WIHR-ah-KOH-chah): As stated before, nuna is the Quechua word for "soul." Located in the qosqo, this is the aspect of creative essence that is the Magdelene pouring out the Form of Manifestation. She is also the Primal Goddess, the birther of all things. Her birthing is Kamasqa, the Sacred Tremor. In traditional Catholicism, this would be referred to as the Holy Spirit, but as we return to a world of the sacred, we recognize this level in its true form as the Magdalene.

These levels of creative being are the essence of the One made manifest, the World Soul acting out the Hermetic axiom, "as above, so below." It is through these levels of Wiracocha's manifestation that we can understand that creation is a participatory action!

We are Creator, and the World Soul is the seat of the generative movement of all life and consciousness. We *are* the Sacred Tremor! Together, Taytanchis, Taytacha, and Nuna Wiracocha make up the great "I am," that which is Creator on all three levels of being.

I then began to practice drawing these concepts into my body when performing any ritual or ceremony. Before I begin, even before the kawsay activation, I bring my right thumb to my forehead and draw a small, invisible cross, stating out loud, "Taytanchis Wiracocha." Then, I bring my hand to my heart, making the same cross, and state, "Taytancha Wiracocha." Finally to my belly, inscribing the cross, and state, "Nuna Wiracocha." This simple movement is a reminder that I am the microcosm of the great macrocosm that is the creative essence of the entire universe. "Mystical movement is not intended to get us to experience extraordinary mental states of altered consciousness," Daniel Odier says in his commentary to *Yoga Spandakarika*, "but rather to plunge us into reality and to get us to discover that the absolute is found nowhere else *but* in this reality."[61]

After practicing incorporating this movement into the shamanic worldview—not just ideologically, but through ritual action and in everyday life—my whole life exploded into completely new vistas of reality I never thought were possible before.

Practicum 22: Vision Quest

As I have said several times, shamanic practice is never-ending. However, many of these practices are a preparation for the moment in which one can pilgrimage into the natural world alone, to be in solitary connection with the World Soul. I recommend undergoing tutelage with an experienced shamanic practitioner within a lineage or apprenticeship program before going on such a pilgrimage. It is important to have that one-on-one support. However, if the reader does not have any options available for such mentorship, here are some recommendations and protocols for going on one's own pilgrimage for a shamanic vision quest.

Recommendations

- Read this enire book first.
- Pick an extended period of time for this experience. At minimum, you will want to be out in the natural world for at least

---

61 Odier, *Yoga Spandakarika*, 23.

twenty-four hours. A vision quest can last up to two or three nights, so plan accordingly, such as during a holiday weekend.

- You will want to be far away from any civilization, in an area where you will not be disturbed. If you do not have access to your own land, there are plenty of federal and state parks you can contact and ask the rangers for the best options available. You may be surprised how helpful and informative park rangers can be if you let them know exactly what you are doing. Be sure you will not be staying in an area where there will be a lot of campers. Isolation is key! Above all, find a place that is sacred to you. A paqowachu normally occurs on the most sacred mountain for the curandero. You do not need to pilgrimage to a mountain if this is not a viable option for you. Find a place of meaning from which you derive great power and medicine.

- Speaking of isolation, *do not take your cell phone!* Some people will still want their cell phone in case of an emergency, but I recommend otherwise. The temptation to connect to the outside world is too great. An incalculable number of people have gone on spiritual pilgrimages for centuries with no phone connection. Do yourself a favor and disconnect. Have some trust in the spiritual process. For emergencies, let a close friend or family member know what you are doing, where you will be, and for how long. Commit to checking in with them when you have finished.

- Fast, if you can, during the pilgrimage. Some people cannot fast due to dietary needs and that is fine; take only the bare essentials to get through the designated time period. Do not deprive yourself of water.

- If you need a tent and camping gear, that is up to you. Be sure to research how to safely interact (or not interact) with the wildlife and flora in your area of choosing. My preference is to go just as I am, with maybe a blanket for a pillow and sleeping bag if it is chilly. We are only talking about exposure to the elements for one night minimum. That being said, pick a time of year that is most comfortable for you in terms of climate.

- Read the protocol below and make a list of all the things you will need. One item of note is your journal so that you can document your experience.

Protocol

1. Spend the week before your pilgrimage in deep meditation and ceremony. Follow the routines in appendix A daily if you can. Abstain from drugs, alcohol, and any unhealthy, greasy foods or sugar for a week to cleanse your system.

2. Bundle as much of your mesa as you can and take it with you. Leave behind any fragile artifacts you may have in your mesa. However, try to at least have enough artes to represent the three campos. You can bunch your artes together in the center of the cloth and wrap them, then place them in a backpack or basket. Find a way that is easy for you to take your mesa with you in travel form. Definitely take your Staff of Individuation.

3. When you arrive to the place your vision quest will take place, find a body of water in which to bathe. Be prepared if you are on a mountain: the water will be freezing! If there is no body of water accessible, you can take an extra jug or bottle of water to cleanse yourself. Imagine this bathing as a baptism, leaving behind your old self and your old life, giving yourself fully over to Pachamama.

4. Offer some tobacco to the fire and to the land, asking permission to be here and perform this ceremony. State your intentions out loud. Listen. If you feel a strong intuition that you should not be there, then leave. Either go to a new spot or pack up and go home. Out of respect for the spirits of the

land, do not perform ceremony in a place that does not want you there.

5. If space allows, draw a circle of cornmeal around your campsite. This will be your container of protection for the duration of the vision quest. If you leave the circle, such as to use the restroom, take a vara with you to stay connected to your ceremonial grounds. As much as you can, stay within the circle.

6. If you have the ability and you are not in a fire hazard zone, create a fire. Follow the safety precautions of the county or park you are in.

7. Unwrap and set up your mesa. Be sure to consecrate the ground accordingly before setting up the artes in their designated campos. Stick any varas that you brought into the ground at the head of their designated campos.

8. Perform your breathing basics, then kawsay activation, the pillar of light, and finally the opening of the account.

9. Before asking for a vision, you will need to create a despacho for the occasion, to satiate the spirits of the land. You can bring your own items for the despacho, but also use some natural elements (such as flowers and seeds) from the land around you. If you forage outside your circle, be sure to take a vara with you to connect you to your protective ceremonial space, and make sure to give an offering (of tobacco, cornmeal, or otherwise) for any plants and other items you retrieve from the land for the depacho. Create a despacho of your own design, both in the spirit of gratitude for being here on this occasion and also in seeking a vision from the World Soul. Make sure the design of your despacho reflects the feeling and intention of your being here.

10. When it is complete, bundle the despacho and touch the bundle to your forehead, heart, and stomach to connect your poq'po to its medicine. Then, with despacho in hand, call out

to Creator, then to the designated saints or deities of each of the three campos of your mesa, and finally to the spirits of the land around you. Stake your claim that this despacho is a gift for them and that in return you wish to receive a message to further your medicine journey on this planet, to help propel your shamanic practice to the next level of evolution. Ask for a vision that will help assist in your soul's growth and show how that growth will be of service to Pachamama and her people.

11. Then, offer the despacho to the fire as an offering to the land. While it burns, mark the sign of the cross on your forehead, heart, and stomach while intoning, "Taytanchis Wiracocha, Taytacha Wiracocha, Nuna Wiracocha." Watch the despacho burn with the utmost focus: you may see something in the fire or smoke relevant to you.

12. For the rest of the pilgrimage, sing songs in praise of Pachamama or life. Drum, rattle, dance. Perform healings on yourself with the artes on your mesa. Journey with each campo to deepen your relationship with them. Pay attention to everything going on around you: the weather, the wildlife, and more. Every little thing on a vision quest is part of the vision itself; it is the message. The most profound vision quests sometimes don't even result in a visionary experience; rather, it is the realization of being alive itself that is the revelation. The end goal of the pilgrimage is to strengthen your partnership with the World Soul and yourself.

13. Feel free to sleep when you must. Do not deprive yourself of the opportunity to receive messages from the dreamtime.

14. After twenty-four hours (or if longer, whenever you feel the ceremony is complete), close out your ceremonial process accordingly. Be sure to offer a final blessing of tobacco or cornmeal to the land before you leave. Make sure you do

your best to leave the space as you found it, with little to no trace that you were there. Do a final bathing before leaving the space or upon returning to where you started at the natural water source.

15. When you return to the world, take the medicine of your experience with you and keep it with you every day. It does not matter how eventful or uneventful it may have been—the experience is yours and yours alone. Do not share your experience immediately; try to give time for integration before speaking of your time alone. Do your best to not immediately connect with the outside world. Give yourself time to slowly process the experience and become acclimated to the new medicine that is now carried within you. Over time, you should try to journal your experience or find some other creative way of expressing it (such as through art or music) before sharing it with anyone else. This is something meant to be yours; honor the experience you gave to yourself and treat it with reverence.

The Soul Within

Do not try to wrap your head around the concept of soul too much. Soul is the poet's cry. Soul is the voice of Billie Holiday or James Brown. Soul is van Gogh's texturized brush stroke. Soul comes from within. A vision quest is a pilgrimage to the outer world of nature so that one can encounter the soul within. You can clearly see the difference between one who is living from soul and one who isn't. The shaman lives from soul. The shaman shines with soul. When one taps into that essence of soul within, the life of the shamanic initiate amps up to a whole new level.

Conclusion

After I trained for years, don Daniel invited me to his lodge one day to have a smoke on the porch. The sounds of the natural world buzzed around us, in the prime of summer, as we puffed on our pipes together. At this point, he had already shepherded me into a space of facilitating San Pedro mesadas and pouring water for inipi (sweat lodge) ceremonies, as well as sponsored me as a sanctioned teacher in the Pachakuti Mesa Tradition. Through his ability to hold space for me, provide safety, and witness my process without judgment, don Daniel had groomed me into a human being who was in solid physical, mental, emotional, and spiritual health. He had truly become my *padre*, my spiritual father in all ways.

"I need to tell you something," he said as he exhaled a plume of tobacco smoke, still smiling as he always did. "I have been watching the signs. My dreamtime has been very consistent. I have been seeing the number nine everywhere, which is a symbol of completion for me. I have gone to the mesa with this and have done many divinations. The answer is clear."

He paused and looked at me through that joyful glint in his eye.

"*Hijo*, it's time for me to retire from the work."

"The work? What do you mean?"

"My shamanic work is ready to move to a different level. I am ready to complete this life of working with clients for healing, of training and initiation. I am well into my elder years. It is time for me to step away from community and go more internal."

I was stunned! We had come so far! What did he mean "retire"? How can someone retire from this? I had grown so much under his tutelage; I wanted more, to keep evolving!

"But, what about my training? There's still so much to learn."

"You will be fine," he chuckled. "You will keep learning. You have everything you need within you."

I didn't like that answer. I wasn't satisfied. Frankly, I was hurt. I really took this personally. How could he abandon me when I needed him so? One doesn't just *quit* being a curandero, do they?

"What are you going to do, then?" I stammered, my gut churning into that familiar twist of panic I felt so long ago.

"The shamanic work, the mesa, will always be with me, a part of me." There was an adamancy that shot through his voice. His eyes widened and his hands patted his chest. "I have been in service to others for long enough. It is time for me to devote the rest of my time on this planet to having my own relationship with soul. It is time for me to do some of the things I have never been able to do, such as painting and sculpture. It is all shamanism. Life is shamanism. I will continue growing my soul—that will never stop."

"But... but what will I ... how will I ...?"

"We will pass the reigns of community over to you and Autumn. You will do fine. Just continue being who you are."

And don Daniel left it at that. We finished our pipes together, exchanging casual conversation, and then I left. I cried in the car the entire way home. I felt betrayed, abandoned, at a loss. The whole world seemed new and scary, like I was a little kid whose father just dropped him off on a busy street corner in the big city. I wasn't ready for this. I wasn't ready to face all the aspects of the shamanic work—and life in general—alone without his guidance.

Don Daniel was a rock for me, a foundation on which I could prop myself up and know the world wasn't going to fall apart. And now he was stepping away from that role.

As the days went on, my sadness increased. Bitterness began to set in. The sense of betrayal and abandonment grew. In essence, I let my sombra ganadera get the better of me, to overcome my senses and way of thinking. As Autumn and I settled into this newfound role, I distracted myself from my grief by drowning in work, cofacilitating with Autumn numerous mesadas, apprenticeships, and healing sessions, as well as writing a book. On top of that, I had a full-time day job and was a father of three. Throughout the next few years, as you can imagine, there was little time for self-care. The stress increased, my health began to fail again, and my relationship with Autumn was becoming constrained by all we had to juggle. Consequently, my shamanic work itself became tiring, a burden rather than something of joy.

Eventually, as with all unregulated growth, the bubble popped. Autumn and I eventually had to come to terms with all we had taken on. It was not an easy process for us. We took our responsibilities seriously. We wanted to honor the lineages that were being bequeathed to us, to honor the ancestors. We held don Daniel and don Oscar and our other teacher, Stumbling Deer, in the highest esteem. Our commitment to the great work they were putting into the world was unsurpassed. In a way, we even felt like missionaries, spreading the good news.

However, with the amount of time and stress all this leadership was causing—and with our kids coming to an age when more focus was on their school activities—we made the decision to step away from it all, as well. We had to put our relationship and our children first. And though it was difficult to do this (as we initially felt like we were shirking our sacred duties), something new began to emerge and blossom within us.

The relationship between Autumn and I had evolved in a new way. Also, our relationship with our mesas and our shamanic activities grew into new vistas of understanding.

During this time, I came across a passage from one of my favorite mystics, Jiddu Krishnamurti, in an interview called "The Circus of Man's Struggle." I was reminded of both my wife and me as I followed Krishnamurti's logic regarding the tendency for human beings to push themselves, to effect change in their environment and the world. He says, "When there is the operation of will, it is a form of resistance; to overcome, to suppress, to deny, to escape—all that is will in action. That means life is then a constant battle."[62] This passage struck me. As we had spent years trying to fill in our time with "changing the world for the better," we were essentially exerting our will. This is not in and of itself a bad thing. But when you are perpetually in "do-it-all" mode, there is no room to breathe. Think of one of the first, and most essential, exercises in this book: breathing basics. Lungs expand and contract, the rhythm of life. They do not just keep expanding and expanding, or they would eventually explode. When you are pushing yourself, essentially one element of your consciousness is dominating another. There is no balance. There will be conflict and disorder; there will be no peace. This, Krishnamurti says, is the circus of the human struggle: the will itself.

The solution, according to Krishnamurti, is to rid oneself of the war among the contents within one's consciousness.[63] As we have worked through the aspects of the campos, the three pachas, and the three sombras, this is exactly what he means. If there is no more will, then there is no more division, no more fragmentation, no more of the conflict between one sombra (aspect of the self) and another. In fact, these aspects of the self only exist as fragments because they *are* in conflict. When they are not in conflict, they no longer exist as fragments, they no longer act as disparate parts, and the fragments disappear when they are not acting against one another.

What does this mean? When Democrats and Republicans are no longer fighting is when there are no more Democrats and Republicans. When Pakistan and India are no longer fighting is when there are no more Pakistan and India. Identity is only assumed when in opposition to another. The moment any fragment tries to assume the authority to change another fragment (even within one's own mind), the fragmentation of consciousness is maintained. If the fragments are the content of consciousness itself, the authority maintains the conflict.

The only way to resolve the issue is when there is no conflict at all, relieving consciousness of the fragments of all authority, of identification.

---

62 Jiddu Krishnamurti, *The Awakening of Intelligence* (New York: HarperCollins Publishers, 1987), 118.

63 Krishnamurti, *The Awakening of Intelligence*, 122.

In the case of Autumn and me and our next level of shamanic life, don Daniel removed himself from a place of authority in our lives. I did not want to accept that at the time, and so tried to fill that void by finding other things in reality to assume authority over me (which ended up creating a life of perpetual conflict). However, in stepping down from the shamanic work, don Daniel ended up teaching me the greatest lesson he would ever teach me: he eliminated the ability for me to look to him for guidance, so that I had to look inward. Not only did he dedicate himself to his own soul growth and happiness, but also by stepping away from being my teacher, he paved the way for me to find my own footing so that I could become my own authority in my shamanic walk. He hadn't "gone away," as I had feared. In fact, Autumn and I visit don Daniel and his wife, Karrie Marie, regularly, as they are like our second family. It was only when I finally came to the space of accepting the loss of don Daniel's tutelage, and sought that authority only within myself, that my shamanic life path evolved into a whole new level of soul alignment.

Kamasqa

One of my most favorite stories of training comes from don Oscar Miro-Quesada. During his training with don Celso Rojas Palomino, don Oscar was shown how to reconstruct don Celso's mesa, filled with numerous artifacts for ceremony. Don Oscar states in his book *Lessons in Courage*, "Rather than simply memorizing the placement of all the medicine pieces or imitating his actions, [don Celso] insisted I deeply commune with each piece, each *arte*, as a conscious being and trusted medicine ally that is imbued with the power of creation in every moment."[64] This is the essence of northern coastal curanderismo. Rather than replicating his maestro's actions, don Oscar was encouraged to create his own flow with the moment.

Kamasqa is the creative potential of the universe, the universe creating itself out of itself. As souls, we are a part of the greater World Soul. Shamanic training culminates not just in the full knowing of this

---

64 Glass-Coffin and Miro-Quesada, *Lessons in Courage*, 22.

realization, but in expressing the creative act itself. Everything you do is Kamasqa, an expression of *Spanda* (the Sacred Tremor).

Create, don't replicate.

Don't allow authority—either from another or in your own mind—to conduct your actions. I spent years allowing others to have authority over me, impacting how I felt about myself, how I dressed, how I acted. It got me nowhere but being in constant psychological turmoil. Anytime I even try to imitate my teachers, the true magick of shamanism is lost. Shamanism is like jazz: you take something familiar, and then you improvise and build it into something that is your own.

This revelation of embodying Kamasqa was even more clear to me after I had attended a ceremony with don Oscar on the majestic peak of Mount Shasta. He and his wife, maestra curandera Cindy Miro-Quesada, had imparted some sacred artes to Autumn and me in a beautiful ceremony. After receiving these sacred items, don Oscar advised us to immediately take a walk in the wilderness to allow us time to process the reception of these gifts. Autumn and I wandered to a nearby creek, its frigid waters flowing from the watershed of the mountain itself. I stood on a rock within the rushing water and cleared my mind, focused only on my breathing and the sound of the gushing stream. After a few moments of peace, a thought came into my mind.

The nature of Kamasqa can be described with this anecdote: Imagine the world, the entire universe even, as a mountain. The snowy peaks of that mountain are where the creative power of the Source, the One Being, within the Hanaqpacha touches the rest of reality. Kamasqa is the process of that snow melting at the watershed, turning into roaring mountain streams, and flowing down the mountain. During this process, the water cuts into the land, forms it, maneuvers it into a flow and new way of being. This is Kamasqa, that flow of creation moving through reality and forming it into existence.

I did not just realize this while standing on this rock, in the running mountain stream. I could feel the flow, the movement. I fully embodied that rushing surge of creation, the Kamasqa flow itself. As I felt that presence of the Sacred Tremor fully in my body, I opened my eyes and looked down into the water. Immediately, I saw a snake swimming in the water, fighting the current, and wiggling its way under the very rock I was standing on!

From then on, one set of circumstances after another seemed to be setting my life up for pure soul alignment: to create, and not to replicate.

This intention was made ever clearer about a year after that when I was approached by an individual from the Lakota lineage who gifted me a chanupa (a sacred pipe) in that tradition. I was expected to follow the rules and protocol of being a pipe-carrier in that tradition. I of course have no problem with upholding the sacred rites of any ancient tradition; however, there were a lot of limitations of these protocols surrounding women and other restrictions that were not comfortable for me. They seemed to make no room for evolution, only harkening back to an era that no longer works in this day and age.

Wanting to respect this tradition, I went to my teacher Stumbling Deer, progenitor of the Stone People's Dance. It just so happened my wife was on her vision quest; Stumbling Deer had set up a tent on the outskirts of the sacred area wilderness in which Autumn was questing in order to monitor and facilitate prayers for her vision. I went to offer my own prayers for Autumn's vision and, after completing them, sat with Stumbling Deer to chat. I shared with him my struggle with carrying this new chanupa, that the rules and protocols seemed to be getting in the way of me even being able to have a relationship with it, as I would my artes on my mesa.

Stumbling Deer—a small, elderly man with long, scraggly hair usually covered with a leather cowboy hat—shifted in his seat and stared into the nearby trees with a weighty glare.

"Now, I'm not going to tell you what to do," he muttered, almost embarrassed to even be imparting advice. "Creator knows I got my own problems. You know I don't follow any certain tradition. The medicine wheel is like my mesa. It's a symbol of the way the world works. And I tried following the way of the Lakota, or the Cherokee, and so forth, but none of them seemed just right to me. I just still couldn't get it. The medicine wheel didn't feel alive.

"And then one day, by myself, just staring at the clouds it all just came to me. The medicine wheel made sense. And that was only because it was mine and nobody else's. I have my own understanding of the medicine wheel. The directions and the elements and the totems may be a little different, but it's all the same. Every tradition has their own way, but it all really comes back to the same thing: your relationship with Creator.

"That's why I never tell people to follow me or the way I do things. Do it your own way. That is the only way it will be right for you. If it belongs to somebody else, it can't be yours. And that's what's important. That's the way I see it and I'm sticking to it!"

From that moment, it was all crystal clear. I returned the chanupa to the Lakota elder, graciously thanking them for thinking of me and trying to include me. Nevertheless, I needed my own relationship with a sacred pipe, if that were ever to come. It needed to be a more natural fit, a Kamasqa-like flow down the mountain. Within a month, a chanupa from an elder in the Stone People's Dance community was brought to the next Stone People's Dance, which I attended as a dancer. It had belonged to another teacher of mine, Gray Horse Woman, who had since gone to live at a nursing home and imparted her sacred items out into the community. My attention, my heart, was immediately drawn to this pipe. One the leaders of the dance, Kevin Gentle Bear, suggested I dance with the pipe. When I did, the connection was clear: I could physically hear Gray Horse Woman speaking in my ear! It was settled: with Stumbling Deer's blessing, I had become the caretaker for this chanupa and still am to this day, a responsibility I take great reverence in.

All it took was for me to allow the Kamasqa to flow through, to be the Kamasqa flow, to forge my own path instead of it being shepherded by others. To relieve myself of the authority of my teachers, of the lineages I honor and uphold, of my own mind. I still honor my teachers. I still honor and uphold these lineages. Yet I do it as Daniel Moler, not as don Daniel Baxley, don Oscar Miro-Quesada, Gray Horse Woman, or Stumbling Deer. And, it turns out, the more Daniel Moler I became, the prouder don Daniel, don Oscar, Gray Horse Woman, and Stumbling Deer became.

Follow Your Flow

In this book I have covered a lot of territory, from the purpose of shamanic training to ritual techniques that will assist you in the process of regaining health and individuation. I recommend taking your time with the material, even if it seems basic. Some of my most magical experiences have come from returning to the basics over and over, revisiting the process with the mind of child. You can make something new again by just eliminating hubris from your mind. No matter how much you learn, you still know nothing. To a shaman, that is a refreshing concept indeed!

I believe we are in a new era of transition for the role of the shaman. The shaman used to be the indigenous witch doctor in the wilds. Yet Pachamama is evolving, and her children are more connected than ever. Roles shift and change as humanity uncovers new ideas and technologies. I believe the role of the shaman in this new world coming our way will not be as inaccessible as it once was. In fact, I believe that initiatory quality of the shaman resides in every single human being, waiting to be born.

True revolution will come to the world when each person focuses on being a conduit of the Creator in their own way. The greatest shamans of ages past have come to be known as Kamasqa themselves, such as the great don Celso Rojas Palomino and don Benito Corihuaman Vargas. This sort of training is known as a "fourth-level" initiation, *Kurak Akulleq*. One who *is* Kamasqa is the embodiment of the creative power of the universe itself. You have the divine right and potential to *be* that Kamasqa.

Throw out all the processes, even the ones I have proposed, and make them your own. Shamanism is about the individual's growth of their own soul, and as soon as you allow anyone else to influence that, you lose your soul. Go on your own journey and don't make it about anyone or anything else. You are your only authority. You are all you need.

As Lao Tzu said,

> *When you have accomplished your goal simply walk away.*
> *This is the pathway to Heaven.*[65]

---

65 Lao Tzu, *Tao Te Ching*, trans. John H. McDonald (New York: Chartwell Books, 2009), 35.

Appendix A

Shamanic Routines

Here are some suggestions for routines you can use in your shamanic practice, with abbreviated versions of the practices in this book. Feel free to improvise on what I have offered or create your own.

Daily Routine

Daily habits can be especially hard, but trying this routine for as long as possible will boost your ceremonial prowess in the long term. Do not beat yourself up if you miss a day or two or can't bring yourself to having a daily routine at all; however, giving it a go will make a big difference in your shamanic capabilities.

Morning Ritual

1. Signs of the Cross (approximately 30 seconds)

    a. Brow: "Taytanchis Wiracocha"

    b. Heart: "Taytacha Wiracocha"

    c. Stomach: "Nuna Wiracocha"

2. Body Stretches (10–15 minutes)

    a. I suggest yoga, sun salutations specifically.

3. Breathing Basics (5–10 minutes)

    a. Focus on breath as the source of life; inhale through the nose, exhale through the mouth.

4. Thought Tracking (5–10 minutes)

    a. Now, focus on your thoughts rather than your breath. Track every thought sequentially.

5. Kawsay Activation (5 minutes)

    a. Inhale kawsay from the earth and through the center of the body, exiting the crown to flow back down around the poq'po, encircling the poq'po in a golden egg.

6. Pillar of Light (5–10 minutes)

    a. Bring in a shaft of light from the center of creation.

        i.   Activate kulli chunpi: "Ñoqa kani" (I am)

        ii. Activate kunka chunpi: "Simi" (the word)

        iii. Activate sonqo chunpi: "Munay" (the love)

        iv. Activate qosqo chunpi: "Nunay" (the living soul)

        v.   Activate chaki chunpi: "Pachamama" (of Pachamama)

    b. Extend the shaft to the center of the earth.

7. Prayerful Benediction: Greet the morning in gratitude and state your intentions for the day.

    a. Suggested Prayer: "Illariy sonqoq pachaman, kallpaq Pachamaman!" (Hail the light of the dawning of the heart and power of Mother Earth!)

    b. Suggested Prayer: "Pachakamaq, Noqaqmi sonqoypi tupakuy, kawsaypi qhawakuy!" (World creator, meet yourself in my heart, see yourself in my life!)

Evening Ritual

1. Return to Power (10–15 minutes)

    a. Breathe in negative moments of the day and exhale through the coccyx into Pachamama.

Ceremonial Routine

Here are some basic protocols for engaging in ceremony. Again, feel free to adjust according to your own needs and ideas.

1. Burn some incense or sage to set the space.

2. Signs of the Cross

    a. Brow: "Taytanchis Wiracocha"

    b. Heart: "Taytacha Wiracocha"

    c. Stomach: "Nuna Wiracocha"

3. Breathing Basics

    a. Focus on breath as the source of life; inhale through the nose, exhale through the mouth.

4. Kawsay Activation

    a. Inhale kawsay from the earth and through the center of the body, exiting the crown to flow back down around the poq'po, encircling the poq'po in a golden egg.

5. Pillar of Light

    a. Bring in a shaft of light from the center of creation, and extend it over both yourself and the mesa.

        i. Activate kulli chunpi: "Ñoqa kani" (I am)

        ii. Activate kunka chunpi: "Simi" (the word)

        iii. Activate sonqo chunpi: "Munay" (the love)

      iv. Activate qosqo chunpi: "Nunay" (the living soul)

      v. Activate chaki chunpi: "Pachamama" (of Pachamama)

   b. Extend the shaft to the center of the earth.

6. Opening of the Account

   a. Extend the cord from the qosqo chunpi to the nuna khuya and harmonize with the mesa.

   b. Activate the pillar of light over campo justiciero; rattle or drum while calling out to patron saints or deities of the campo to empower your mesa, as well as calling artes of that campo into account. Do the same for the campo medio and then the campo ganadero. Suggested call: "I call the powers of the [prospective campo] into account. I call forth the power of [patron saint or deity] to fill me with your essence, to guide my mind, heart, and hands on the field of the mystic. Teach me humility and devotion to all creation. I call forth the power of [name of arte] and your ability to [healing power of arte]. Thank you for your service and for guiding my mind, heart, and hands."

   c. Spray agua de florida three times over each campo.

7. When finished, retract the cord of light from the mesa and return it to your qosqo chunpi. Take a deep breath in and hold it for three seconds while you contemplate the beauty of your creation in the mesa, then exhale a strong phukuy back into the mesa itself as a blessing of gratitude.

8. Perform the ritual (shamanic journey, despacho, healings, etc.).

9. Close the ceremony.

   a. Bless and cleanse the mesa with extra agua de florida or sage.

   b. Call out to the sacred powers of the mesa in gratitude for their support.

   c. Clap one time to seal the good work done.

Appendix B
Shamanic Calendar

Shamanic magickal practice is dependent on nature's calendar. The cycles of the celestial bodies—specifically the sun and the moon—are imperative to observe in terms of timing for ceremony. These are the primal heavenly forms that dictate our physical existence on this planet. Without them, we would not have life. This is why the sun and moon are often revered in most indigenous societies. Here are some suggestions for the types of ceremony you want to follow in respect to the celestial phase.

Moon

Moon phases are particularly relevant for magick or individual ceremonial processes.

New Moon: Planting seeds; new beginnings; setting intentions for a new cycle

Waxing Moon: Maturation; growing into one's self-expression and creativity

Full Moon: Fruition of one's desire; abundance and celebration

Waning Moon: Moving into inner work; restoration and self-care

Sun

Sun cycles are excellent times for despachos or community ceremonies.

Spring Equinox: Planting new life; growth and renewal

Summer Solstice: Celebration of the outer light; thanksgiving

Autumnal Equinox: Conservation and honoring the harvest

Winter Solstice: Celebration of one's inner light mastering the darkness

Eclipses

Though in ancient times eclipses were often seen as terrifying omens, they have a different connotation in the modern shamanic worldview. Eclipses are a time to surrender to the majesty of the cosmos; this is a time for a complete realignment in one's life path and perspective, a chance to reorient one's trajectory into a higher evolutionary potential.

Appendix C
Shamanic Resources

Where to go from here? The following is a list of resources for you to deepen your shamanic practice.

Shamanic Music for Ceremonies and Journey Work

* *Ancient Mother* by On Wings of Song and Robert Gass
* *Buddha Nature* by Deuter
* *Canyon Trilogy* by R. Carlos Nakai
* *Ch'aska Punku* by the Sāmi Brothers
* *Dream Tracker* by Byron Metcalf, Dashmesh Khalsa, and Steve Roach
* *Helpers, Guides, and Allies* by Byron Metcalf
* *Icaro Canto Shamanico* by Tito La Rosa
* *Inca Quena* by Inti Raymi
* *Kiva* by Steve Roach, Michael Stearns, and Ron Sunsinger
* *Love Is Space* by Deva Premal
* *Mantram* by Byron Metcalf, Steve Roach, and Mark Seelig
* *Medicine Wheel* by On Wings of Song and Robert Gass
* *Medicine Work* by Byron Metcalf and Rob Thomas
* *Nuna Kallpa* by the Sāmi Brothers
* *Ofrenda a la Pachamama* by Tito La Rosa

* *Prophecy of the Eagle and the Condor* by Tito La Rosa
* *Qeswachaka* by Pachatusan Inkari
* *Sacred Land* by Pachatusan Inkari
* *Shamanic Trance Dance* by Byron Metcalf
* *The Gathering* by Inlakesh
* *The Precipice of Choice* by Byron Metcalf
* *The Serpent's Lair* by Byron Metcalf and Steve Roach
* *The Shaman's Heart* by Byron Metcalf
* *The Song of the Tree* by Lis Addison
* *Trance Spirits* by Steve Roach and Jeffrey Fayman, with Robert Fripp, and Momodou Kah
* *Tree of Life* by Loren Nerell and Mark Seelig
* *Wachuma's Wave* by Byron Metcalf, Steve Roach, and Mark Seelig
* *Wifala* by Kike Pinto
* *Winaypaq* by Pachatusan Inkari

Shamanic Training

If you would like to receive shamanic training, there are a variety of resources available for seekers. Although I feel it is best to receive training directly from a shamanic lineage, there are many programs that exist for the average person that provide great value to the tradition of modern shamanism. These are just a few:

Shamanic Soul Journeys

www.danielmolerweb.com/shamanic-soul-journeys

My wife and I recorded the journeys in this book, specifically from chapters 6 and 7, as well as some of the other exercises to help guide you in the practicums. Enjoy!

The Heart of the Healer

www.heartofthehealer.org

The shamanic web portal into the lineage of the Pachakuti Mesa Tradition offers numerous ventures into monthly ceremonies and events, as well as opportunities to experience the Pachakuti Mesa Tradition: Cross-Cultural Shamanic Arts for Personal and Planetary Renewal, a five-part apprenticeship that aligns the traditional teachings of Peru and the wisdom of its heritage with the needs of the present day.

Spirit Wisdom Healing

www.spiritwisdomhealing.com

Located in beautiful Mount Shasta, Alan Waugh is best-selling author Graham Hancock's number-one recommended shaman healer. Alan offers not only healing services but also classes in numerous shamanic practices.

Earth Flower Wisdom

www.earthflowerwisdom.com

Heather Weingartner not only offers shamanic training, healing, and ceremonial facilitation but also creates some of the best despacho supplies on the planet.

Living the Ceremony

www.livingtheceremony.com

Curandero Matthew "Mateo" Magee, author of *Peruvian Shamanism*, has learned a variety of modalities from many cultures but focuses a lot on northern coastal curanderismo practices. He offers private sessions and training.

Lodge of the People

www.lodgeofthepeople.com

The website of my wife, Autumn, and me, where we offer ceremonies, healing services, and shamanic training.

Glossary

Alineación: Aligned with the campo medio of the mesa, an alineación is an "alignment" of the person's well-being, a reorienting of mind, heart, and body into a holistic unity. It is a remembering of one's True Self, an Individuation.

Apu: Literally, "lord" in Quechua, though it is most commonly used to describe the power and spirit of a mountain.

Ayni: A system of sacred reciprocity, specifically in giving back to Mother Earth for the abundant life she provides.

Campo: The prime forces of the universe represented on the mesa as corresponding fields, generally portrayed as three vertical fields upon the cloth of the mesa extending from top to bottom: one on the left (campo ganadero), one in the middle (campo medio), and one on the right (campo justiciero).

Campo Ganadero: The campo on the left side of the mesa, otherwise known as the field of the magician. The purpose of the campo ganadero is to contain negative forces and leverage their power for a constructive outcome in harmony with the other forces on the mesa. The curandero also uses the campo ganadero to dispatch negative energies or malevolent forces.

Campo Justiciero: The campo on the right-hand side of the mesa, otherwise known as the field of divine justice. This field embodies the mystical quest of seeking connection with the Divine, generally associated with white magic or beneficial energies. The healing powers of this campo raise the potential of an individual and help them create their own future.

Camp Medio: The middle field of the mesa, also known as the field of equilibrium. This campo is not so much a field in its own right as it is a fusion of the campo ganadero and campo justiciero. This is where the two opposing forces of the universe are stabilized into a cohesive union or balance.

Chavín: A pre-Incan civilization dating back as far as 1000 BCE. It is well noted in northern coastal curanderismo that this civilization is one of the prime influencers of using the huachuma (San Pedro) medicine as a ceremonial practice. Much of the iconography of this culture has continued to be an inspiration for curanderismo to this day.

Chavín de Huántar: The primary ceremonial temple of the Chavín. This complex is highly important to the northern coastal curanderismo lineage and contains much of the vital curanderismo iconography, including *Ángel-Atigrado*, the Huachuma God frieze (figure 31).

Chunpi: Literally, "belt" in Quechua, although it can also refer to the energy centers of the body. Also known as a "chakra" in Eastern spiritual practices.

Curanderismo: A system of folk healing in the Americas, particularly prevalent in Central and South American countries, that normally incorporates indigenous healing practices, often focusing (but not limited to) spiritual and herbal techniques. This is sometimes referred to synonymously as "shamanic healing."

Curandero/a: A practitioner of curanderismo or shamanic healing.

Despacho: An offering of ayni made to Pachamama and the spirit guardians of the natural world. This practice originates from the indigenous Quechua people of Peru and involves the building of a mandala-like design with natural materials on paper, which is then wrapped and disbursed either by fire or burying in the ground.

Hanaqpacha: Also known as the upper world, the place where Creator and all the angelic beings of more refined energies of existence reside. In Peru, the Hanaqpacha is often related to the tops of the mountains, the roof of the world.

Huachuma: Also known as San Pedro, a mescaline-containing cactus that grows in the lower regions of the Andes Mountains. This cactus acts as a psychoactive stimulant, a catalyst to activate the curandero's power for divination and healing.

Individuation: A concept highly promoted by psychoanalyst Carl Jung, individuation is the integration of disparate parts of the psyche, returning the self to a state of wholeness. For the shamanic practitioner, individuation is not just a process but a way of life.

Kamasqa: The flow of creation into the world that comes from the Source of All Creation (God, Goddess, etc.). It is the task of the curandero or shaman to be a direct conduit of Kamasqa, to channel this energetic flow into their healing practices.

Kawsay: An invisible force that is the essence of life itself and sustains and vitalizes the poq'po, often stored in and able to be drawn from the body of Pachamama.

Kaypacha: Also known as the middle world, this is the plane of existence, which comprises the here and now, the material reality you interact with on a moment-to-moment basis.

Levantada: A ritual raising of the recipient's spirit. Associated with the campo justiciero of the mesa, a levantada uplifts the recipient from their current situation and boots them into a forward momentum to live their life's purpose.

Limpia: The ritual practice of cleansing one's poq'po, or energetic body, extracting any density associated with trauma or some other illness. This healing practice is associated with the campo ganadero of the mesa.

Mesa: The Spanish word for "table." This word is used often in both Central and South American countries as a term for the shamanic altar used in curanderismo and other folk healing traditions.

Northern Coastal Curanderismo: A lineage of folk healing originating in the northern coastal regions of Peru, focused on healing practices using the mesa and herbal remedies, specifically through the use of huachuma medicine.

Nuna: The Quechua word for "soul."

Pacha: The Quechua word for "world," though it holds an attribution of both time and space. Sometimes it is used in reference to an era or a dimension of space-time.

Pachamama: The Quechua term for "Mother Earth," the living embodiment of our home planet and mother to us all.

Pachakuti Mesa Tradition: The cross-cultural shamanic tradition originated by respected curandero don Oscar Miro-Quesada from Peru. The term *pachakuti* is a Quechua word meaning "world reversal" and refers to the time of transformation we are experiencing now on Pachamama. Known colloquially as PMT, this tradition uses a mesa, an altar of self-exploration and personal growth to foster one's relationship with the self and universe to restore balance and harmony with the world.

Paqo: A shamanic healer-priest of the Quechua indigenous peoples of Peru. A paqo is responsible for paying ayni to Pachamama as well as tending to the overall health of the community.

Poq'po: The energetic field or "bubble" of the human body. The poq'po is composed of both energy and mind, generating an integral link between the physical body and the unseen dimensions of the shamanic realms.

Quechua: An indigenous people who live high in the Andes of Peru. They have an agrarian culture and are sometimes attributed by anthropologists to be the descendants of the Inca. The language of the Quechua is known as *runasimi* ("people speak"). Often the term *Quechua* can refer both to language and the people.

Sombra: Literally, "shadow" or "shade" in Spanish. Sombra refers to the idea of an image cast upon another surface. The sombra is not only a reflection of one's psyche but also the projection of one's astral self. The sombra is the image cast by the shaman when traveling through pachas of the cosmos.

Sombra Criandera: The aspect of oneself that nurtures the curandero upon their path of shamanic practice, encouraging them toward evolution. Other traditions call this the higher self, that which is concerned with transcendent reality.

Sombra Ganadera: The apparatus of the soul that remembers and reacts to the past. Other traditions refer to this as the lower self, and most often it resides in a subconscious state of the mind where suppressed memories are stored.

Sombra Primera: The "prime shade" or "first shade," the part of oneself concerned with relationships and being in this world. The sombra primera reminds us to be grounded; to honor the schedules of society and the boundaries of community is the principal aim of the sombra primera's function. Residing in the campo medio, the sombra primera acts as the mediator between all realms.

Sonqo: Literally, "heart" in Quechua.

Ukhupacha: Also known as the lower world. However, the Quechua word *ukhu* is more of a reference to the interior spaces of the world and even within oneself. The Ukhupacha can normally be understood as the place of heavy or dense energies and the darker things of existence.

Bibliography

Abbott, Edwin A. *Flatland: A Romance of Many Dimensions*. New York: Signet Classics, 2005.

Bardon, Franz. *Initiation into Hermetics*. Translated by Gerhard Hanswille and Franca Gallo. Salt Lake City, UT: Merkur Publishing, 2016.

Barnstone, Willis, and Marvin Meyer, ed. *The Gnostic Bible: Gnostic Texts of Mystical Wisdom from the Ancient and Medieval Worlds*. Boston, MA: Shambhala, 2003.

Burger, Richard L. *Chavin and the Origins of Andean Civilization*. London: Thames and Hudson, 1992.

Bly, Robert. *A Little Book on the Human Shadow*. San Francisco: HarperSanFrancisco, 1988.

Campbell, Joseph. *The Hero with a Thousand Faces*. Princeton, NJ: Princeton University Press, 1973.

Chapman, Alan. *Advanced Magick for Beginners*. London: Aeon Books, 2008.

Dass, Ram. *Be Here Now*. San Cristobal, NM: Lama Foundation, 1971.

Echols, Damien. *High Magick: A Guide to the Spiritual Practices That Saved My Life on Death Row*. Boulder, CO: Sounds True, 2018.

Elford, Jaymi. *Tarot Inspired Life: Use the Cards to Enhance Your Life*. Woodbury, MN: Llewellyn Publications, 2019.

Eliade, Mircea. *Rites and Symbols of Initiation: The Mysteries of Birth and Rebirth*. Translated by Willard R. Trask. New York: Harper and Row, 1958.

———. *Shamanism: Archaic Techniques of Ecstasy*. Translated by Willard R. Trask. London: Penguin Books, 1989.

Fortune, Dion. *The Training & Work of an Initiate*. San Francisco: Weiser Books, 2000.

Glass-Coffin, Bonnie. *The Gift of Life: Female Spirituality and Healing in Northern Peru*. Albuquerque: University of New Mexico Press, 1998.

Glass-Coffin, Bonnie, and Oscar Miro-Quesada. *Lessons in Courage: Peruvian Shamanic Wisdom for Everyday Life*. Faber, VA: Rainbow Ridge Books, 2013.

Harpur, Patrick. *Daimonic Reality: A Field Guide to the Otherworld*. London: Viking Arkana, 1994.

———. *The Philosopher's Secret Fire: A History of the Imagination*. Chicago: Ivan R. Dee, 2002.

Heaven, Ross. *The Hummingbird's Journey to God: Perspectives on San Pedro, the Cactus of Vision & Andean Soul Healing Methods*. Hampshire, UK: O Books, 2009.

Hine, Phil. *Condensed Chaos: An Introduction to Chaos Magic*. Tempe, AZ: New Falcon Publications, 1995.

Hunt, Valerie V. *Infinite Mind: Science of the Human Vibrations of Consciousness*. Malibu, CA: Malibu Publishing, 1996.

Joralemon, Donald, and Douglas Sharon. *Sorcery and Shamanism: Curanderos and Clients in Northern Peru*. Salt Lake City: University of Utah Press, 1993.

Jung, Carl G. *Memories, Dreams, Reflections*. Edited by Aniela Jaffé. Translated by Richard Winston and Clara Winston. New York: Vintage Books, 1989.

Krishnamurti, Jiddu. *The Awakening of Intelligence*. New York: Harper-Collins Publishers, 1987.

Lawlor, Robert. *Voices of the First Day: Awakening in the Aboriginal Dreamtime*. Rochester, VT: Inner Traditions, 1991.

Magee, Matthew. *Peruvian Shamanism: The Pachakúti Mesa*. Kearney, NE: Morris Publishing, 2005.

McKenna, Terence. *The Archaic Revival: Speculations on Psychedelic Mushrooms, the Amazon, Virtual Reality, UFOs, Evolution, Shamanism, the Rebirth of the Goddess, and the End of History*. San Francisco: Harper Collins, 1991.

Moler, Daniel. *Shamanic Qabalah: A Mystical Path to Uniting the Tree of Life & the Great Work*. Woodbury, MN: Llewellyn Publications, 2008.

Morales, Jessica I. "The Heart's Electromagnetic Field Is Your Superpower." *Psychology Today*, November 29, 2020. https://www .psychologytoday.com/us/blog/building-the-habit-hero/202011 /the-hearts-electromagnetic-field-is-your-superpower.

Mueller, Pam A., and Daniel M. Oppenheimer. "The Pen Is Mightier Than the Keyboard: Advantages of Longhand over Laptop Note Taking." *Psychological Science* 25, no. 6 (2014): 1159–68. https:// linguistics.ucla.edu/people/hayes/Teaching/papers/Mueller AndOppenheimer2014OnTakingNotesByHand.pdf.

Odier, Daniel. *Yoga Spandakarika: The Sacred Texts at the Origins of Tantra*. Translated by Clare Frock. Rochester, VT: Inner Traditions, 2005.

Olson, Carl. "The Existential, Social, and Cosmic Significance of the Upanayana Rite." *Numen* 24, no. 2 (1977): 152–60.

Polia, Mario. "Andean Cosmology and Cosmography in the North-Peruvian Shamanic Mesa." In *Mesas & Cosmologies in the Central Andes*, edited by Douglas Sharon. San Diego, CA: San Diego Museum of Man, 2006.

Rabjam, Schechen. *The Great Medicine That Conquers Clinging to the Notion of Reality: Steps in Meditation on the Enlightened Mind.* Boston, MA: Shambhala, 2007.

Roessingh, Hetty, "The Benefits of Note-Taking by Hand." BBC. September 10, 2020. https://www.bbc.com/worklife/article/20200910-the-benefits-of-note-taking-by-hand.

Sharon, Douglas. *Shamanism & the Sacred Cactus: Ethnoarchaeological Evidence for San Pedro Use in Northern Peru.* San Diego, CA: San Diego Museum of Man, 2000.

————. *Wizard of the Four Winds: A Shaman's Story.* Self-published, CreateSpace, 2015.

Skillman, R. Donald. *Huachumero.* Ethnic Technology Notes, vol. 22. San Diego, CA: San Diego Museum of Man, 1990.

Strom, Jill. *The Cura Convergence: Healing Through Science and Spirit.* Bloomington, IN: Balboa Press, 2017.

Talbot, Michael. *The Holographic Universe.* New York: HarperCollins, 1991.

Tzu, Lao. *Tao Te Ching.* Translated by John H. McDonald. New York: Chartwell Books, 2009.

University of California, Los Angeles. "Study Shows How Serotonin and a Popular Anti-depressant Affect the Gut's Microbiota." *Science Daily.* September 6, 2019. www.sciencedaily.com/releases/2019/09/190906092809.htm.

Walsh, Roger. *The World of Shamanism: New Vision of an Ancient Tradition*. Woodbury, MN: Llewellyn Publications, 2007.

Wilcox, Joan Parisi. *Masters of the Living Energy: The Mystical World of the Q'ero of Peru*. Rochester, VT: Inner Traditions, 2004.

Williams, J. E. *The Andean Codex: Adventures and Initiations among the Peruvian Shamans*. Charlottesville, VA: Hampton Roads, 2005.

To Write to the Author

If you wish to contact the author or would like more information about this book, please write to the author in care of Llewellyn Worldwide Ltd. and we will forward your request. Both the author and the publisher appreciate hearing from you and learning of your enjoyment of this book and how it has helped you. Llewellyn Worldwide Ltd. cannot guarantee that every letter written to the author can be answered, but all will be forwarded. Please write to:

Daniel Moler
℅ Llewellyn Worldwide
2143 Wooddale Drive
Woodbury, MN 55125-2989

Please enclose a self-addressed stamped envelope for reply,
or $1.00 to cover costs. If outside the U.S.A., enclose
an international postal reply coupon.

Many of Llewellyn's authors have websites with additional information and resources. For more information, please visit our website at http://www.llewellyn.com.